The Herb Society of America's

ESSENTIAL GUIDE TO GROWING AND COOKING WITH HERBS

The Herb Society of America's

....

ESSENTIAL GUIDE TO GROWING AND COOKING WITH HERBS

edited by
KATHERINE K. SCHLOSSER

LOUISIANA STATE UNIVERSITY PRESS

BATON ROUGE

Published by Louisiana State University Press

Manufactured in the United States of America
First printing

Designer: Barbara Neely Bourgoyne
Typefaces: Myriad Pro and Whitman
Printer and binder: Edwards Brothers, Inc.

Botanical drawings are by Elizabeth R. Neely. All photographs are courtesy of
Katherine K. Schlosser.

Library of Congress Cataloging-in-Publication Data
The Herb Society of America's essential guide to growing and cooking with herbs /
edited by Katherine K. Schlosser.
    p. cm.
  Includes bibliographical references and index.
  ISBN 978-0-8071-3255-5 (cloth : alk. paper) 1. Cookery (Herbs) 2. Herbs.
I. Schlosser, Katherine K. II. Herb Society of America. III. Title: Essential guide to
growing and cooking with herbs.
  TX819.H4H4545 2007
  641.3'57—dc22

                                 2006100112

The paper in this book meets the guidelines for permanence and durability of
the Committee on Production Guidelines for Book Longevity of the Council on
Library Resources. ∞

Disclaimer: The Herb Society of America is a nonprofit, educational organization
dedicated to promoting the knowledge, use, and delight of herbs through
educational programs, research, and sharing the experience of members with the
community. Since we are not medical practitioners, it is the policy of The Herb
Society of America not to advise, recommend, or prescribe herbs for medicinal
use. Information is provided as an educational service, and The Herb Society of
America, Inc., and LSU Press cannot be held liable for its content. Please consult a
health care provider before pursuing any herbal treatments.

To Jim Adams and Chrissy Moore

Contents

The Herb Society of America and the National Herb Garden

The National Herb Garden (NHG), within the United States National Arboretum, is a treasure and a jewel in the crown of The Herb Society of America (HSA). The Herb Society of America is very proud to have been the force behind the creation of the Garden, and to have continued a close relationship with the Garden's curator and staff in the twenty-five years since its inception. In 1939, Anne Burrage, one of the founders of the HSA, first voiced the aspiration that "some day we have a garden in the National Arboretum." It took forty-one years, but we did it.

The HSA's support for the National Herb Garden is multifaceted. For a number of years, we have funded an intern to assist the Garden's curator and to help develop educational programs at the Garden. Income from an NHG endowment and individual donations partially make up this funding. In addition, the National Herb Garden committee of the HSA undertakes special fundraising projects to assist with the NHG intern's salary. This book is one of those projects. We hope that it will raise awareness of the NHG throughout the United States.

The NHG, like the National Arboretum, may be toured without charge. It is now possible to rent the Garden for events such as weddings or large parties. A lovelier place for an early evening stroll to enjoy the colors, textures, and scents of herbs cannot be found.

The Herb Society of America, a nonprofit organization, was founded in 1933 by seven women with a serious interest in herbs and botany. The Society is now comprised of some 2,300 members. Its logo, a circle around seven sprigs of thyme, was designed by one of the founders, Florence Bratenahl, who was also responsible for the Bishop's Garden at the National Cathedral in Washington, D.C. The seven sprigs of thyme represent the seven founding members, designed after a woodcut from John Gerard's *Herball* (1597). The HSA motto, "For use and for delight," was taken from John Parkinson, a seventeenth-century herbalist and apothecary to King James I of England.

In the nearly seventy-five years since the founding of the HSA, research and learning about herbs have continued to be of primary interest. As our mission statement affirms, "The Herb Society of America is dedicated to promoting the knowledge, use, and delight of herbs through educational programs, research, and sharing the experience of its members with the community." Our Research Grant program accepts applications annually for grants covering a variety of subjects. We recently began a Grant for Educators program to challenge individuals, groups, or small businesses to develop and deliver learning experiences to the public. In the Seed Exchange program, members gather and clean seed, which is made available for purchase by both members and the public. The Promising Plants program profiles little-known and underused plants. We also maintain a series of Plant Collections, which are listings of all the herbal plants registered with the HSA and held by members or groups of members.

The Society has an annual conference with lectures by well-known herb enthusiasts. Members are themselves lecturers, teachers, researchers, authors, crafters, and avid gardeners. Our annual publication, *The Herbarist*, includes articles by members, grant recipients, and others interested in herbs. A quarterly newsletter also contains articles of interest to members. Our national headquarters, located in Kirtland, Ohio, is run by a professional staff. An extensive library is located there, and the staff assists members in research. Our website, www.herbsociety.org, offers a wealth of information for herb lovers, including a Family Herb Corner.

Membership in the HSA is open to anyone interested in herbs, with two main categories: unit members and members at large. Members often support one or more public gardens and sponsor educational events. For membership information, contact The Herb Society of America at 9019 Kirtland-Chardon Road, Kirtland, OH 44094 (440-256-0514), through the membership section of our Web site, or by e-mail (membership@herbsociety.org).

The Herb Society of America is delighted to present this informative and entertaining guide. We hope that you enjoy the recipes included here, and that you are inspired to embark on adventures of your own in growing and cooking with herbs—in short, to use the information to your own delight.

Anne H. Abbott
President, 2006–2008
The Herb Society of America, Inc.

The National Herb Garden: A Garden for the People

On the warm evening of June 12, 1980, hundreds of people gathered at the U.S. National Arboretum (USNA) in Washington, D.C., to celebrate the dedication of the largest designed herb garden in the world, the National Herb Garden. While the opening of the Garden received widespread publicity, newspapers could not begin to cover the whole story. Many of the attendees had raised money to support the Garden; others had researched plants for the extensive beds. Yet even some of them did not realize what a tremendous effort had been expended in the Garden's debut that night.

The idea of a national herb garden was conceived fifteen years earlier, in the summer of 1965, when The Herb Society of America (HSA) held its annual meeting at the University of Virginia in Charlottesville. While walking the university grounds, HSA president Edna Cashmore told Betty Rea, chair of the newly formed Greater Washington Unit (now the Potomac Unit), that she thought it would be wonderful to have an herb garden in Washington, D.C., perhaps at the White House. Rea's reply was a practical one: if there was a garden at the White House, few people would have access to it. She also pointed out that the Secret Service probably would not allow HSA members to enter the White House grounds with buckets and pruners in hand to care for the garden. Instead, Rea suggested locating the garden at the USNA. At the next meeting of the HSA board of directors, Cashmore proposed the idea of a national herb garden, and it was met with enthusiasm. Cashmore, Rea, and fellow HSA member Margaret Brokaw-Smith subsequently met with Dr. Henry T. Skinner, then director of the USNA, about the possibility of a garden. While Dr. Skinner fully backed the idea, he warned that no funds were available to pay for such an endeavor. For a few years, the Garden remained only a dream.

Plans and fundraising began with fervor in the early 1970s. Elsetta Barnes, an HSA member and designer of the Western Reserve Unit's herb garden at the Garden Center of Greater Cleveland (now the Cleveland Botanical Garden), developed the initial concept for the Garden. Betty Rollins (HSA president, 1972–1974) and Dr. John Creech (director of the USNA, 1973–1980) selected the Garden's final placement in a meadow across from the Arboretum administration building.

Many HSA units across the country raised money for the Garden by holding luncheons, garden tours, plant sales, symposia, and craft sales. Their efforts hit a snag, however, because congressional regulations prevented the Agricultural Research Service (ARS), the branch of the U.S. Department of Agriculture that oversees the USNA, from receiving private monies. During the presidency of Genevieve Jyurovat (1974–1976), the HSA thus established an official relationship with the ARS, enabling the acceptance of funds for the NHG. An HSA National Herb Garden committee was formed, consisting of Dottie Hood, Caroline Cadwalader, Joanna Reed, Nancy Howard, and Audrey O'Connor. Upon the recommendation of Creech, the committee decided to hire Sasaki Associates of Watertown, Massachusetts, to design the Garden. A young landscape architect, Tom Wirth, was put in charge of the project. Using Barnes's concept of the Garden as a starting point, Wirth soon completed a detailed plan.

Wirth recalled his experience designing the National Herb Garden as "the best working relationship I have had with a garden club. The Herb Society was very decisive." He frequently traveled to Washington to work on design details with USNA chief horticulturist Skip March, Creech, and the National Herb Garden committee. As he remembered, "The site and program of the Garden inspired what the eventual design would be." The Garden was aligned to fit into the bank at the meadow's edge. The history of growing herbs was also very important to this project, so the Knot and Rose Gardens were incorporated into the overall design. Stating that "the plants are the focus of this garden," Wirth built the theme gardens at an elevated angle for optimal plant viewing. "This also gave people the feeling that they were in the gardens, not just looking at them," he added.

In consultation with the National Herb Garden committee, Creech determined the themes of the ten specialty gardens, which represented a broad spectrum of herbs and herbalism. The plant lists for the gardens were compiled by the following individuals: Dioscorides Garden, Dr. Fred Meyer, USNA; Dye Garden, Faith Swanson and Virginia Rady, Western Reserve Unit; Early American (Colonial) Garden, Susan Plimpton, New England Unit; Native American Garden, Holly Shimizu and Ruth Smith, Potomac Unit; Medicinal Garden, Dr. Heber Youngken, New England Unit; Culinary Garden, Henny Truitt, Philadelphia Unit; Industrial Garden, Helen Whitman, New York Unit; Fragrance Garden, Joanna Reed, Philadelphia Unit; Asian Garden, Dr. John Creech, USNA; Beverage Garden, Madalene Hill, South Texas Unit, and Joanna Reed. Ruth McDowell, New England Unit, designed the knot, and the Rose Garden plant material was chosen by Hester Crawford, Western Reserve Unit.

Thanks in large part to supportive donations from the McIlhenny family—of Tabasco renown—of Avery Island, Louisiana, the old compost area at the Arboretum became the curator's office and growing area. (The McIlhennys have continued to support the Garden and send a yearly donation of live, mature *Capsicum frutescens*, their famous Tabasco pepper plants, to display in it.)

When Rea became HSA president in 1976, the National Herb Garden fund contained $140,000. Before work on the Garden could begin, however, the HSA needed a total of $400,000 in hand. Ruth and Roland Remmel, of Little Rock, Arkansas, agreed to take on the formidable task of fundraising. They were great champions of the NHG and took their efforts far and wide. By the following summer, funds for the Garden had reached $200,000. Then, as fate would have it, Rea met Secretary of Agriculture Bob Bergland while attending a summer Youth Garden event at the Arboretum. She told the secretary about the National Herb Garden project and asked him if the Department of Agriculture could give any financial help. After reviewing the plans, Secretary Bergland recommended that Rea meet with Representative Jamie L. Whitten of Mississippi, who was the head of the House Appropriations Committee. Whitten asked Rea if she would be willing to testify before a congressional subcommittee. She agreed. Before the day arrived, Rea brought a copy of her prepared testimony and a tussie-mussie—a small bouquet of herbs and flowers—to each House and Senate member on the committee. Her testimony was persuasive. The committee voted to give the remaining $200,000 necessary for the National Herb Garden.

Construction of the NHG began on December 15, 1978. That morning Bill Scarborough of the USNA facilities crew called Rea to tell her they were going to begin by bulldozing the path around the theme gardens. It was a rainy, cold day, but Rea came out to the Arboretum, placed a tussie-mussie on the bulldozer, and had the pleasure of riding the bulldozer around the oval. Meanwhile, specific plant selections and garden designs were researched and finalized by HSA members Joanna Reed, Madalene Hill, and Nancy Howard.

In February 1980, the NHG's first curator was hired. Holly Shimizu, a former woody-plant instructor for the U.S. Department of Agriculture, was selected for the position. She remembers getting the call from Skip March, who said, "Congratulations to the new curator of the National Herb Garden." Her first assignment as curator was to procure all the plants to be planted throughout the gardens. "It was a challenge finding big plants and obscure plants. Skip March was a big help with this task," Shimizu recalled. Many other HSA members also helped with the plant material, especially Joanna Reed, Nancy Howard, and Joy Logee Martin.

Finally, the evening of June 12 arrived. A tent with food and champagne was set up on the lawn behind the USNA director's office. Just before the dedication of the Garden, a champagne toast was offered in the director's office with all of the past presidents of the HSA and Anne Burrage, a founding member of The Herb Society. The dedication ceremony, held on the terrace outside the administration building, began with a patriotic musical opening by the U.S. Marine Band. Following greetings and introductions by USNA director Dr. John Creech, Burrage presented the National Herb Garden to the American people. Joan Mondale, wife of Vice President Walter Mondale, accepted the Garden on behalf of the American people. Secretary of Agriculture Bob Bergland and Representative Jamie L. Whitten also addressed the audience. Joan Mondale planted the last shrub in the Knot Garden, and the Garden was officially open.

Once the excitement of the opening died down, Shimizu found that HSA members were still available for support. Henny Truitt, Pennsylvania Unit, was a gifted garden designer and kindly assisted her with planting schemes. USNA employee Albert Brown, a talented gardener, became her assistant. He took pride in the Garden and contributed a great deal to its cultivation, having a special fondness for the Rose Garden.

Because the Garden received a great deal of publicity, Shimizu was able to meet and learn from many people visiting from all over the world. As she said, "The Herb Garden was ahead of its time. Herbs were new and unique to the American public." Her biggest challenge was making the Garden beautiful as well as educational. She figured out the right combinations to make the plantings attractive, massing and interspersing annuals, perennials, flowers, and textures to show off the plants in the best way possible. As she put it, "Plants are defined as herbal because they are useful, not by the way they grow."

In January 1988, Shimizu left the National Herb Garden for the U.S. Botanic Garden, where she became assistant director. "Leaving was awful, like putting a child up for adoption," she remembered. Janet Walker was then hired as curator. As she recalled, "I was on cloud nine. It was an absolute high point in my life, like having a baby." Walker began her job on July 5, 1988. Kathy Wolfe, Walker's first intern, began the next day. During the interim, Albert Brown and volunteers Catherine Russell and Betty Moller oversaw the continuous planting and garden maintenance.

By this time, the Garden was ten years old and starting to show signs of wear. The gravel paths had washed out, and broken trellises and water pipes needed repair. Moreover, the Knot Garden continually lost plants due to poor drainage. Walker worked diligently with the Arboretum Facilities Unit to get these problems fixed. The Rose Garden trellises were repaired, the irrigation systems were updated, and drainage problems in the Knot Garden were corrected, thanks to financial help from HSA units.

Walker felt especially lucky to have the assistance of the Potomac Unit, which produced *The National Herb Garden Guidebook*. She was the content editor and Dick Ober was the senior editor for the book. As Walker said, "This was a massive undertaking, but a very fun way to learn and refine the plant lists."

In 1989 the HSA National Herb Garden committee was formalized and made a permanent part of the HSA structure. Laura Viancour was the first chair of this committee, which was made up of HSA members within driving distance of Washington, D.C. They raised money for the Garden's biggest need: an intern. They also worked together on herbal and educational programs and conducted an herbal-tree drive to complete the original design for the Garden. Dorothy Bonitz was the next chair, when the committee held its first major fundraiser. Other fundraisers have followed, allowing the NHG summer internship to be extended to ten months.

In 1996, Walker realized that this physically demanding job in the very sunny Garden was taking a toll on her. She thought nothing was as interesting as herbs and the stories they tell, so she began concentrating on the education and interpretation side of horticulture. She began work on a master's degree in museum education, and in August 1996 took the position of Education and Visitor Services Unit Leader at the USNA.

In October of that year, I was asked to be acting curator of the National Herb Garden. Prior to that I had been the assistant to the curator of the Fern Valley Native Plant

Collection at the Arboretum, and nothing excited me more than the chance to work in one of my favorite gardens. My first visit to the Herb Garden had been in 1991, as a student intern at Longwood Gardens. Janet Walker had led a tour of the Garden, and I remember being entranced by what I saw, wishing that someday I, too, might be able to work there. Now I had realized my dream. Although I had studied plants for most of my life and had worked in herb gardens since I was thirteen years old, the diversity of plant material in the Garden was humbling. I knew if I was to have a chance at the job of curator, I would really have to prove myself.

With the help of my assistant, Kari Iddings, we worked to ensure that all tender plants would survive the winter and the gardens were put to bed. I took the opportunity of being in charge to do things I felt needed to be done. A birch tree was removed from the birch border, the hedge around the Rose Garden was lowered to improve air circulation in that garden, and the curved garden beds at the entrance to the Garden were converted into showy plantings of annual herbs to make the site more inviting. I also began the rejuvenation of the diseased boxwood hedge surrounding the theme gardens.

In January 1997, I began a wonderful working relationship with the National Herb Garden committee, under the leadership of its new chair, Bernice Pivarnik. They continued to support the National Herb Garden internship by selling polo shirts with the HSA logo and a needlepoint kit of the Knot Garden created by Katherine Schlosser of the North Carolina Unit. Sandy Salkeld deHoll served as chair of the committee from 2001 until 2005, when Katherine Schlosser assumed the chairmanship.

In late April 1997, I was officially offered the job as curator of the National Herb Garden. I accepted with great excitement; it was one of the happiest moments of my life. That autumn, my assistant, Kari, took a new position at the Arboretum, and the following summer the enthusiastic Chrissy Moore (a previous Herb Garden intern) became my assistant.

Shortly after I became acting curator, I was asked to sit in on plans to renovate the Garden. Its age was really beginning to show, and repairs were desperately needed to improve accessibility to the physically challenged. Over the past seventeen years edging and bricks had heaved, causing trip hazards, and the gravel had worn down, making wheelchair access difficult. The irrigation system needed to be modernized, and lighting needed to be installed so the Garden could be used in the evenings. Over the next two years ARS engineers, the Arboretum Facilities Unit, and I worked with the landscape architectural firm of Rhodeside and Harwell to come up with an acceptable and functional design for reconstruction. During the summer of 1998, NHG staff and volunteers carefully removed nearly one thousand plants to prepare for the renovations. On November 2, 1998, the National Herb Garden was closed to visitors for the first time since its opening in 1980.

The renovation was done swiftly, efficiently, and with minimal damage to the plantings. On March 19, 1999, the NHG quietly reopened to the public. On April 29, a celebration entitled "A Garden for All" took place. At this event, the Garden was formally reopened, with remarks by Dr. Tom Elias, director of the U.S. National Arboretum; Joyce Brobst, president of The Herb Society of America; Richard Rominger, Undersecretary of Agriculture; and Vincent Orange, a member of the Washington, D.C., city council. Many members of the HSA, along with other supporters of the National Herb Garden, attended.

Like Shimizu and Walker before me, I get a great deal of pleasure working with all of the people that make the National Herb Garden the special place it is, including the HSA National Herb Garden committee members, other HSA members who donate their time, knowledge, and financial support, and Garden docents and volunteers. The docents and volunteers come in weekly and work through all kinds of weather to create the beautiful garden everyone enjoys.

On June 12, 2000, the Garden reached its twenty-year milestone. On June 17, as part of their annual meeting, over three hundred HSA members and invited guests gathered for a luncheon in the NHG meadow to celebrate the occasion. Remarks were made by Dr. Tom Elias, HSA president Joyce

Brobst, HSA president-elect Mary Wohlleb, Sandy Salkeld deHoll, Betty Rea, Deputy Secretary of Agriculture Richard Rominger, and me. The guests included Tom Wirth; ARS administrator Floyd P. Horn; Dr. H. Marc Cathey, a former director of the USNA; and Skip March, former chief horticulturist of the USNA.

This garden, which began as a lofty dream fifteen years before it opened, has become one of the most influential gardens in American horticulture. Much has happened in the Garden in the past twenty-five years, and I expect just as much to happen in the next twenty-five. A special debt of gratitude is owed to all who have contributed their time, talents, and efforts to create the magnificent horticultural legacy known as the National Herb Garden.

Jim Adams

Curator, 1997–2005

Acknowledgments

This book gathers information from some of America's most respected herb authorities, all members of The Herb Society of America. They include Jim Adams, Madalene Hill, Rexford H. Talbert, Arthur O. Tucker, Lorraine Kiefer, and Scott Kresge. Barbara Brouse, Lori Schaeffer, Sandy Salkeld deHoll, Caroline Amidon, and Joyce Brobst also contributed research and articles.

A complete list of those generous members of The Herb Society who shared their favorite recipes is included at the end of the book, though their names deserve to be on the cover. Also deserving of thanks for their tireless commitment of time and energy are the many members of The Herb Society who tested and retested the recipes. Members of the U.S. National Arboretum staff, who have always been supportive of the relationship between The Herb Society of America and the National Herb Garden, also eagerly submitted and tested recipes. Their support for this project, and for all of the activities at the National Herb Garden, is greatly appreciated.

Special thanks go to Gloria McClure, who serves as the Botany and Horticulture committee chair for the HSA. It was Gloria who adopted this project when things looked bleak, infusing new optimism into our plans for the successful publication of the book. Rita Sillivan-Smith, former Botany and Horticulture chair, also championed the book throughout her term on the HSA board of directors. Thanks, too, go to Alisa Plant and the staff at LSU Press, whose vision and enthusiasm saw the book through the review and publication process.

Then there are the family members, especially my husband Steve, daughters Stephanie and Jennifer, son-in-law Boyd Stanley, and grandchildren Josh, Madison, and Carter, who patiently reviewed the work in progress, helped test many recipes, and put up with five years of books and papers scattered around the house. My sister Mimi Westervelt and her daughter Jessica pitched in when needed to help with organizing files, recipes, and correspondence. My brother, Eldon Karr, of the Architects' Design Group in Roanoke, Virginia, assisted with converting photographs to black-and-white images. Rex Talbert kindly and knowledgeably reviewed botanical names and engaged me in thoroughly interesting conversations on various topics as the project progressed. Art Tucker was always available to answer sticky questions of nomenclature. Anne Abbott's advice and gentle behind-the-scenes support was unfailing. Jim Adams's assistance was invaluable; he contributed articles, personal experiences, enthusiasm, and support for the project at every step of the way. Chrissy Moore's support was also unwavering as recipes were gathered, tested, and selected.

Herb Society of America members who have served on the National Herb Garden committee during the years this project has been underway have consistently provided enthusiasm and assistance, many of them sharing recipes and helping test recipes: Sandy Salkeld deHoll, Devah Brinker, Scott Kresge, Pat Johnsen, Jill Friestad, Lorraine Kiefer, Barbara Brouse, Anne Abbott, Rita Sillivan-Smith, Lori Schaeffer, Donna Baumgartner, Phyllis Burton, Barbara Angstadt, Peggy Conway, Kathy Bepler, Bernice Pivarnik, Betty and Ed Rea, Janet Walker, Liz Miller, Carol Chewning, Jeanne Pettersen, Sara Holland, Billi Parus, Jack and Kathy Donohoe, and Louise Taylor Smith.

The proceeds of this book will go into a fund at The Herb Society of America that provides the National Herb Garden with a full-time intern. Selected annually, the intern assists the curator with everyday garden chores and takes on an education project that fits the mission of both The Herb Society and the National Herb Garden. These projects have included the development of guides to the various gardens, creating plant labels for all of the gardens, and research to supplement plant records. Over the years the Garden has seen many talented interns and has benefited greatly from the time they spend with us. Our interim curator, Chrissy Moore, at one time served as an intern.

Members of The Herb Society of America have always generously supported the National Herb Garden, including regular and significant contributions to the intern fund. By purchasing this book, readers also contribute to that fund.

Katherine K. Schlosser

I | The Culinary Garden

Growing and Using Herbs

The Culinary Garden within the U.S. National Arboretum's Herb Garden contains sixty-three herbs, ranging from *Alliums* (onions, chives, and garlic) to *Zingiber* (ginger). This guidebook offers detailed information—including horticulture, recipes, and history—about each of these herbs. While not a comprehensive collection of culinary herbs, the Culinary Garden contains both familiar plants and a few slightly more exotic ones that you may want to try in your own garden. Also included in this book is information on each of the areas within the National Herb Garden. We hope not only to promote the culinary use of herbs, but also to foster a greater awareness of and appreciation for the Garden.

WHAT IS AN HERB?

The classic definition of an herb is any plant used for flavoring, food, fragrance, or medicine that is without a woody stem and that dies to the ground after flowering. This seemingly neat and tidy definition does not take into account some plants that are quite commonly known and used as herbs, yet have woody stems and do not die back—for instance, rosemary, sage, and lavender, as well as some trees. Many first-time visitors to the National Herb Garden are surprised to see twenty-five species of trees scattered throughout the Garden, sometimes assuming that they are there as structural or decorative elements. In fact, they are just a sampling of the trees that we use for food, flavoring, and medicine.

At the National Herb Garden, the definition offered by Henry Beston in *Herbs and the Earth* (1935) governs plant selections: "In its essential spirit, in its proper garden meaning, *an herb is a garden plant which has been cherished for itself and for a use* and has not come down to us as a purely decorative thing."[1] More recently, members of the National Herb Garden committee have recommended the adoption of the following definition:

> The term "herb" refers to seed-bearing, generally fleshy annuals, biennials, and perennials, aromatic or useful shrubs, vines, and trees. The defining characteristic for these plants is their usefulness, past or present, including their value for flavoring, medicine, ornament, economic, industrial, or cosmetic purposes. For the educational purposes of this garden, spices, traditionally defined as aromatic parts derived from the bark or seeds of a plant, may also be included within appropriate theme areas, depending upon the history and uses of the spice and the appropriateness of the plant to the garden.[2]

This definition allows us to include some trees, shrubs, vines, and roses in the Garden, complementing the fragrant little plants we commonly associate with the word *herb*.

GROWING HERBS

This guidebook provides basic horticultural information for each of the plants within the Culinary Garden, including general light and soil requirements and hardiness information. Hardiness refers to the average minimum low temperatures in which a plant will survive as a perennial (see table). Annuals are plants that are expected to die back at the end of the growing season. The plants selected for the National Herb Garden are those that successfully grow in its zone 7 climate. Some plants—such as lemongrass, lemon verbena, and pomegranates—are grown in the Garden but are taken into the greenhouse for the winter.

A map outlining hardiness zones in the United States is available at the USNA website: www.usna.usda.gov/Hardzone/ushzmap.html. Maps are also readily available in libraries and

Hardiness Zones

Zone	Avg. annual minimum temp.
1	-50° F.
2	-50° F. to -40° F.
3	-40° F. to -30° F.
4	-30° F. to -20° F.
5	-20° F. to -10° F.
6	-10° F. to 0° F.
7	0° F. to 10° F.
8	10° F. to 20° F.
9	20° F. to 30° F.
10	30° F. to 40° F.
11	above 40° F.

garden centers. Recent developments in hardiness mapping have divided zones into *a* (indicating the lower temperature limits within a zone) and *b* (indicating the higher temperature limits within a zone).

It is wise to take note of hardiness zones, but use them as general guidelines rather than as rules. Whether or not a plant will survive the winter in the ground depends on several things: the nature of the plant itself, the temperature range for any given year, the soil type and pH level (acidity), and the existence of microclimates—little areas within a garden that are warmer or cooler (or drier or wetter) than surrounding areas. Protection by walls, shrubs, or trees (which may hold warmth and protect a plant from winds) can create a microclimate as effectively as landform, proximity to water, and a host of other environmental conditions. An easy way to determine whether a plant can survive in your garden, even though it is described as hardy for a zone above or below that in which you live, is to try it. If you have—or create—a microclimate that mimics the conditions found in a plant's native habitat, your chances of success with that plant will be improved. Follow the advice of National Herb Garden staff: push the envelope a bit and try plants that garden books suggest are out of your zone.

For most herbs, drainage is almost as important as hardiness zones. Heavy clay soils subject roots to rot and suffocation. Amending the soil with compost and even digging down twelve to eighteen inches and adding a layer of gravel at the bottom of your planting area should help loosen the soil. Water then will be able to transport needed nutrients, and oxygen will allow the roots to breathe. Sandy soil can be equally difficult because it allows water to drain too fast, depleting not only water but nutrients. Amending sandy soil with lots of organic matter, such as compost or leaves, will help hold water in the planting area.

Most herbs grow well in soil that is in the mid-range on pH scales (around 6). If you are having difficulty with a plant, have already amended the soil, and know that it is getting the proper amount of light, water, and nutrients, you should check the acidity of the soil. Inexpensive soil test kits are available at most nurseries, or you can take a soil sample to your local cooperative extension office. Take soil samples from several areas of your garden, as the acidity can vary from spot to spot. Amend the soil as indicated from your test results, adding more or less lime as necessary. "Chicken grit," a product available in many feed and seed stores, is an inexpensive way to add a slow-release lime to soil.

FRESH OR DRIED HERBS?

Fresh herbs are almost always preferable to dried herbs for cooking. The most important deciding factor is aroma. If an herb, fresh or dry, smells good, use it; if there is little or no aroma, why bother? If you follow that rule of thumb, you may find that the herbs available dried in grocery stores, notably chives and parsley, have little to offer other than adding a touch of green to your dishes. It's much better to rely on fresh chives and parsley for flavor. Some herbs will, in fact, dry well, and modern spice and herb companies have excellent equipment for drying them with minor loss of flavor, but you may need to adjust the amounts when cooking. A long-held tradition is to substitute fresh for dry at a three-to-one ratio: three parts fresh herb for one part dry herb, or one tablespoon fresh herb for one teaspoon dry herb.

This simple rule cannot always be trusted, since different herbs contain different levels of volatile oils, which are retained through the drying process at different rates. In most cases, the oils are concentrated upon drying, so that less volume of the herb is necessary to get the flavor desired. Herb sprigs collected from a single plant can vary in intensity of flavor based on where on the plant you collect. Leaves closer to the growing tip are likely to have more oil glands and thus to be more flavorful than leaves closer to the base of the plant, which are older and may have already lost some of their volatile oils. The age of the plant can also have an effect on intensity of flavor. Basil, for instance, is more flavorful when harvested before the plant begins to flower, at which time some say that the leaves take on a slightly bitter taste. For that reason, many gardeners regularly prune their basil plants to keep them from flowering during the growing season. Not all herbs are affected by flowering. Lavender, for example, is harvested only after the flower buds have formed and begun to open, for it is the bud that is used rather than the leaves.

The flavor you get from dried herbs, no matter how carefully they are processed, will be different from that of fresh herbs, especially fresh herbs direct from your garden. The best rule to follow in cooking is, again, to use your nose and your palate. Start with a small amount of herb, fresh or dried, and add more to taste. In most dishes, it is best to add the herbs near the end of the cooking time, as the oils will evaporate rather quickly on heating. Some of the stronger herbs—such as rosemary, sage, and bay—will stand up to longer cooking times, however, and can be added earlier in the cooking process. In general, dried herbs can be added earlier than fresh herbs. For your health and comfort, remember to remove bay leaves at the end of cooking, as they are tough, fibrous, and can cause gastrointestinal distress if consumed. Unless finely minced, lemongrass and lemon verbena should also be removed before serving a dish, as they too are tough and difficult to digest. With a little experimenting, you will soon discover whether you need to add more or less of an herb the next time you prepare a recipe. Follow the standard three-to-one ratio if you must, but when it comes to seasonings, most recipes are simply guides. You may easily adjust amounts to suit your own tastes.

Purchase dried herbs in small amounts, and in whole-leaf form when you can. Kept in glass containers in a cool, dry, dark spot, dried herbs will keep for six months or more. Fragrance is by far the best guide for determining shelf life. Like coffee beans, if they do not elicit an "Ahhh" when you open the container, they are likely to disappoint when you use them.

Fresh is best, but dried is better than none! In fact, lavender buds are best used dried. Fresh bay leaves are best for dessert dishes, but dried are great in long-simmering soups and stews.

ABOUT SPICES

A common question concerns the shelf life of spices, and the answer is relatively simple. Ground spices lose their flavor faster than whole spices, as more surface area is exposed to air, even in a tightly closed jar. Spices' volatile oils begin to evaporate just as soon as they are ground. You may be able to keep some for six months, perhaps a year, but their quality will deteriorate. If you purchase ground spices, check them periodically. If you don't get that strong, familiar fragrance the moment you open your jar, it's time to replace the spice.

If you have not tried whole spices, start with a few whole nutmegs. Inexpensive tin nutmeg graters are available in most grocery stores; you can also find antique versions in silver, pewter, or bone. All are simple and allow you to grate exactly the amount you need. Try a recipe calling for fresh nutmeg, or just grate a little over some green beans, spinach, or a dish of vanilla ice cream. You won't need as much as you are accustomed to using, and you aren't likely to go back to the commercially ground version. The difference is amazing.

Grinding cloves at home is a little more complicated, but if you have a coffee mill that you can dedicate to herbs, give it a try, grinding just what you need for a given recipe. Mills that use grinders rather than blades produce the most satisfactory results, as they produce less heat, which destroys some of the cloves' volatile oils. You can also use a mortar and pestle, grinding the cloves to a powder. Both these methods may give you a coarser grind than that to which you are accustomed, but the flavor will be great. You will find that you can keep whole cloves and nutmeg for years.

Use your judgment about other spices. It is possible to grind peppers to create your own paprika, but the volatile oils released into the air can cause respiratory distress and burning eyes. Since very fine paprika is available commercially, spend the money to buy new batches regularly. The variety available in supermarkets is usually bland. If you want sweet, spicy, or smoky paprika, try an upscale grocery store or look online for a vendor.

Whole or ground, spices are best kept in glass containers in a cool, dry spot. HSA member Scott Kresge recommends keeping your whole spices in the freezer, removing just the amount needed for a recipe, toasting the spices lightly in a frying pan, and then grinding them immediately.

HARVESTING HERBS

The recipes in this book usually recommend fresh herbs, which may be collected at any time of day and kept in a jar of water, as you would a bouquet of flowers, until ready to use. If you gather your herbs in the morning for use later that night or within the following few days, store them in the refrigerator wrapped lightly in paper towels to absorb any extra moisture. Some people feel that the best time of day to harvest herbs is in the morning, before the sun has time to heat up and release some of the plants' volatile oils.

Herbs are easy to harvest. For plants with small leaves, such as thyme, cut a sprig or more about six inches long. Wash and dry the sprig; then, holding the stem at the tip, lightly grasp the stem and pull backwards toward the base. The small leaves will pop off in your hand (or over a plate). Discard any small pieces of woody stem. Small leaves can be used without further preparation, or they can be chopped if desired.

Larger-leafed herbs, such as basil, tarragon, oregano, mint, and sage, can be handled in a similar manner, or their leaves can be plucked individually. Large-leafed herbs can be used whole, or they can be cut. A mezzaluna (usually a two-bladed chopping device that rocks back and forth) or a pair of sharp kitchen scissors will do the best job. Basil does best when cut with scissors, as using a knife often leaves a little blackening along the edges of the leaf. Stack the leaves to make quick work of the job.

Dill and fennel leaves can be snapped off close to the stem, then simply snipped with kitchen scissors.

Chervil, parsley, cilantro, and lovage can be cut in bunches, cleaned, and chopped with a knife or mezzaluna.

Cut chives when they are about six to eight inches tall. Grasp a small handful and cut them nearly to the ground. After washing, simply snip them to the desired size with kitchen scissors.

Cut sprigs of rosemary to the desired length, removing no more than about a third of the length of a stem. Wash and dry the sprigs, then snip the leaves off into small pieces while holding the stem in your hand. Rosemary sprigs can also be used whole in soups and stews. Just pop the sprig into the simmering pot and remove it before serving.

Tough leaves, such a lemon verbena, must be minced or even run through a small food processor to get pieces small enough to use. When appropriate, use the leaves whole and remove them before serving. To get the flavor without worrying about the fibrous nature of the leaf, make a strong "tea" or simple syrup using the leaves and then substitute it for part of the liquid in the recipe.

When using lemongrass, cut a stalk from the plant very close to the base, being careful not to cut your hands on the sharp edges of the leaves (especially if you run your hand from the tip of a leaf to its base). Use the lower, whitish portion of the stalk; clean and mince or process. This is another tough, fibrous herb, so the best way to use it is to steep or sauté it while whole and remove it from the dish before serving.

Use only clean herbs and vegetables in your recipes. We recommend following the advice of Arthur Tucker and Thomas DeBaggio: clean your herbs with a spray of 3 percent hydrogen peroxide and then a spray of household vinegar.[3] Both of these items are available in any grocery store, and you can use a simple household sprayer. Wash your herbs to dislodge any visible dirt and insects, spray lightly with the peroxide, and spray again with the vinegar. Allow the herbs to sit for a while, then rinse them once again in cool and clear water before using. This process will help to destroy any E. coli bacteria that might be present from the soil. This is especially important if you purchase fresh herbs and don't know how they were collected or processed. Never use fresh herbs from the grocery—or from your garden—without first washing them.

The best advice is to grow your own herbs, whether in a large garden or in a small container outside your kitchen door.

Herbs in the Culinary Garden

The herbs growing in the National Herb Garden's Culinary Garden all have a long history of use for flavoring foods, each providing a unique taste and aroma to foods that are sometimes bland. Many of these plants are so closely associated with the cuisine of a particular country or region that they are immediately recognized even by the young, who readily make the connection between pizza and oregano. Who can smell fresh basil without thinking of tomatoes, or dill without thinking of fish? Following are short descriptions of each of the plants in the Culinary Garden, along with a little horticultural information about them and some suggestions for using them in your kitchen.

Each of the herbs described below is listed first by its common name followed by its botanical name. Common names lead to considerable confusion, as the same plant may be known by a different name based on location or tradition. Botanical names are reviewed and recorded by the International Botanical Congress. This organization maintains the International Botanical Code on Nomenclature, which contains rules for naming plants. Botanical names change from time to time, but they are the standard names recognized worldwide. A botanical name is generally a two-part name, identifying first the genus and then the specific epithet. For example, the name assigned for garlic is *Allium sativum* L. A name or initial following a specific epithet indicates the person credited with first identifying the plant—in this example, the eighteenth-century botanist and taxonomist Carl Linnaeus.

Plant classification is a way to group plants based on similarity of physical characteristics. Categories within the system are general at the top and increasingly more specific toward the bottom. In the descriptions below, the botanical name is followed by the family to which the plant belongs. Also provided are the country or area of origin for the plant, the hardiness of the plant, and general light and soil requirements for growing the plant.

AMARANTH, PURPLE AMARANTH, RED AMARANTH

Amaranthus cruentus

Family: Amaranthaceae

Origin: Central America

Hardiness: annual

Light/Soil: full sun/well-drained soil

Amaranth is a powerhouse of a plant. It is striking in size—up to six feet tall—and grows in a rainbow of colors from green to red to purplish bronze. It packs a punch for nutritional value too, with seeds that are 16 percent protein. The seeds are used as a cereal, ground into flour, or sprouted. Not a true grain, amaranth is a broad-leaved plant with a flower head of feathery plumes.

Native to Central America, amaranth has spread widely in tropical and subtropical areas of the world, and it has a long history of cultivation for food, medicine, and use in religious ritual. Pre-Columbian Aztecs mixed the seeds with honey and formed the mixture into idols that sometimes resembled mountain deities or human leaders, which were broken into pieces and ceremonially eaten. Spanish conquerors, with a distaste for idol worship, forbade the planting of amaranth, hoping to end the practice that they felt too closely resembled the Christian eucharist.

The plant is easily grown from seed sown directly in the garden when the ground is warm. Not fussy at all, amaranth will grow in sandy, clay, or loam soils. The seedlings need moisture, but as the plant matures it will tolerate dry conditions. In order to produce showy flower heads and a bountiful crop of seeds, the plant does need lots of sunshine. The seedheads will mature in about 110 days, and they are ready for harvest in late summer. Harvested plants are left to dry in the field, and the tiny seeds are separated by threshing, which yields as many as forty thousand seeds per plant.

Amaranth products are widely available, making it unnecessary to thresh our own amaranth. It can be found in the form of cereals, pasta products, and breads in many grocery stores. Amaranth flour is also available and can be mixed at a one-to-four ratio with white flour for use in breads and baked goods. For flatbreads, amaranth flour can be used full strength. Boiling equal parts of seed and water for ten to fifteen minutes yields a substance similar to grits, which may then be added to soups or stews or eaten as a cereal.

Young amaranth leaves are edible when boiled and are eaten much like spinach. They can also be used in soups, casseroles, and rice dishes. Amaranth is also grown in the National Herb Garden's Dye Garden. The plant produces a reddish color that was used by Hopi Indians to color their traditional piki bread for kachina ceremonies, which honored the friendly rain gods. Piki is a paper-thin bread made with green juniper ashes, sunflower oil, blue cornmeal, and water. The breads were quickly cooked on hot stones and rolled to serve.

ANISE, ANISEED

....

Pimpinella anisum
Family: Apiaceae
Origin: Asia
Hardiness: annual
Light/Soil: full sun/light,
    moist soil

Anise, or aniseed, is one of those spices seldom receiving the attention it deserves. Known primarily for its seeds, which are really fruits, anise provides a spicy, sweet licorice flavor to breads, cakes, biscotti, and beverages. The seeds are so readily available that most of us don't give much thought to their source, which happens to be a lovely garden plant.

Anise grows to about eighteen inches in height, with finely divided leaves and umbels of tiny, creamy white flowers. It needs well-drained, slightly sandy soil, full sun, and 120 frost-free days to set fruit, from which you will be able to gather one to two tablespoons of seeds per plant.[1] Anise is an annual plant that you can easily grow from seed sown after the soil has warmed. Regular watering is required if your garden is in a period of drought. If the plant gets spindly, tie the main stem to a small stake in order to keep it upright. It is easy to confuse members of the Apiaceae family, which includes poison hemlock, so be absolutely certain that you are harvesting the correct plant before consuming any part of it. While waiting for the seeds to develop, harvest a few leaves to sprinkle on salads or use them as a garnish on soups or meat (especially pork and lamb) stews.

Anise has a long history of culinary use, having appeared on the tables of ancient Greeks and Egyptians. In *A Modern Herbal* (1931), Maud Grieve suggests that the little spiced cakes called *mustacae* (which included anise) served at the end of Roman feasts to aid digestion may have been the origin of the spiced wedding cakes that we serve today.[2] Dioscorides included anise in his books, recognizing it as an effective remedy for coughs and bronchial infections, asthma, and as a carminative. Anise has been used to flavor dental preparations and has even been claimed as an aphrodisiac. It is probably best-known today for its use in flavoring liqueurs such as ouzo and Pernod, as well as candies known as licorice. One of the most unusual claims about anise is that a bit of its distilled oil wiped onto a fishing lure will increase the chances of a successful freshwater catch.[3]

ARUGULA

Eruca vesicaria subsp. *sativa*

Family: Brassicaceae

Origin: Mediterranean

Hardiness: annual/self-seeding biennial

Light/Soil: full sun/rich, moist soil

Arugula is called *rocola* in Italy and *roquette* in France; it is sometimes known as "rocket." If you like a pungent flavor in your salad, plan to grow arugula in early spring. As long as the weather stays cool, its small leaves are wonderful when cut and tossed in a salad. When the weather gets hot, arugula will flower quickly, much as radishes do; its flowers then make a spicy garnish for soups and salads. Left to reseed, it will come up for a fall crop of tasty greens. Some gardeners like to seed it successively over several weeks for a harvest that lasts almost all year long. Frosts hardly bother the plant at all, so seeding in March and April in many areas works well.

To plant the seeds, hoe or turn the soil in a garden row. Rake the soil well and mix in some compost. Rake once more and make an indentation in the soil, into which you sprinkle the seeds. Gently tamp the seeds into the soil, leaving them uncovered, and water well. A good, rich soil with lots of compost and regular watering will keep this plant looking and tasting good. You can also mix the seeds with flowers in a flowerbed.

For the best flavor, harvest leaves when they are three inches tall. The plants will continue to grow if some leaves are left. They add a peppery and nutty flavor to a salad. These greens can also be used on meats and fish or in sandwiches. Older leaves of arugula, large and slightly bitter, can be chopped and added to soups, stews, vegetable sautés, or casseroles.

ASAFOETIDA

Ferula assa-foetida
Family: Apiaceae
Origin: Middle East and India
Hardiness: zone 7
Light/Soil: full sun/moist soil

Asafoetida is unusual in its method of preparation and is unfamiliar to most Americans, though many have consumed it in the form of Worcestershire sauce, in which it is an essential ingredient.[4] The high content of sulfur compounds in asafoetida gives it a strong odor of garlic. It has long served as a substitute for garlic and onions in cultures that shun those herbs, for it adds an earthy depth of flavor to otherwise bland dishes without leaving unpleasant aftereffects.[5]

In the garden, the soft green leaves of asafoetida have a lacy look, almost like southernwood. The plants reach a lush and elegant seven feet when in bloom, with umbels of small yellow flowers. Asafoetida will grow in most soils, but it does best when consistently moist. Once the plant is mature, it can be tapped for resin. The soil around the plant's crown is removed to reveal the top of the root. An incision is made in the root, from which a malodorous resin seeps. The resin is scraped away and allowed to dry in a lump. The fleshy root may be tapped again, or it can be pulled from the ground and sliced to release the resin.

Asafoetida is sold in small resinous lumps or in powdered form. As a powder, asafoetida is less pungent, though still strong enough to make one wonder who first added it to food. A small lump of resin—no more than the size of a pea is adequate for a large pot of food—is dropped into a couple of tablespoons of hot olive oil, which allows the resin to melt and infuse the oil with flavor. As the asafoetida cooks, its flavor mellows, and it no longer produces the strong odor that gives rise to one of its common names, "devil's dung." Remove the oil from the heat and use it, a few drops at a time, as a flavoring agent in the dish you are preparing. Powdered asafoetida sometimes includes wheat as a filler, but it may be handled in the same manner. Asafoetida is a classic ingredient in Indian dal dishes, which are recipes centered on legumes and often combined with cumin. In Middle Eastern countries, asafoetida is a traditional ingredient of meatballs and pickles.

Asafoetida is believed by some to have been a lesser-quality substitute for silphion, a fennel-like plant of culinary value to Romans but most highly valued for its reputed effectiveness as a birth-control substance. Silphion was so highly revered that it appeared on Roman coins. By the second century BCE, however, it was extinct, possibly because of overharvesting.

BASIL

Ocimum spp.

Family: Lamiaceae

Origin: Africa, India, Malaysia, China, Europe, Australia, South America

Hardiness: annual except in some frost-free areas

Light/Soil: full sun/well-drained, rich soil

There is little in the garden that is more sensual than brushing past a basil plant, running your hands through its soft green leaves and releasing their warm, sweet fragrance. It makes tending the garden a pleasure, and, given proper sun and moisture, it is such a prolific producer of leaves that you will have plenty to use fresh and to prepare for use when the ground freezes.

There are about sixty-four species of *Ocimum*, all native to the tropics and subtropics, and thus frost-tender. They are shrubby plants, growing from eighteen inches to a reported six and a half feet tall, and they require full sun, good drainage, and plenty of moisture.[6] The plants root easily from cuttings placed in water, so you can multiply your crop quickly and inexpensively. Pinching off the blossoms as they begin to form will keep the plants producing leaves throughout summer and into early fall. Basil plants may be harvested as soon as they begin to reach their mature height, if you can wait that long. Just be sure to leave enough of the plant that it can continue to grow. If the plant flowers, you can use the blooms too—try tossing a few into your salads, soups, or baked goods.

The fragrance of various cultivars ranges from anise, cinnamon, clove, and thyme to lemon, camphor, and floral tones. Cinnamon basil goes well with chocolate, lemon-scented cultivars are wonderful with fish, and anise-scented basils are good with fruits and desserts. The basil most commonly sought is *O. basilicum* (sweet basil). Cultivars include 'Lettuce Leaf', 'Italian', 'Genoa Green', and 'Purple Ruffles'. These are best when eaten fresh, pairing nicely with tomato dishes. There is little better in this world than a sandwich of homemade whole wheat bread, thick slices of homegrown tomato still warm from the garden, a little mayonnaise, and a big handful of fresh basil. 'Greek Columnar' (*O.* ×*citriodorum*), also known as 'Lesbos' and 'Aussie Sweetie', gives quick and fragrant structure to a garden, as well as being a great source for pesto. 'Dark Opal' is a lovely choice for herb butter: try mixing a stick of softened butter with 'Dark Opal' basil, a little honey, and a few chopped cranberries. Spread on toast or biscuits, it makes a mouth-watering treat.

Plant lots of basil in all of its variety—you won't be disappointed. Once you have grown your own, you will wonder why anyone bothers with the dried basil available in grocery stores.

BAY LAUREL

Laurus nobilis

Family: Lauraceae

Origin: Asia

Hardiness: to zone 8

Light/Soil: full sun/average soil

A classic symbol of victory for heroes and athletes, bay laurel has won the hearts and taste buds of cooks and bakers. Native to Asia Minor, the leaves of this evergreen tree are used in savory as well as sweet dishes. In North America, bay laurel prefers hot summers, growing in full sun or very light shade. Because it is not reliably hardy in zones 7 and colder, many people grow it in a container and over-winter it in a cool, dry space with plenty of light.

Whether in the ground or in a pot, bay laurel flourishes in a loose, well-drained soil. It can easily be trained into a standard or other topiary shapes. Bay leaves may be harvested at any time of the year and used fresh or harvested in summer to be dried. Fresh leaves usually have a stronger flavor than dried. The leaves can be powdered or crushed, but they are most often used whole and added to a dish. They should be removed before serving because their large size and rough texture makes for an unpleasant eating experience and can even cause injury if ingested.[7]

According to ancient belief, a bay laurel tree planted next to a doorway prevented evil spirits from entering a house. The tree also protected the house and its inhabitants from the danger of thunder and lightning storms. Also, it was believed that people who carried a sprig of bay laurel were protected from evil sprits.

BLACK CUMIN

Nigella sativa

Family: Ranunculaceae

Origin: western Asia, the
Middle East

Hardiness: annual

Light/Soil: sun/loamy soil

Growing in a sunny spot in the Culinary Garden at the National Herb Garden is a lovely plant two to three feet tall, with wispy leaves and pretty five-petalled white flowers with blue veining. As pretty as *Nigella sativa* is, it is the seeds of black cumin that have attracted the attention of herbalists and cooks for many centuries. The seed capsule has five compartments, each topped with a little spike. When mature, the capsules open to spill out their treasure of tiny black triangular seeds.

The raw seeds have little aroma, but their flavor is released when rubbed lightly. Toasting or roasting intensifies their flavor, which many find reminiscent of oregano. Native to western Asia, the seeds are an important part of medicinal and culinary traditions in the Middle East, Europe, and more recently the United States. Some claim that an obscure plant mentioned by the prophet Isaiah in the Old Testament is black cumin: "For the fitches [*N. sativa*] are not thrashed with a threshing instrument . . . but the fitches are beaten out with a staff."[8] The Prophet Muhammad recommended the use of black cumin as a remedy for every illness except death.[9]

Turkish flatbread is traditionally sprinkled with black cumin before baking, and it is often an ingredient of five-spice and garam masala blends. Black cumin is also often added to vegetable dishes.

Plant the seeds in the garden after the last frost, then thin the plants to four to six inches apart. In warmer climates (zone 7 and higher), it will reseed.

The common cottage garden flower, Love-in-a-Mist (*N. damascena*), is closely related to black cumin and also has edible seeds. They lack the flavor of *N. sativa*, however, so enjoy them for the flowers and look for black cumin for use in the kitchen.

CAPERS

Capparis spinosa

Family: Capparaceae

Origin: Mediterranean and
Middle East

Hardiness: zone 9

Light/Soil: full sun/well-drained,
light soil

Capers thrive in hot, dry climates. In the United States, the best locations for growing these small shrubs are California and the Southwest. With a little coaxing, however, they can grow in other parts of the country. In zones 8 and lower, they can be grown either in a protected spot or in a container or trough. They need excellent drainage, and once established are extremely drought tolerant. In colder regions, temperatures hovering close to freezing will kill the plants if they are exposed for more than a few days.

Grown in the garden or in a container, capers make lovely specimens that can grow to a five-foot-high mounding shrub. The branches are long, with a sprawling habit, and look best trailing down a wall or over a rock. The plants have small, dark-green, rounded leaves that give an interesting texture to a garden. Because the flower buds are picked for their tasty pickled flavor, the flower is seldom seen. However, if a bud escapes the harvester, a two-inch or larger, white, delicate flower with dark pink or purple stamens opens. Plants are difficult to grow from seed, as germination is sporadic and can take anywhere from two weeks to four months. Propagation is much easier and more reliable from cuttings.

Most people are surprised to hear that capers are not a fruit or vegetable, but actually a flower bud. The tight buds are harvested from late spring through early autumn and pickled in vinegar and brine in the same manner as cucumbers. Commercially, the smaller buds, known as Nonpareilles or Surfines, are more valuable. Larger ones are known as Capucines or Communes.

In the National Herb Garden, capers are most often grown in a trough so they can be brought into the greenhouse for the winter. On some occasions, the troughs are on display in the Entrance Garden.

CARAWAY

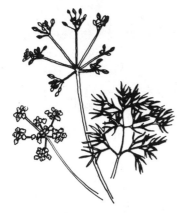

Carum carvi

Family: Apiaceae

Origin: Asia, central Europe

Hardiness: zones 3–9

Light/Soil: full sun to part shade/
rich, well-drained soil

Caraway is a lovely, fern-leafed plant. In late spring it is covered in lacy white flowers. There are two forms of caraway, an annual and a biennial; the more common is the biennial.

The biennial, planted in late spring to midsummer, will grow and form clumps of leaves. The following spring it will send up flower spikes that will ripen into flavorful caraway seeds. A large plant will yield about a third of a cup of caraway seed.[10] Annual forms can be sown in early spring and will be ready for harvest in mid- to late summer. The annual form is not as flavorful as the biennial, but it is preferred by commercial growers because of higher seed yields and ease of harvesting. Biennial forms tend to have dark brown seeds, while the seeds of annual forms tend to be light brown or blond. The seeds of biennials are the more flavorful, having a higher oil content.

For either type, seeds should be harvested as the older seeds begin to ripen and dry. Seeds will continue to ripen once the seedhead is picked, so dry the seedheads on screens that can catch seeds or else hang clusters of seedheads upside-down in a paper bag for a week or more to catch falling seeds. A few seedheads should be left in the garden to allow the plant to self-sow.

Rye bread and sauerkraut—staples of German and Austrian cuisine—are the most well-known foods associated with caraway. Perhaps because of this, caraway is known in many languages as German cumin.

CARDAMOM

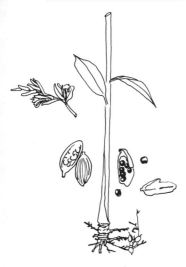

Elettaria cardamomum
Family: Zingiberaceae
Origin: India
Hardiness: frost sensitive
Light/Soil: sun to part shade/
 rich, moist soil

Several related plants are called cardamom, all of which have slightly different flavors, but only *Elettaria cardamomum* has culinary importance. It differs from other cardamom species by having a eucalyptus—not a camphor—scent. Although the leaves give off a delightful smell of cardamom when rubbed, it is the seed that is used for flavoring. Green seed pods are the most flavorful but lose their intensity quickly. They should be left whole until they are needed, at which time they should be freshly ground. Peel off the tight papery skin from a few cardamom pods, releasing the fragrant seeds, which can be ground or used whole according to the recipe. Ground seeds lose flavor even more quickly than whole seeds, so if you purchase ground cardamom, do so in small amounts that you will use quickly.

Cardamom grows in the warm, shady, rain forest in the mountainous regions of India and Sri Lanka. This large tropical plant will grow to six feet tall and will only survive outdoors in the warmest parts of North America. In colder climates, cardamom makes a handsome container specimen, which needs to be wintered indoors. However, cardamom rarely flowers when grown in a container, thus never producing seed. No matter where it is grown, cardamom prefers to be kept slightly pot-bound, moist, and shady. In the National Herb Garden, two large specimens can be seen growing in pots placed under the grape arbors.

Cardamom is an essential flavoring for curries and Arabian coffee. It is also used in spiced teas and mulled wine, and it makes an excellent flavoring for creamy desserts, such as bread pudding.

CHERVIL

Anthriscus cerefolium

Family: Apiaceae

Origin: southern Europe

Hardiness: zones 3–8

Light/Soil: spring and winter
   sun, light shade in summer/
   rich, well-drained soil

The sheen of chervil's pale green, lacy leaves make it tempting to use this herb as a garnish in much the same way that parsley is used. Its distinct flavor—similar to parsley, with a hint of anise—reveals its true value, that of a delicate seasoning for early spring vegetables, eggs, poultry, and fish. Chervil is native to the southern regions of Europe but has been adopted by many cultures. It is a classic of French cuisine, appearing in blends of fines herbes and sometimes substituted for parsley in bouquet garni and herbes de Provence.

Chervil is most attractive in the garden in early spring and the fall, growing best in cooler temperatures and with some protection from the strong summer sun. Seeds sown directly in the garden in the fall or very early spring will produce plants that reach twelve to eighteen inches in height, during which time they can be harvested for fresh use. As summer temperatures rise, the plants will send up flower stalks that can reach twenty-eight inches, with umbels of tiny white flowers. The plants then produce seeds, which are dropped to the ground, lying dormant until cooler temperatures arrive. Provide evenly moist, well-drained soil, and plenty of sun in the spring for a good crop of fresh chervil.

As is true with many herbs, chervil quickly loses its flavor when dried or exposed to long cooking times. When using fresh chervil in cooked dishes, add it five to ten minutes before serving. The flavor of chervil is preserved nicely in vinegars and can be used to make pesto. Simply process fresh chervil leaves, grated pecorino cheese, pine nuts, garlic, and olive oil. The resulting pesto will have a delicate flavor and is delicious in soups, fish dishes, and eggs.

Chervil is a classic ingredient of béarnaise sauce, and it is delightful tossed into spring salads. It does the same things for food that parsley does, but with a lighter, more delicate touch.

CHILE PEPPERS

Capsicum spp.

Family: Solanaceae

Origin: South America

Hardiness: annuals except in
    frost-free areas

Light/Soil: full sun/well-drained
    soil

In the Chile Pepper Collection at the National Herb Garden, within a border stretching about forty feet, are peppers that will please the palates of chile aficionados, from the "Yeow!" of the orange habanero (*C. chinense*), with a Scoville rating nearing 300,000 units, to the almost cool poblano pepper (*C. annuum*), with a 1,000-unit Scoville rating. (The Scoville scale measures the pungency, or heat, of various peppers.) In addition to heat, true chile fans are in search of complexity of flavor, which ranges from sweet and fruity to smoky and earthy.

Capsaicin is responsible for the bite in chiles, and it can range from 0 to 500,000 or more Scoville units. The Scoville scale is a subjective measure of capsaicin content based on human testers and has recently been replaced with a more objective measure, based on high-performance liquid chromatography.[11] 'Red Savina' and 'Chocolate' habaneros (*C. chinense*) have the highest heat ratings.

When selecting peppers, keep in mind that dried chiles are usually hotter than fresh. Heat levels can be affected by the climate in which the plants are grown, with cooler temperatures significantly reducing the heat. Chiles are also known to vary from pod to pod on the same plant. To reduce heat just a bit, remove the veins that hold the seeds. The seeds themselves have little to no capsaicin, but the placenta in which they grow have the highest content in the plant. Removing the veins allows more of the subtle flavor of the chile to infuse your food, with less of the heat. If you love the heat, toss a whole chile (or two or three) into your dish.

Chiles have been popular flavorings for a long time; archaeological evidence dates their use in cuisine as far back as 7500 BCE.[12] Native to South America, they worked their way north and were quickly adopted in Central America and Mexico. Christopher Columbus was indirectly responsible for the movement of *Capsicum* species to Europe. Although the physician on Columbus's voyages, Alvarez Chauca of Seville, was interested primarily in black pepper, cinnamon, and nutmeg, he did take note of the spicy peppers favored by the natives.

Heat Rating of Chiles

Cultivar	Species	ASTA rating*	Cultivar	Species	ASTA rating*
'Cherry'	C. annuum	1	'Rocotillo'	C. chinense	7
'Anaheim'	C. annuum	2	'Tabasco'	C. frutescens	8
'Ancho'	C. annuum	3	'Rocoto'	C. pubescens	8
'Floral Gem'	C. annuum	5	Scotch bonnet	C. chinense	9
'Jalapeno'	C. annuum	5	'Habanero'	C. chinense	10
'Serrano'	C. annuum	6			

*ASTA rating (10 = hottest)

Seeds of the plants were taken to Spain in 1494, where they were adopted into the gardens of the wealthy.[13] Chauca described chiles as useful in "dressing meats, dyeing, and other purposes, as well as a medicine."[14] *Capsicum* species quickly spread across the globe, influencing regional cuisine dramatically. There are some areas—notably Thailand, Sri Lanka, Jamaica, and the Sichuan province of China—known for their fiery foods. Western Europe and most of North America were slower to acquire a taste for chiles, but they have achieved almost a cult status among enthusiasts.

Chile plants are readily available in nurseries. They can be grown from seed, but they require a little patience as they take up to two weeks to germinate. Germination is speeded by soaking the seeds for three days prior to sowing, and by providing temperatures of 70° to 80° F. The plants need full sun and regular watering once fruit is set. Most chile plants require at least 130 days to produce a crop, and those should be warm, sunny days with a temperature range of 72° to 90° F. for the best-quality chiles with the highest heat.

Chiles may be used fresh from the plant, dried, frozen, or preserved in vinegar. When working with chiles, wear gloves and do not touch your eyes, as the capsaicin will burn. If you eat a chile that is too hot for your taste, drink milk or eat some yogurt or sour cream. Water won't help, nor will bread or carbonated beverages. If you would like to try working your way up the heat scale, try some of the chiles above.

CHIVES AND GARLIC CHIVES

Allium spp.

Family: Lilaceae

Origin: Asia, Europe, North America

Hardiness: to zone 5

Light/Soil: full sun/well-drained soil

Chives are one of the easiest herbs to grow and one of the simplest to use. Their delicate, onion-like flavor makes them a must for every kitchen, and they are best used fresh. Outdoor plants begin to grow early in the spring, and the grass-like leaves can be harvested almost immediately. They should be harvested from the outside of the clump and can be picked by hand or cut with scissors. In late spring the clump will send up purple flowers on thick stems. The flowers can be picked as well and eaten fresh or used to flavor vinegar. When harvesting flowers for use, choose only young flowers that have not yet begun to set seed. To keep a fresh supply of chives available for easy picking all summer, cut the entire clump back to the ground after the flowers have started to fade and some of the leaves have begun to yellow. There are several cultivars available that offer brighter or larger flowers, such as 'Forescate', which has large, bright pink flowers. Another cultivar, 'Sterile' (Profusion™), boasts flowers that do not set seed, making them more desirable to be used fresh.

Garlic chives, a lesser-known species, are just as easy to grow and as useful as chives. Garlic chives are the Asian counterpart to chives and have a delicate garlic flavor. Blooming in late summer, the large, white flowers are edible when young and tender, before the seed matures. The plants have a tendency to spread by seed in a garden so picking the flowers before the seed ripens is recommended.

CILANTRO, CORIANDER

Coriandrum sativum

Family: Apiaceae

Origin: Mediterranean

Hardiness: annual

Light/Soil: sun to part shade/
moderately rich, moist soil

If you like salsa, guacamole, or stir-fry, chances are you like cilantro. This plant, which is suddenly popular in many styles of cooking, is really an ancient herb. It dates back to biblical times and was a main seasoning in Chinese, Mediterranean, and even Greek cooking. Egyptians used it and often buried their dead with the seeds.

Cilantro is sometimes a bit tricky and gardeners are not always successful in growing it. The best way to ensure success is to plant successively—to plant a few plants and then sprinkle some seeds around them. Harvest the plants when they are about six inches high so that they will not go to seed. When the seedlings begin to emerge, wait two weeks and then sprinkle a few more seeds where there is space. Every couple of weeks thereafter, sprinkle a few more seeds. The plants like a moderately rich soil with good drainage. They will grow in full sun or part shade, but remember to keep the plants, especially seedlings, watered well. Do not allow them to dry out and wilt. The oldest plants may be allowed to go to seed, and then the ripe seeds will fall and sprout.

Cilantro is sometimes called Chinese parsley, but the seeds of the plant are called coriander. Use the seeds for a delicious surprise in banana bread. The seeds are only used when dry and usually are ground except in pickles. They are used in fruits, breads, sausage, and as an important ingredient in curry powder.

CUMIN

Cuminum cyminum

Family: Apiaceae

Origin: Asia or Egypt

Hardiness: will withstand
light frost

Light/Soil: full sun/moist,
not wet, soil

Cumin deserves to be more frequently used in American kitchens. Its warm, earthy fragrance has long been appreciated by cooks in Latin America, Asia, and North Africa, but it has only recently been widely used in North America and Europe. It often gets an undeserved reputation as a hot spice because it is frequently used in dishes with chiles, black peppers, and mustards. It is an ingredient in curries, garam masala, and tandoori blends.

Cumin has been cultivated for thousands of years. Its small, crescent-shaped seeds (which are actually fruits) are roasted and lightly rubbed between the palms of the hands to release their fragrance.[15] The seeds can also be ground, making their use easy, but causing them quickly to lose their flavor, so if you purchase ground cumin, look for small packages. If you grow your own, grind only what you need.

The cumin plant is small, growing on average to about sixteen inches, with umbel-like flowers and thin, feathery leaves. It is an interesting specimen for the garden, though a bit finicky, so you shouldn't count on a large harvest. Tucker and DeBaggio advise home gardeners to grow cumin in a container.[16] Unless you grow a lot of plants, you are better advised to rely on commercial producers for your supply.

Toast cumin seeds in a dry sauté pan over medium heat for just a minute or two. Remove from heat and crush lightly in a mortar using a pestle. Toss the seeds into soups, stews, and meat dishes. Their flavor adds wonderful depth to beans, lentils, and potatoes.

DANDELION

Taraxacum officinale

Family: Asteraceae

Origin: Eurasia

Hardiness: zones 3–10

Light/Soil: full sun/moist to
dry soil

As funny as it seems, those of you with a natural lawn can pick a wonderful batch of greens for a delicious soup or salad in the spring! Both dandelion and violet leaves are rich in vitamins and have restorative properties for promoting good health. To many, the dandelion is a legendary jewel because of centuries of its use against infections, as well as for liver and memory problems.

Dandelion wine has long been consumed as a healthy tonic year-round because it preserves the therapeutic qualities of the blooms. Beverages made from dandelion root and countless dishes made with the plant's green leaves can be found in a number of cookbooks.

Most people would laugh if someone admitted to planting this common weed in their garden, yet today's supermarkets buy vast amounts of dandelion from farmers who grow it for market. Dandelion gets its name from a corruption of the French *dent de lion,* which means "teeth of the lion," because of the configuration of the jagged periphery of its leaves. High in vitamin A, vitamin C, and iron, this green is also low in calories and fat.

Dandelion is most readily available in spring and can be harvested for tender salad greens. Always try to pick the youngest leaves before blooms appear. Only harvest from lawns that are free of chemical pesticides and far from roads where there is much traffic. Be sure to wash the greens well before you use them.

Dandelion greens are around most of the season. While tender young leaves in the spring are great eaten fresh, the larger and more mature leaves can be blanched in boiling water until tender and then sautéed in butter or olive oil. They can be served over pasta or as a side dish, or simply given a squeeze of lemon juice and enjoyed with crusty buttered bread and cheese. Any leftover greens can be tossed into an omelet or casserole. Most supermarkets have them both in and out of season.

DILL

Anethum graveolens

Family: Apiaceae

Origin: Eurasia

Hardiness: annual

Light/Soil: full sun/well-drained
soil, moderately moist

Dill is a medium-sized annual, with ferny foliage and umbels of yellow flowers that produce oval seeds. It grows best when given a rich soil and adequate water; it also is happiest when nights are a bit on the cool side.

Seeds can be planted in early spring, followed by another planting about two weeks later. Dill is a short-lived annual, bolting quickly to flowering when summer heat begins. Sow the seed where you intend the plant to grow, for dill does not transplant well. Use the delicate, feathery foliage in cucumber salads, with cheese, and in fish, egg, and potato dishes. The foliage can also be used to flavor vinegar, and it is essential in making dill pickles.

Once the plant has flowered, check it frequently for the development of seeds. When the seeds have formed, tie a small paper bag over the seedhead to catch the seeds when they fall. The seeds can be used in breads and stuffings, soups and stews, and savory condiments.

Dill and fennel seeds were known as "meeting seeds" in the colonial era because they were carried in the pockets of churchgoers and chewed to quiet rumbling stomachs as sermons wore on. Some Indian restaurants keep a small bowl of dill or fennel seeds on hand for patrons, who may chew a few to assist with digestion at the end of a meal.

When summer heat begins to wane, you can try a second planting of seeds. A moderate fall may give you time for a second crop of dill foliage. Be sure to plant plenty of seeds, spring or fall, as the caterpillar of the lovely swallowtail butterfly will offer mighty competition for the pungent foliage. As with parsley, plant one for yourself and one for the caterpillars!

EDIBLE FLOWERS

Edible flowers make any meal a party. The confetti of petals in a salad delights the eyes as well as the palate. Although they are most often used as a garnish on top of cakes or floated in punch or wine, many flowers can be filled with delicious herbal dips and cheese spreads and served as an appetizer. They are also good in or on tea sandwiches, and some blooms can be dipped in batter and fried. Plant some edible flowers in your herb or kitchen garden for color as well as a culinary adventure.

Calendula, *Calendula officinalis*

Although an annual, this plant reseeds and is a dependable resident of the herb garden. It is long-lived in some climates. Scorching summer heat will render it weak, but trimming and a little mulch will help it limp along till fall temperatures revive it. Seedlings will also bloom in the fall, often till December. The golden blooms look great as a garnish in all types of desserts, and their sunny petals add color and flavor to many dishes. Used often in rice dishes, this plant is sometimes called "poor man's saffron." It colors butter and frostings and has long been used for a dye.

Allowed to reseed in an area along with other annuals, it often becomes part of the "cottage look" of an herb garden. Sow both in the spring and the fall or allow plants to self-sow. Deadhead some of the blooms to ensure the plant will remain strong.

Carnations, Pinks, *Dianthus* spp.

These are annuals, biennials, and perennials. Many have a spicy, clove-like fragrance and are very good for garnish on cakes or in salads. They can also be added to wine for a beverage reminiscent of the Middle Ages.

Lavender, *Lavandula* spp.

Lavender blossoms make a pretty garnish on cakes, cookies, and in fresh fruit dishes. Add a few blossoms to a glass of champagne or sprinkle a few on top of a summer salad. Layering sugar and lavender buds will create a delicately flavored sugar to use in tea or frostings.

Nasturtiums, *Tropaeolum majus*

The bright and peppery flavored bloom of this annual is so tasty! The plants love cool weather and look best before the summer sun heats up. They like sunlight and bloom best if they are not overfed, which causes them to produce too many leaves. Nasturtium blossoms are delicious in salads or filled with an herbal dip, avocado mix, or cheese.

Pansies, *Viola tricolor* (Johnny-Jump-Up)

A delightful bloom to float in punch or wine or to toss in salads. Full of vitamin C, this tiny flower is a cousin of the larger garden pansy, which is also edible and a great bloom to top salads or cakes. Pansies are a good winter or early spring plant because they like a cool garden in which to grow. In some climates they thrive almost year-round.

Rose, *Rosa* spp.

All roses are edible, but if you plan to eat them, plant only varieties that will do well without chemicals. For pure elegance and romance, nothing is more beautiful than a rosebud atop a cake. But don't discount the fact that rose petals are good in salads, jams, jellies, and a myriad of other recipes. After washing the bloom, cut off the white at the base of the petals, as it is bitter. Many of the old-fashioned roses produce hips, which can be used along with petals in teas and conserves. In most forms, the rose is a good source of vitamin C. Use mini-roses on cakes or desserts along with the leaves of scented geraniums for wonderful decorations.

Scented Geraniums, *Pelargonium* spp.

Pelargonium blooms add a mild floral taste to desserts, many kinds of punch, and teas. The leaves can be used in cakes and puddings or to decorate cakes.

Squash Blossoms, *Cucurbita* spp.

The robust blooms of all squash and pumpkins can be stuffed with cheese, or dipped in batter and fried. They can also be sliced and sautéed in oil and garlic with some vegetables.

Sweet Woodruff, *Galium odoratum*

Select several stems of the small, whorled leaves of sweet woodruff to create a traditional Mai wine, using white wine and strawberries, with a few violets to sprinkle on top. Steep the woodruff in the wine for several hours; then remove it and add the other ingredients.

Sweet woodruff grows best in shade with humus soil. If it is happy where planted, it will soon form a dense ground cover with tiny, star-like, white flowers in the spring. Because of its coumarin content, sweet woodruff's Generally Recognized as Safe status recommends its use only in alcoholic beverages.

Violets, *Viola odorata*

Another relative of the pansy, this flower is wonderfully fragrant when grown in a garden. Its wild cousins, which grow almost anywhere, can also be used for salads, fruit soups, and cookies. Wild violets have the same color and beauty but not the perfume of garden violets. Use the leaves of wild violets along with dandelion leaves in a chicken broth, or with spring vegetables (such as sugar peas, asparagus, carrots, or celery) for a wonderful spring dish. Top each bowl with a sprinkle of violet blooms upon serving.

Most violets grow well in a semishaded, woodsy environment. It is a good companion for sweet woodruff since both like the same conditions. Try not to plant *V. odorata* where common violets abound, as they might mix, weakening the fragrance of the cultivated blossoms.

Miscellaneous Herb Blooms

The flower of any culinary herb is edible. You may use the blooms as a garnish on any dish or in salads. Most can also be used in herb vinegar.

FENNEL

Foeniculum vulgare

Family: Apiaceae

Origin: Africa, Asia, Europe

Hardiness: zones 4–10

Light/Soil: full sun/light,
  well-drained soil

Fennel, a short-lived perennial, is a tall, wispy plant that grows five to seven feet and has umbels of tiny yellow flowers, making it an attractive addition to the back of a perennial border. All parts of the plant are edible; it has a cool, sweet flavor reminiscent of anise. A popular vegetable and flavoring herb for hundreds of years, fennel has naturalized in northern and central Europe, North America, and Australia.

Grow fennel from seed sown directly in the garden in early spring, when temperatures reach the upper fifties and the soil begins to warm. Its deep taproot makes fennel difficult to transplant, so sow the seed where you want the plant to grow. Much like parsley, its close relative, fennel's seeds will germinate better if soaked in a jar of water for two days before planting. Some gardeners advocate adding a teaspoon of vinegar to the jar. Fennel does best in well-drained, slightly alkaline soils in full sun. It is not hardy where winters are cold and wet, nor is it reliably hardy in heavy clay soils, where it is best treated as an annual. It will grow well and reseed, sometimes freely, to zone 7.

The dark-green, thread-like leaves may be harvested for use at any time, and they are especially good with seafood and vegetables. Bronze fennel (*F. vulgare* 'Purpureum') is as beautiful in the garden as it is in the kitchen. Its ripe fruits, commonly called seeds, are harvested at the end of summer. Collect them by placing a cut flower head into a paper bag. The seeds will drop into the bag as they dry. Fennel seed is a staple of Italian sausage and Chinese five-spice powder. Toasting the seeds will remove some of their sweetness and make them more savory.

Florence fennel (*F. vulgare* var. *azoricum*) grows a bulbous base that is used steamed or boiled as a vegetable; it is also sliced or grated raw in salads. This annual grows to about three feet tall and prefers cool weather.

For centuries, cooks in Italy have collected fennel pollen on warm sunny days, when wild fennel is at its peak of flower and fragrance. An unusual spice, fennel pollen is used to impart its intense flavor to meats and vegetables. Some say that this pricy spice is not fennel pollen at all, but rather the ground flower heads of the plant (which would include some pollen). Regardless of its nature, like saffron, its collection is labor intensive, which makes it expensive and sometimes hard to get. If you can find it, try fennel pollen mixed with a little butter and drizzled over freshly steamed vegetables. If you cannot find fennel pollen, ground fennel will serve the same purpose.

FENUGREEK

Trigonella foenum-graecum

Family: Fabaceae

Origin: southern Europe, Africa, Asia

Hardiness: annual

Light/Soil: full sun/moist soil

Fenugreek is a member of the pea family, as is obvious by its flowers and leaves, which appear almost clover-like. This plant has been used since the ancient Egyptians, Greeks, and Romans, but it is still not well known in the United States. Its ground seeds are an essential ingredient of Indian curries, and its dried leaves have been incorporated into regional herb blends. Unbeknownst to many American consumers, a maple-flavored syrup can be made from fenugreek seeds, which have also been used in candy, ice cream, and other foods.

Fenugreek tends to be a short-lived crop, especially in the hotter areas of the United States, and it should be treated as an annual. As soon as the soil is warm, soak seeds overnight before planting them. This will speed up the germination time, allowing the plants to mature and produce seeds before the hottest part of the summer arrives. The plants do best in moist, well-drained soil. Like other members of the pea family, fenugreek is a heavy feeder and needs rich soil. Top dress with compost for the first part of the growing season and apply an all-purpose fertilizer throughout the growing season.

Fenugreek is rarely seen growing in herb gardens in the United States. That does not mean it is not worthy of cultivation. Try this gem in your garden, and you will be pleasantly surprised.

GALANGAL

Alpinia spp.

Family: Zingiberaceae

Origin: southeast Asia

Hardiness: zones 8b to 11

Light/Soil: part shade/rich,
well-drained soil

Greater galangal (*Alpinia galanga*), commonly known as galangal or galanga, is a popular spice throughout southeast Asia and is especially typical in the cuisine of Indonesia, Malaysia, and Thailand. The rhizome, which looks very much like ginger, has a slightly pinkish tint and a warm taste similar to ginger, but with overtones of cardamom. Like ginger, galangal is harvested in late summer for use as a fresh spice; it can also be cleaned of its roots, sliced thickly, and dried for future use. Dried galangal is usually reconstituted in water before being chopped and added to recipes.

Galangal makes its presence known in the garden, serving as a good architectural element. With twenty-inch-long lanceolate leaves arranged much like a ginger plant, and three- to four-foot racemes of the palest green orchid-like flowers, the plant can reach six feet in height. Galangal is tropical in origin and hardy only in warm climates, though it may be grown as an annual in cooler regions. It prefers well-drained soil in partly shady conditions, and it loves humidity. Attempts to grow galangal outside of its natural range will likely disappoint cooks, for the plant's rhizomes are harvested after four to six years, but in most of the United States, the plant does not survive beyond its first year.

Lesser galangal (*A. officinarum*) is slightly smaller in stature than greater galangal, with rhizomes of an orange color and a hot, peppery taste. Lesser galangal is more important for its medicinal qualities; it is often used for digestive upsets, pain, fever, and infections. It, too, is a tropical plant in need of rich, well-drained soil and some protection from the sun.

Greater galangal doubles its exotic appeal when combined with lemongrass, garlic, and hot peppers. It is used in soups, vegetables, and meat stews, as a flavoring agent for vinegars and liqueurs, and is sometimes added to Chinese five-spice blends. A traditional fried rice dish, nasi goreng, is dependent on galangal's spicy warm flavor.

GINGER

Zingiber officinale

Family: Zingiberaceae

Origin: eastern Asia, tropical Australia

Hardiness: zone 7b

Light/Soil: part shade to full sun/moist but well-drained rich soil

A visit to your local market will present you with two choices for ginger: fresh whole or powdered dry ginger root. Yet it is not the root, but rather the rhizome of *Zingiber officinale* that brings a spicy, flavorful warmth to both sweet and savory dishes. Native to Indomalaysia and eastern Asia, much ginger is now exported from India, though some say that Jamaican ginger is the best. Ginger is perennial to zone 7b, prefers full sun or just a little shade, and will grow to about four feet in most areas.

Ginger is easily grown and can even be started from a rhizome purchased at the market. Select one that appears reasonably firm and fresh, and plant it shallowly in good soil in your garden or in a container. In late fall, cut back the dead leaves and carefully extract the rhizomes. Scrub off the dirt and you are ready to cook. Fresh ginger has a very spicy, pungent bite and is a bit more tender than what is often available at the market.

Fresh ginger may be peeled (use the edge of a spoon for easiest peeling) and then sliced, minced, or grated. Fresh ginger dropped into a pot early in the cooking process will lose some of its bite. Added late in the cooking process, it will yield a fuller flavor. Candied ginger is a great remedy for nausea, and one of its byproducts is ginger syrup—which you can use to make ginger ale or to marinate fresh fruits.[17] You can also use the syrup as a flavoring agent in cakes and cookies.

Dried, powdered ginger is what is most often used for baking: it is the traditional ingredient in ginger cakes, gingerbread, and a wide variety of other baked goods. Dried, powdered ginger is also an ingredient of some curry powders, Chinese five-spice powder, and tandoori blends. Add a little to soups or stews for an aromatic and slightly mysterious flavor.

HORSERADISH

Armoracia rusticana

Family: Brassicaceae

Origin: eastern Europe

Hardiness: to zone 5

Light/Soil: full sun/moist, can
    withstand some drought

Few of us have the experience of eating freshly grated horseradish. Thought to be of Mediterranean or eastern European origin, it was most likely first used medicinally. Happily, it soon made its way into the kitchen, where it has been a staple seasoning, especially in central and eastern Europe, since at least 1000 BCE.

To grow your own horseradish, prepare a sunny bed in early spring and plant pieces of the root in well-drained, moist soil. The leaves will grow to spectacular lengths, up to thirty inches long, making a bold statement in your garden. In the fall, however, take care to dig up all the roots that you can; otherwise you will have a persistent horseradish crop that defies eradication. Horseradish is hardy to zone 5, but its roots are best used in a plant's first and second years, as they get tough beyond that point.

To use fresh horseradish, wash and peel the root, then grate it carefully, using only as much as you need. The root is full of strong-smelling volatile oils, which may cause some breathing discomfort, so take the same precautions you use when chopping an especially pungent onion. Store the remaining horseradish root in the refrigerator until you need it again. If you prefer, you can grate all of your horseradish, mix it with a little vinegar and salt, and store it in the freezer.

Horseradish loses much of its pungency when heated, so the best recipes will add it at the end of cooking. It is also used as a sauce or cold condiment. If a recipe calls for cooking horseradish with other ingredients, taste the finished product. You may want to stir in a little extra fresh horseradish just before serving.

HYSSOP

Hyssopus officinalis
Family: Lamiaceae
Origin: Mediterranean
Hardiness: to zone 5
Light/Soil: full sun/average
to slightly dry soil

The tall spikes of deep royal-blue flowers of hyssop announce midsummer in the garden, attracting long-tongued bumble-bees, cooks, and herbalists. This bushy plant will grow to nearly three feet tall, but it is easily clipped to maintain a full appearance; it can also be trained into a border for a knot garden. Hyssop's narrow leaves are bitter. Some detect a slight undertone of mint; others claim the plant develops "a skunk-like odor on hot summer days."[18] Another authority contends that the fragrance of the flowers improves upon drying.[19]

Hyssop is not a commonly used herb, but for the adventurous it can be an interesting addition to salads and fruit dishes, or it can be cooked with game and meat stews. It has also found favor as an ingredient in certain liqueurs—Benedictine, for example—and in some herbes de Provence blends.

Hyssop has Generally Recognized as Safe status, but its essential oil has the potential to cause convulsions or even death. Tucker and DeBaggio note, "For a human weighing 150 pounds, that comes out to be 0.31 ounce and 3 ounces, respectively," referring to the quantity of the essential oil required to produce toxicity and death.[20] The leaves and flowers of hyssop have a history of use as an antiseptic in the treatment and cleansing of wounds.

Full sun and average to slightly dry soil will keep your plants healthy. They will reseed, but the seeds are slow to germinate; you can increase your number of hyssop plants more easily by root division in the fall. You can also root softwood cuttings taken in early spring. By taking cuttings, you are essentially pruning your plant, giving it a fuller, more compact appearance. Deadheading the spent flowers will keep the plant blooming and will help maintain the shape of the shrub.

The purple-blue of hyssop, as well as its stately size, make it a good choice for the back of a garden bed or for hedging. Whether or not you use its flowers and leaves in your cooking, you will be happy with the appearance of *Hyssopus officinalis* in your garden.

LAVENDER

Lavandula spp.

Family: Lamiaceae

Origin: Greece, Italy, France, Spain

Hardiness: to zone 5

Light/Soil: full sun/somewhat dry

In past generations, linens were sometimes carefully draped over lavender bushes to dry after being washed. As the sun beat down on the wet linens, they picked up the scent of the lavender beneath them. To this day, lavender water is used in the final laundry rinse in elegant establishments, and lavender sachets are still tucked into dressers.

Lavender has also been appreciated for its medicinal value. In *The Herball* (1597), John Gerard prescribed lavender for bathing the temples of those with "light migram or swimming of the braine."[21] Nicholas Culpeper's *The Complete Herbal* (1649) suggests that lavender "is of especial use for pains in the head and brain, following cold, apoplexy, falling-sickness, the dropsy or sluggish malady, cramps, convulsions, palsies and faintings."[22] Used as a remedy for skin problems, insomnia, and madness, it was also carried into sickrooms to ward off disease. Its oil was extracted and used as an antiseptic.

With all of lavender's household and medicinal uses, it is not a surprise that some enterprising cook brought the herb into the kitchen, where it is used in beverages, as an ingredient of herbes de Provence blends, and in a variety of sweet dishes.

Lavandula angustifolia is the best choice for culinary purposes. The flowers should be harvested just before opening and dried before use. The leaves have a somewhat medicinal fragrance and are not recommended for cooking.

Lavender is hardy to zone 5. It requires full sun, excellent drainage, and good air circulation. In North America, especially in areas with high humidity, a mulch of white sand or gravel is recommended. This will reflect light and heat into the plant, mimicking its growing conditions in the wild, and also discouraging disease.

LEMON BALM

Melissa officinalis
Family: Lamiaceae
Origin: Africa, Asia, Europe
Hardiness: zone 5
Light/Soil: part shade to full
sun/moist soil

This easy-to-grow, hardy perennial reaches about eighteen inches tall in the sun or shade, where it makes large clumps of nice-looking, crinkly foliage that smells like lemon. The flowers are nondescript, but they seed wonderfully, over time turning the clump into a lush bed. Grow lemon balm under shade-loving trees and shrubs as a useful ground cover or in a little sun for a glorious, rich, green bed. The more you pick, the better it grows.

For centuries, lemon balm has been used for a wide variety of ailments; it also makes a refreshing lemon beverage. It has been used as a relaxing agent and as an aid to restful, nightmare-free sleep. Lemon balm added to wine "comforts the heart and driveth away all melancholy and sadness," according to Gerard's 1597 *Herball*.[23] It can be made into salves to treat wounds, and it "was the principal ingredient in Eau de Carmes, a favorite scent before the introduction of Eau de Cologne."[24] Use the fresh leaves in salads, in tea, in baked goods, and even in your bath to release their sweet fragrance.

A square-stemmed plant, lemon balm is related to mint, and it spreads almost as rapidly, though not as vigorously. It will grow in vacant lots, in fields, under trees, or just about anywhere. It does best in slightly moist soil that is rich in humus, and with a few hours of sun each day.

Cut a few leaves and place them in a cup, cover them with boiling water, allow them to steep for several minutes, and enjoy a lemony tea. For a summer drink, combine a few stems of lemon balm, lemon thyme, and lemon verbena in a pitcher of hot water, allow them to steep for a few hours, and then add lots of ice and a slice of lemon. The resulting drink is refreshing on a hot day.

LEMONGRASS

Cymbopogon citratus

Family: Poaceae

Origin: perhaps southeast Asia

Hardiness: annual

Light/Soil: full sun/moist,
    well-drained soil

Lemongrass, like cilantro, is an herb used for flavoring that is relatively new to the culinary scene in the United States. Within the past thirty years, it has become much better known, and it is now a sought-after plant for the garden. It is a favorite in Asian and Thai cooking and is also delicious steeped in water for a hot tea or iced beverage. It will grow beautifully outdoors in a large pot sunk in the ground that can be lifted in the fall and brought indoors. Lemongrass can also be planted directly in the garden, where it will be a magnificent plant, but it usually will not survive the winter in a zone colder than zone 8.

Lemongrass is a member of a small group of very aromatic grasses found in tropical southeast Asia. It will grow in a clump up to six feet high if conditions are perfect. It is now quite popular and is grown in Florida commercially for its oil, which is often used to flavor lemon candy.

Like many herbs, lemongrass does not want to be overfertilized, so a time-release fertilizer, used sparingly, works best. It needs good light when indoors, but it can take full sun or part shade outside in the summer. It must be put outdoors in the summer to grow well and develop its full flavor.

Cut the leaves of mature plants and use them fresh all summer. The best part of the leaves is the lower portion, which is usually a much paler green than the rest of the leaf. Chop the leaves very finely or remove them before serving a dish, as they are tough and can be difficult to digest. Treat them as you do bay leaves.

Dry or freeze the leaves in late fall for winter use if you do not plan to bring the plant indoors. Be sure the leaves are completely dry before storing them or they will mold.

LEMON VERBENA

....

Aloysia citrodora

Family: Verbenaceae

Origin: Argentina

Hardiness: to zone 8

Light/Soil: full sun/moist, rich soil

This shrub-like plant has the most lemony scent of all the lemony herbs. It is a beautiful plant, but it will not usually survive the winter outdoors north of zone 8. A cool or unheated sunroom or greenhouse is best in northern climates. Collect its leaves during the summer, when its growth is rampant. Dry the leaves to use in cakes, muffins, or cookies. You can combine seven to ten leaves in a blender with any liquid in a recipe, from melted butter to eggs, milk, or water. Then simply add the resulting green slurry to your recipe. The zest or juice of a lemon will further intensify the flavor. Lemon verbena, like any lemon herb, always tastes best when used in a recipe with butter.

There are many plants that have a citrus fragrance, and some have a taste close to lemons. Two chemical components, citrate and limonene, give these plants their lemony fragrance. Some of the lemon-scented herbs are lemon balm, lemon basil, lemon catnip, lemon gem marigold, lemongrass, lemon mint, lemon thyme, lemon geranium, and lemon verbena. Each has their own unique fragrance and taste, some spicy and some fruity. The flavor of lemon verbena is very intense; all other lemon herbs pale beside it. Brushing up against the plant in the garden is enough to release its fragrance and make your mouth water.

A surefire way to have lots of lemon verbena leaves for tea, potpourri, or baking is to grow the plant in a large pot or tub. Be sure it has good drainage and a loamy potting soil. Feed the plant a spoon of a slow-release fertilizer in early summer and again in midsummer.

Plants that get full and lush over the summer can be cut back severely before being brought in for the winter. Their leaves can be dried on a screen and stored in a jar until needed for tea, jams, or muffins.

LOVAGE

Lovage is a tall and sturdy perennial plant that commands attention in any herb garden. Its aromatic leaves and stems are best described as being on the sweet side with a hint of celery. Early in the season its tender leaves can be chopped and used in many dishes, as well as in salads. Both the stalks and the leaves can be used in cooking, and they add a wonderful flavor to many foods. They are good paired with chicken or potatoes, as well as other meats or starches. Lovage was used in many European countries as a salt substitute during World Wars I and II.

Lovage does well in a heavy, rich, moist soil. It is a perennial that depends on a cool summer and adequate moisture in order to survive for a good many years. A generous amount of compost topped with mulch works well in warm, sandy areas.

Add chopped lovage and a cup of parsley to homemade chicken soup. It is a great way to use this herbal giant of the garden.

Levisticum officinale

Family: Apiaceae

Origin: eastern and western Europe

Hardiness: to zone 5

Light/Soil: full sun/moist, rich soil

MINT

....

Mentha

Family: Lamiaceae

Origin: Europe

Hardiness: to zone 5

Light/Soil: full sun to part
shade/rich, moist soil

The genus *Mentha* includes more than nineteen pure species that have repeatedly crossed, resulting in two thousand named species and their hybrids. Because of this extensive hybridization, most mints do not reproduce true from seed. This is a minor problem, as they are notorious for spreading via their underground runners.

Many, though not all, of the mints benefit from rich, moist soil in full to part sun. Ten to fourteen hours of daylight is required for flowering and good oil yield. Rotating plant locations will help to prevent wilt and leaf rust. Many home gardeners prefer to keep mints in containers, thus controlling their spread; cross-pollination can leave you with a garden-variety mint with little fragrance.

Cultivated mints generally fall into two major groups: those with a spearmint fragrance and those with a peppermint fragrance. 'Madalene Hill' is a form of the species *M. ×gracilis* unique in its "doublemint" fragrance, which combines the flavors of spearmint and peppermint, making it a desirable culinary mint. 'Kentucky Colonel' (*M. spicata*, sometimes called *M. cordifolia*), the wrinkled-leaf form of spearmint, is most often used in mint juleps. Among the peppermints, favorites include 'Orange Mint' (*M. aquatica* var.), which has a citrus-like fragrance, and 'Mitcham' (*M. ×piperita* var. *piperita*). 'Mitcham' is often sold as black peppermint. It smells like chewing gum and holds up well in dessert recipes, candies, and teas.

MUSTARD

Brassica spp.

Family: Brassicaceae

Origin: Middle East, southern and eastern Asia

Hardiness: will withstand frost

Light/Soil: full sun/average soil, slightly moist

Brilliant gold fields seen across America in the summertime are often mustard. Native most likely to the Middle East and parts of Asia, mustard species have found a happy home in North America, seeding freely and found along roadsides, in abandoned fields, and in cultivation.

The virtues of mustard as a vegetable, seasoning, and medicinal plant have long been known. Archaeological evidence indicates that mustard seeds were chewed with meat in Asia and parts of Europe in the period before 10,000 BCE, and they were a staple of Sumerian (Babylonian) diets as far back as 2500 BCE.[25] Romans were fond of the spice, which was included in recipes found in a first-century cookbook by Apicius. By 900 CE mustard was a cultivated crop in Europe, where it may have been brought by Romans—or, later, Arabs—as they traveled through the Iberian peninsula.[26] Medieval European recipes included mustard as a seasoning in, for example, dried fish dishes.[27] Indian curries, before the sixteenth-century introduction of chile peppers from South America, depended on mustard to create a hot blend.[28]

The spicy warmth of mustard found favor as a medicinal as well. In the sixth century BCE, Pythagoras advocated its use as a remedy for scorpion bites, and it was also recommended by Hippocrates about a hundred years later. In the first century CE, Pliny included mustard in forty of his remedies and "announced that lazy women would turn into ideal housewives if they were fed mustard."[29] Used in poultices, which were layered over cloth and applied to aching backs or congested chests, mustard relieved pain. A mustard footbath eased an aching head and provided relief from a cold.[30] Applied directly, mustard can cause blistering of the skin; it has thus lost favor for such external treatments. Folk remedies included some unusual uses of mustard, including the belief that scattering its seeds around the perimeter of a house would keep evil spirits away. Danes fed mustard to "frigid" women to make them "change [their] ways."[31]

Most of all, mustard has been enjoyed as a seasoning, bringing a pungent warmth to foods. The addition of turmeric to mustard blends gives it the familiar bright golden color that we associate with hot dogs. As W. M. Gibbs notes, "Turmeric is treated more as a constituent of the mustard than as a foreign substance—a fact which makes it appear almost a commercial necessity."[32]

Traditional English mustard is a blend of white (*Sinapsis alba*—still a mustard, but a separate genus) and brown mustards (*B. juncea*).[33] French mustard is often brown mustard, as is Chinese.

Using the mustard flour readily available in markets makes home preparation of mustard a simple and pleasant task. Add cold water and blend to make a paste, allowing the mustard to sit for fifteen to thirty minutes to develop its flavor. Adding vinegar or lemon juice to the mixture will stop the development of heat, and you can add herbs and spices to create your own unique blend. Tarragon and champagne vinegar is a tried and true combination.

Whole or coarsely ground mustard seeds are added to sausages, and whole seeds are included in most pickle recipes. The young leaves and flowers of *B. nigra* can be added to salads.

B. juncea, brown mustard, is more commonly grown commercially than *B. nigra*, black mustard, simply because harvesting black mustard is more labor intensive.[34] Both can be grown in home gardens. *B. juncea* grows to about four feet tall with stalks of bright yellow flowers. *B. nigra* is a slightly smaller plant. Both can be grown from seed sown in early spring. Successive planting over a three- to four-week period will provide a good supply of salad greens over the summer.

Gather seed pods before they open in summer, placing them in a paper bag to dry and catch the seeds. Store the dry seeds in a tightly covered jar. Grind the seeds in an electric spice mill, or just crush them with a mortar and pestle to make a coarse-grained mustard. Creating your own mustard blends is easy and allows you plenty of room for creativity, as well as a chance to use many of the other herbs in your garden. Keep your mustards stored in the refrigerator once they have achieved the heat level that you prefer.

NASTURTIUM

Tropaeolum majus

Family: Tropaeolaceae

Origin: South America

Hardiness: annual

Light/Soil: full sun/well-drained, average soil

If you want a bright, cheerful garden, you cannot do much better than nasturtiums. These South American natives have big flowers in a range of colors from bright yellow to deep red. Some are solids, while some have flashy splotches of contrasting color. The leaves are a real standout, too, looking much like miniature water-lily pads; some are variegated, which adds even more color. Best of all, the plant is edible. Its leaves add a spicy zest to salads and sandwiches, its flowers make a peppery garnish, and its buds can be pickled as a substitute for capers.

Nasturtiums grow well from seed. Be sure the soil is warm before putting the seeds out, and water them only until they are established. The plants are fairly drought-tolerant and will produce flowers best in average soil. Too much fertilizer will produce a great display of leaves but few flowers.

When the flowers begin to bloom, pick them freely. They make a beautiful garnish, either atop a salad or lining a plate. Stuff them with an herbed cream-cheese blend or chicken salad for a stunning appetizer, chop them into a cheese spread for sandwiches, or toss a few blossoms into vinegar for color and zest. They not only look great, but they add spiciness to otherwise bland foods.

These flowers are simply gorgeous as they spill out of flower boxes, tumble from containers, or spread across your garden border. Give them room and let them grow, enjoying their beauty, and then take a few into the kitchen for a little summer in your salad bowl. If you are really ambitious, you can toast the ripe seeds and grind them to use as a pepper substitute.

OREGANO

Origanum spp.

Family: Lamiaceae

Origin: southern Europe, Mediterranean, northern Africa

Hardiness: some to zone 6, some only to zone 9

Light/Soil: full sun/well-drained loam

There are a number of plants for the herb garden that have the characteristic scent of oregano. If you want to grow one of these and plan to use it in recipes, our best advice is to shop with your nose. Rub the leaves of the plant to see if they release oregano's familiar, pleasing, and spicy fragrance. Be aware, however, that many plants—over fifty species of disparate genera other than *Origanum*—have the characteristic fragrance of oregano. For example, Cuban oregano is a pretty plant with a spicy, oregano-like odor, but it is a *Plectranthus* and lacks Generally Recognized as Safe status.

The genus *Origanum* is popular in many ethnic cuisines and has been naturalized in many parts of the world. Different common names have been given to the same plant, and the same name has sometimes been applied to different plants, causing confusion in identification. To complicate matters further, labels are often insufficient or even contradictory.

To begin, all marjorams are *Origanums*, though not all *Origanums* are marjoram. The best culinary marjoram (*O. majorana*) has a flavor milder and sweeter than that of the oregano essence associated with Italian and Greek cooking. This more typical oregano plant can be either *O. vulgare* subsp. *hirtum* or *O. onites*. Both plants are commonly called "Greek oregano" unless you are in Turkey, where they are just as possessively labeled "Turkish oregano."

If you are looking for an ornamental oregano, try the hybrid cultivar *O. rotundifolia*, 'Kent Beauty'. Although of no use as a culinary plant, it is a floral beauty, with trailing pink-tinged creamy bracts that almost completely hide the small corollas.

Because of their Mediterranean origin, all *Origanums* are best suited to a hot, dry climate. Where the winters are wet and cold they struggle to survive. They are woody-stemmed plants, mostly upright (although some, such as 'Kent Beauty', are trailing), and they tend to get leggy if left unclipped. This means that you are free to clip regularly once you have found the *Origanum* you prefer. Many *Origanums* are hardy to zone 6 and will often reseed in your garden.

PAPRIKA

Capsicum annuum

Family: Solanaceae

Origin: South America

Hardiness: annual

Light/Soil: full sun/moist to
slightly dry soil

Paprika is a flavorful, vibrant spice, adding subtle, warm, earthy notes to many meat and vegetable dishes. Paprika is often thought of as a Hungarian spice, but it is actually native to the Americas.

If you garden, chances are that you have at some time grown the primary ingredient for paprika—peppers. Almost any type of pepper can be made into paprika, though Americans are most familiar with sweet paprika, made from red bell peppers. In Hungary, Spain, or South America, you might find a more pungent paprika, which is sometimes made from chile peppers.

To produce paprika, red peppers are dried and then ground two or more times, usually without the seeds and veins. Sweet Hungarian paprika is considered the best. Making your own paprika is not recommended, especially if you are using a hot pepper, since the process releases large amounts of volatile oil and dust into the air and could make breathing difficult. Because paprika is a spice that is finely ground, it begins losing its flavor right away. For best results, replace your paprika every six to eight months.

The flavor of paprika is released upon heating; when it is sprinkled on cold foods, it is little more than a garnish. When cooking with paprika, add it at any time to soups, stews, or liquid dishes. If you are cooking it along with onions or as the base of a rub for meats, watch it closely. Peppers have a high sugar content, so the paprika will burn quickly.

PARSLEY

Petroselinum crispum

Family: Apiaceae

Origin: southeast Europe, western Asia

Hardiness: will withstand frost, biennials

Light/Soil: part shade to full sun/moist, rich soil

Parsley is one of the few herbs that remains green, lush, and healthy in a pot on a windowsill over the winter. The more you pick it, the better it grows. All it requires is a deep pot for its carrot-like root and a cool, bright home. In the garden, parsley plants will send forth a burst of growth as soon as the snow melts and there are a few mild, sunny days. Untouched by cold, this biennial lasts for about eighteen months outside. But once it blooms its life cycle is finished, and it must be allowed to reseed or else be replaced by a new plant.

Parsley was used by ancient Greeks and Romans as a popular garnish for foods. According to legend, they believed that if it was eaten between courses, the wine they drank would not make them drunk. During the Middle Ages this beautiful herb was used in monasteries as an edging in herb gardens, where it was also grown for its medicinal properties.

In order to have an abundance of parsley, sow seeds in the fall, in the early spring, and again in midsummer. Because of parsley's long taproot, it is not easy to transplant seedlings from the garden. The seeds take so long to germinate that legend says that parsley must go to the devil and back nine times unless it is planted on Good Friday. Others say to plant it on St. Patrick's Day. Both dates are in early spring, a time when the seed has a cool period in which to germinate. To speed up germination time, soak seeds in a jar of tepid water to which is added a teaspoon of vinegar. After three days, drain and rinse the seeds and plant them directly in the garden. Given sun, a good soil, moderate food, and water when needed, parsley is very easy to grow. It will thrive in most gardens, but remember to plant twice what you will need, as butterflies lay eggs in parsley and use it as a host food.

Parsley is a great source of vitamin C, as well as serving as an efficient breath freshener. It is used in soups, stews, gravies, and salads, as well as with meats and potatoes. Be generous with this green herb in tomato dishes, and especially in spaghetti sauce, for a fresh, delicious, gardeny taste.

PINK, CLOVE PINK

Dianthus caryophyllus
Family: Caryophyllaceae
Origin: Mediterranean
Hardiness: zone 5
Light/Soil: sun/well-drained soil

Clove pinks are charming little plants with a long history of use, both medicinal and culinary. Theophrastus (371–287 BCE) called them *dios anthos,* or "god's flower," an indication of the reverence with which they were held. The term *pinked* (as in pinking shears) comes from these little flowers, so called because of the serrated edges of the petals.[35] "Clove" comes from, of course, the sweet, clove-like fragrance of the flowers. Tucker and DeBaggio recommend the old hybrid 'Gloriosa', when you can find it, for the most intensely fragrant flowers.[36]

Pinks are easy to grow, requiring lots of sun and well-drained soil. Divide them every year or so to keep them from dying out from the center, and keep the beds free of weeds to avoid diseases. The gray-green, narrow, linear leaves will grow only to about eight inches, but the flowers stalks will reach out above the plants, holding the flowers as much as eighteen inches high. They produce pink to red and purple flowers in early summer, with perhaps another blooming later in the season. They make excellent cut flowers, bringing beauty and fragrance to the table.

Use pinks as a garnish, removing the bitter white base of the petals, or sprinkle them onto fruit salads. You can also make syrup from the petals, or toss one or two into a glass of wine to mimic ancient customs.

POPPIES

....

Papaver spp.

Family: Papaveraceae

Origin: southwest Asia

Hardiness: reseeding annual

Light/Soil: sun to part shade/
    moist soil

Poppies look like gorgeous chiffon skirts in many hues. When in riotous bloom, they have the power to mesmerize. There are many different kinds of poppies, but the one most used for culinary purposes is *Papaver somniferum*, the bread poppy. Its tiny gray-black seeds, which have a nutty flavor, are used on breads and rolls, and they are also used for the poppy-seed filling in Czechoslovakian kolaches.

The cultivation of *P. somniferum* goes back more than six thousand years; it was recorded on Sumerian clay tablets as a medicinal plant. It has been valued for its soporific and pain-relieving qualities. It is the plant from which both morphine and codeine are derived, and its addictive qualities are so strong that it is a tightly controlled plant, illegal to grow in this country. *P. somniferum* has long been recognized for its healing powers, and it appears in the works of both John Gerard (*The Herball,* 1597) and John Parkinson (*Theatrum Botanicum,* 1640). Lady Rosalind Northcote notes that both men "commend it as a medicine that 'mitigateth all kinde of paines,' but say that it must be used with great caution."[37] Fortunately, the seeds of *P. somniferum* pose no danger and are readily available in grocery markets.

The Flanders poppy, or corn poppy, *P. rhoeas,* is the symbol of Memorial Day, on which members of the military who gave their lives in service to their country are honored. *P. rhoeas* are scarlet red with a black center, and they have been used as a memorial symbol from at least the end of World War I.

Regardless of their medicinal and culinary properties, all poppies are beautiful garden gems. Beautiful upright annuals, poppies can grow three to four feet tall in good soils. They do best in the full sun, but in hot climates they benefit from afternoon shade. They do best with a consistently moist soil. The plants have serrated and deeply lobed, bluish-green leaves that are three to six inches long.

Poppy seeds drop when they are fully dried and the pod splits or falls, releasing the seeds. When they germinate, the seedlings look like tiny little thready pieces of green. These seed leaves soon grow into a basal rosette of leaves that look like a tiny cabbage or collard plant. In early spring, a leafy stalk with a single nodding bud emerges. It opens into a bowl-shaped flower that can be as large as four inches across. Flowers come in red, white, pink, purple, or mauve, and they are usually double. Large bluish-green seedpods follow the short-lived blooms.

The seeds of the opium poppy are free from opium and can be sprinkled on cakes and bread. Overindulgence, however, could leave a trace result in one's medical tests. The seeds are also added to birdseed, and they yield a pale yellow oil that can be used for various technical purposes. Among other ways, it is used by artists as a drying oil. All other parts of this pretty poppy are toxic, so do not ingest them.

POT MARIGOLD

Calendula officinalis

Family: Asteraceae

Origin: Europe, northern Africa

Hardiness: annual to perennial
in warm climates

Light/Soil: full sun/average soil

The bright yellow and orange flowers of the pot marigold are common in cottage and country gardens. Native to southern Europe, it truly thrives in cool, temperate zones. The petals are pungent and spicy, but this traditional medicinal is used for culinary purposes as well.

Historically, calendula has been used to heal wounds, on internal and external ulcers, as an antiseptic, and to improve blood flow. Infusions of the petals have been used to lighten and brighten hair, and dried petals are used in soaps. In the kitchen, they are used in fish and meat soups, rice dishes, salads, and for coloring cheese and butter. Since medieval times, entire flowers have often been used as a garnish.

Calendula is a hardy annual in warm climates and will reseed in the garden. It prefers well-drained soil in a sunny locale, although in southern gardens it may need a bit of shade in the late afternoon. Adding compost will help this flowering beauty produce lush, thick foliage and abundant flowers. Mix calendula in your perennial border, vegetable garden, and window boxes and containers, where it will add an amazing splash of color through most of the summer, after which you can use it in the kitchen or dress up your plates the next time you entertain.

ROSEMARY

Rosmarinus officinalis
Family: Lamiaceae
Origin: Mediterranean
Hardiness: zones 7–10
Light/Soil: sun/well-drained

Native to Mediterranean regions, it is often assumed that the name *Rosmarinus* is from Latin, referring to *ros* (dew) and *marinus* (of the sea). Unfortunately, this romantic interpretation is not likely an accurate one. Another, more likely, possibility is that the word stems from the Greek *rhous* (shrub) and *myron* (balm).[38] Whatever the origin of the word, rosemary is a delightful herb to have in our gardens and kitchens.

Rosemary is one of the exceptions to the adage that dried herbs are less flavorful than fresh. When rosemary is dried, its pungent oils are concentrated, making it easy to add too much. Measure carefully, and start with less than you think you might need. You can always add more if needed. Dried rosemary can be tough and unpalatable, so chop it finely before adding it to recipes.

Fresh rosemary is the best choice for cooking. Cut the tender tips of the plant, wash them carefully, and snip the leaves into your favorite recipes. The essential oils of rosemary are quite stable, which means you can add the herb early in the cooking process and it will not lose its flavor. Again, however, be careful not to add too much.

You may add a sprig of rosemary to soups or stews, simply removing the sprig before serving. You get all of the flavor and none of the sometimes tough leaves. You may also cut longer stems, including some of the woody parts of the plant, and use them as skewers for vegetables or meats to be cooked on the grill.

Rosemary has long been recognized for its medicinal properties. It was included in a first-century herbal by Dioscorides, who recommended it as a tonic before exercising. Writing in the late 1500s, John Parkinson praised it as an antiseptic, an anti-inflammatory, and for such maladies as headaches and convulsions. James A. Duke has recommended trying rosemary for a number of ailments, including Alzheimer's disease, arthritis, cataracts, depression, and body odor.[39]

Nicholas Culpeper recorded the use of rosemary for civil as well as physical purposes, citing its use in courts of justice. Rosemary was relied upon to fight against "the contagion of the pestilence from which poor prisoners too often suffered."[40] It was also thought to help improve the memories of those in the courtroom.

A symbol of friendship, loyalty, and remembrance, rosemary was often carried at weddings and funerals. Sprigs of gilded rosemary (sprigs dipped in scented water) were carried at weddings by bride and guests alike, and a bouquet of rosemary tied with ribbons was presented by the bride to her groom on the wedding morning. At funerals, mourners tossed a sprig of rosemary on the casket of loved ones, and a sprig was sometimes placed in the hands of the deceased. An often-quoted literary reference to rosemary is from Sir Thomas More (1478–1535), who wrote, "As for Rosmarine, I lett it runne all over my garden walls, not onlie because my bees love it, but because it is the herb sacred to remembrance, and, therefore, to friendship; whence a sprig of it hath a dumb language that maketh it the chosen emblem of our funeral wakes and in our buriall grounds."[41]

Rosemary is still considered a stimulating herb. It is used in soaps and shampoos, and it is also touted as a memory booster. Some people drink a cup of rosemary tea or pin a fresh sprig of rosemary to their clothes to revive their spirits during a long day.

Rosemary is hardy in zones 7–10. North of zone 7, it is often grown as an annual or brought indoors for the winter. If brought inside, it needs to be near a cool, sunny window, with good air circulation. Even then, it is likely to suffer until it can again be taken outside and put in the ground. In zones 7–10, rosemary will grow as a woody shrub. Some cultivars, such as 'Arp' and 'Herb Cottage', grow to five feet tall and three feet wide, while others, such as 'Blue Boy', are quite small. There are prostrate, or trailing, cultivars ('Dancing Waters', 'Alida

Hyde', 'Blue Lady', and 'Cascade') that do best as perennials in zone 8 and 9. They can also be used as container plants, in which case the branches will spill over to the ground.

Rosemary responds well to trimming, so use it frequently in the kitchen. It is pleasant to take a few cuttings to add to winter bouquets, and it will add a warm, piney fragrance to dull winter days. It is one of our more versatile herbs.

SAFFRON

Crocus sativus

Family: Iridaceae

Origin: cultivated, perhaps from
    C. cartwrightianus[42]

Hardiness: to zone 6

Light/Soil: full sun/well-drained

Although crocus are usually thought of as spring blooms, the fall-blooming *Crocus sativus* is the plant from which we obtain the spice called saffron. Since *C. sativus* is the only edible crocus, it is often grown in herb gardens as a conversation piece. Few cooks count on growing their own saffron because it takes about seventy-five thousand blooms to make a pound of saffron. Since only the threads or stigmas of the blossoms are used, its harvest is a very time-consuming procedure. Commercially, saffron is picked from each flower by hand. If you want to try to harvest your own saffron, you might have the best luck if you use a pair of tweezers to pull out the three red stigmas in each bloom, laying them on a screen or a paper towel to dry. They will add a sharp taste as well as a rich golden color to foods.

Like all members of their family, *C. sativus* plants like part shade but will also do well in the sun. They need a moist but well-drained garden soil, where they will be able to assume a dormant state during the summer. The foliage is green and grass-like in the spring, but it disappears once the weather becomes warm. Allow the foliage to grow as long as it is green, because it is feeding the bulb and making the bloom that will appear in late fall. If the fall is very dry, water the bulbs every week or so. The blooms often appear suddenly after a rain.

Most commercial saffron is grown in the Middle East, but some other saffron-producing countries are Greece, Spain, Turkey, Iran, India, and Morocco. It is valued for rice, soups, cakes, breads, and many fish and meat dishes.

SAGE

Salvia spp.

Family: Lamiaceae

Origin: Mediterranean

Hardiness: to zone 7, but some
    can't withstand frost

Light/Soil: full sun/well-drained
    soil

Although there are over eight hundred species of *Salvia* growing on every continent except Antartica, only one—*Salvia officinalis*—is of importance in the kitchen. This is the plant that we call sage and that we associate with poultry, stuffing, and sausage. It is native to Spain, France, and south-central Europe.[43]

Common garden sage is a woody, sun-loving perennial. It grows most attractively if pinched regularly during its first year of growth to promote branching. Its fleshy leaves are generally a soft green, with a pebble-like appearance and a distinct, warm aroma. There are several popular cultivars of *S. officinalis,* each with a slightly different taste and appealing qualities as garden plants. 'Aurea' has gold-tinged leaves but little flavor; 'Tricolor' has green, purple, and white leaves. 'Purpurascens' is a beautiful garden plant, and many cooks prefer its flavor to common sage. 'Rubriflora' has pink flowers. Finally, according to Tucker and DeBaggio, 'Woodcote Farm' is a good culinary plant.[44]

Since *S. officinalis* is hardy to zone 5, perhaps to zone 4 in a protected spot, there is little reason to rely on the dried sage found on most grocery shelves. With its strong, musky odor and fuzzy leaves, dried sage is powerfully strong. If you live north of zone 5 and must rely on dried sage, use it sparingly.

Fresh sage, on the other hand, is delightful. It transforms a simple grilled cheese sandwich into a gourmet lunch. Try a leaf or two of fresh sage in soups or stews, tucked under the skin of chicken or turkey, or chopped into breads or beans; it will make you a convert to fresh sage straight from the garden. Because it has a strong flavor, it tends to overwhelm more delicate herbs, making it almost pointless to try to combine it with basil, summer savory, salad burnet, or chives.

Attractive and sometimes fragrant, most *Salvias* are not valuable as culinary plants, although some have a history of medicinal and spiritual uses by Native Americans. There are many fruit-scented salvias, which are often used in herbal infusions or as a garnish, but most of them do not have Generally Recognized as Safe status. Plant them for their beauty and fragrance in the garden, for potpourri, or for use in floral arrangements. For use in recipes, stick with *S. officinalis*, common sage.

SAVORY

Satureja hortensis, S. montana

Family: Lamiaceae

Origin: Mediterranean

Hardiness: to zone 6

Light/Soil: full sun/moist to
slightly dry soil

The warm, slightly spicy flavor of savory has made it a culinary favorite for centuries. Vaguely reminiscent of thyme, and with a peppery bite, it is a delicious addition to soups, stews, and especially beans.

There are two primary species of savory grown for use in the kitchen: summer savory (*Satureja hortensis*) and winter savory (*S. montana*). Summer savory is an annual, growing to about eighteen inches, with pinkish lavender flowers. It tends to be a little floppy, so cut it freely and use the trimmings in the kitchen. Summer savory has a mildly piquant flavor that works well in a white bean salad. It is a summertime natural with a variety of vegetables, both fresh and cooked, and with eggs. A lemon-scented savory (*S. biflora*) is also an annual and can be used in both savory and sweet dishes.

Winter savory, an evergreen perennial hardy to zone 5, has a stronger flavor than summer savory and is most likely responsible for savory's time-honored reputation as a pepper substitute. It forms a low mound with white flowers in late summer. Winter savory can be used in the same dishes as summer savory, as well as with meat dishes and recipes that require longer cooking times. Both savories require full sun and well-drained soil to thrive.[45] Summer savory is easily started from seed in early spring. In some gardens, summer savory will reseed itself for a crop the following year. Summer savory can be dried for use over the winter, but if you are in zones 5–9, use your summer savory fresh and rely on winter savory in the cold months.

According to gardening tradition, summer savory rubbed gently over a bee or wasp sting will stop the pain. The experience of many herb gardeners is that bees are far more interested in flowers than in what you are doing, but this remedy might be worth a try if you find yourself at the stinging end of a bee.

SCENTED GERANIUMS

Pelargoniums

Family: Geraniaceae

Origin: southern Africa, cultivated

Hardiness: to zone 9

Light/Soil: full sun/well-drained loam

The scented pelargonium, commonly known as scented geranium, has been used for fragrance and flavoring since the 1700s. Fresh leaves from a plant on your windowsill or in your garden will add a special touch as a garnish or as an ingredient in many dishes or beverages, including cakes, salads, jellies, butters, ice creams, sorbets, liqueurs, teas, and fruit punch. The dried leaves are great additions to potpourri. Some pelargoniums are hardy to zone 7 or 8, and all are hardy in zone 9. They can easily be grown from cuttings placed in well-drained, sterile potting soil. Best plant growth is achieved in a sunny location with well-drained soil.

While many species and cultivars of scented pelargonium are used in cooking, the three most commonly sought for culinary use are peppermint (*P. tomentosum*), rose (*P. 'graveolens'*, also known as *P.* 'Rosé' or *P.* 'Old Fashioned Rose'), and lemon (*P.* 'Mabel Grey').

Always make sure the plant you purchase has a good strong scent, because scents will vary from plant to plant. Your recipes can be enhanced by its flavors if you alternate layers of scented pelargonium leaves with sugar or flour, allowing them to blend for several days to a week before use.

P. tomentosum is definitely the best mint-scented pelargonium to use in culinary endeavors. The "chocolate" in *P.* 'Chocolate Peppermint', a hybrid of *P. tomentosum,* refers to the brown color in the center of the leaf, which has no chocolate flavor.

Other rose- and lemon-scented varieties of pelargonium that can be used for cooking include *P.* 'Cinnamon Rose', *P.* 'Rober's Lemon Rose', *P.* 'Bitter Lemon', *P.* 'Frensham', and the tiny-leafed, lemon-scented *P. crispum.* Our Victorian ancestors floated leaves of *P. crispum* in finger bowls.

Experiment and enjoy the variety of flavors this group of plants offers.

SESAME SEEDS

....

Sesamum orientale

Family: Pedaliaceae

Origin: southeast Asia

Hardiness: annual

Light/Soil: full sun/moist soil

A sun-loving annual, *Sesamum orientale* requires three to four months with temperatures above freezing to produce seeds. Growing to about five feet tall, with narrow four-inch leaves close to the stem, sesame is an easy plant to grow in the garden, tolerating dry conditions and performing well in slightly sandy soil. In cooler climates, start the seeds indoors about six weeks before you move them to the garden in order to allow the plants time to produce seeds. When mature, the upright seed pods, which grow in the axils of the leaves, are a delight to children and adults alike when they pop open, releasing their long-treasured seeds.

Sesame is one of the first seasonings mentioned in recorded history, appearing twice in a twelfth-century BCE Assyrian creation myth. According to this myth, the gods drank sesame wine the night before they created the earth. Indeed, the myth credits a god with filling the earth's storerooms with "sesame, emmer, abundant grain." (Emmer, *Triticum dicoccoides,* is an ancient cereal grain.)[46]

For literally thousands of years, sesame has been an important economic crop. Its tiny seeds have from 45 to 63 percent oil and are 25 percent protein.[47] The oil has a continuing history of use in culinary, medicinal, beauty, and industrial applications.

Prized primarily for their sweet, nutty flavor, which is intensified by light toasting, sesame seeds are used in breads, cakes and cookies, vegetables, curry dishes, and confections. Tahini, a paste made from ground sesame seeds, is a major ingredient of hummus. Pressed, the seeds release a warm-flavored oil that is the basis of many dressings, marinades, and sauces.

Sesame seeds are straw-colored, red, or black. All are nutritious, flavorful, and store well because they contain a natural antioxidant called sesamol. This is a fun plant to grow in the home garden, but unless you plant a field of sesame, don't expect a large crop of seeds to harvest for year-round use. Just enjoy the plants, using what seeds you manage to save as a bonus.

SOCIETY GARLIC

Tulbaghia violacea

Family: Amaryllidaceae

Origin: South Africa

Hardiness: zone 7–11

Light/Soil: full sun/well-drained,
rich soil

Society garlic acquired its name from its reputation for providing a garlicky taste without clinging to the breath. The plant is a lovely choice for the border of a garden, as its flat, narrow leaves form large clumps of four to nine leaves, which grow to about twelve to fifteen inches long. A flower stalk emerges from the center of the plant in midsummer, growing to about eighteen inches tall; it is topped with an umbel of six-pointed, star-like pink flowers, each a little less than an inch across. Society garlic flowers sporadically through the fall, producing triangular black seeds that can be saved for planting the following spring. It can also be left to reseed on its own. It will spread from its tuberous roots, but it is not aggressive, forming a dense border of bright green leaves and pretty flowers.

The leaves and flowers, both with a strong garlic scent when bruised, have been used in salads and other dishes in much the same way as chives. If you really want a garlic flavor, you are better advised to use garlic chives (*Allium tuberosum*) or true garlic (*A. sativum*).

Society garlic has also been used to repel ticks and mosquitoes, as a snake repellent, as an aphrodisiac, and for coughs and colds. Its best use, however, is as an ornamental perennial border plant that can withstand heat and drought.

SORREL, FRENCH SORREL

Rumex scutatus

Family: Polygonaceae

Origin: Asia and Europe

Hardiness: zones 4–8

Light/Soil: sun to part shade/ tolerant of most soils

The word *sorrel* is derived from the French "surele," which translates as "sour." There are two sorrels that are commonly used in cooking: French sorrel (*Rumex scutatus*) and garden sorrel (*R. acetosa*). Both plants are represented in the Culinary Garden, and both have acidic leaves with a slightly lemony flavor. French sorrel is more highly favored, however, because it is milder. The sour taste of sorrel leaves is due to their high levels of oxalic acid, so people with a tendency to kidney stones, arthritis, or gout should consume them only in small amounts.

French sorrel has round, bright green leaves; very different from the arrow-shaped leaves of garden sorrel. It grows to about eighteen inches, with fleshy, large spinach-like leaves that easily snap off their succulent stems. Sow the seeds in moist soil in a sunny spot. It is not necessary to bury the seeds or to mulch the ground in which they grow. Once they start growing, thin the seedlings to produce one plant per twelve inches. During the growing season, harvest the leaves regularly and cut back the flower stalks to keep the leaves tender. Toward the end of the growing season, allow a few stalks to flower and set seed, as the seeds will drop and produce a new crop for the following season. You may also want to divide your plants every four years to keep them from getting too crowded.

Sorrel's young, tender leaves provide an interesting tang when used fresh in salads. Save the larger leaves for use in traditional sorrel soups, or blanch them quickly in boiling water and freeze for later use. Cook only what you need, as sorrel does not keep well once prepared.

Sorrel is an important ingredient in many French and Polish dishes, often cooked in a cream sauce as an accompaniment to salmon or veal. Sorrel also pairs nicely with eggs, goat cheese, and poultry. It is a popular salad herb in Britain, Ireland, Scandinavia, and China. The leaves have been used for many centuries. They formed a part of the cuisine of the ancient Egyptians, and they were used in the medieval era to make vinegar.

When you use sorrel, make sure you use stainless steel equipment, as the leaves can discolor your pots and knives.

TARRAGON

Artemisia dracunculus

Family: Asteraceae

Origin: Asia, Europe, North
America

Hardiness: to zone 5

Light/Soil: full sun/very
well-drained soil

Appreciated in cuisine from castle halls to country kitchens, tarragon is a somewhat elusive plant, not always easy to grow. Best used fresh, it is worth buying at the market if it is not growing in your garden.

French tarragon is a hardy perennial often termed sterile, as it has no blooms. Do not be fooled by the "seeds" offered as culinary tarragon; they are not from this plant but may be Russian tarragon (*A. dracunculus* subsp. *dracunculoides*), which has a balsam-like odor. French tarragon is propagated by cuttings and division. A reliable nursery should provide plants with the characteristic thin, light green leaves that offer a flavor and fragrance of anise when crushed or rubbed.

The fleshy, spreading roots of this plant do best in a rich, friable soil that is filled with compost and well-drained. Light mulch will help when the soil is thin and sandy. A cool climate with at least a month or two of freezing weather allow the plant a period of dormancy, which is needed for good growth. Humid summers will sometimes cause the plants to become weak and turn brown.

Container tarragon can be brought indoors in late winter for forcing (creating an environment in which the plant will grow outside its normal season). It will need good air circulation in a cool room with a sunny window to start a new growth cycle. Pick the leaves often to encourage sturdy growth. You can use them with chicken, eggs, cheese, vinegar, and sauces.

THYME

Thymus spp.

Family: Lamiaceae

Origin: primarily Mediterranean

Hardiness: to zone 6

Light/Soil: full sun/moist to
dry soil

The genus *Thymus,* comprising several hundred species that have a great diversity in color, form, and fragrance, is fascinating for both their beauty and their utility. Moreover, the study of the genus provides the intellectual challenge of delineating the various names attached to the plants.

Common thyme, *T. vulgaris,* is the plant most often used in the kitchen. It also is favored in medicine, having been used primarily as an antiseptic and muscle relaxant. It also has been used as a digestive aid, astringent, and nerve tonic. Thymol, the characteristic chemical constituent, is a common ingredient in oral hygiene products.

T. vulgaris is an upright perennial, growing to about twelve inches tall, with white to pale lavender flowers. Other thymes have a low, creeping habit, making them a bit more difficult to harvest but adding interest to the front of borders. The smallest of the thymes, *T. praecox* and *T. serpyllum* (rarely if ever found in cultivation in the Western Hemisphere) are wonderful for rock gardens.

T. vulgaris 'Narrow-leaf French' is a classic culinary choice due to the predominance of the essential oil thymol, which produces the distinct thyme fragrance. *T. vulgaris* 'Orange Balsam', with its characteristic piney, citrus-like fragrance, works very nicely in fruit salads. *T. vulgaris* 'Fragrantissimus' contains geraniol, which imparts a rose geranium scent that blends well in pound cakes and rice pilaf. Lemon thyme (*T. ×citriodorus*) contains citral, which gives it an essence that perfectly complements vegetables, chicken, and fish. The chemical carvacrol gives *T. pulegioides* 'Oregano-scented' its characteristic flavor, making it a good choice for Italian or Middle Eastern dishes. The decumbent Caraway thyme (*T. herba-barona*), only a few inches tall, owes its fragrance to the same chemical, carvone, that flavors caraway and dill seeds. It is consequently a good choice for use in sauerkraut, breads, and in making herbed vinegars to use with soups and greens.

Leaf colors of the thymes vary from dark to light greens and include variegated forms with silver or gold edges. All require full sun, well-drained soil, and good air circulation. Many thymes are hardy to zone 6.

TURMERIC

Curcuma longa

Family: Zingiberaceae

Origin: southern Asia

Hardiness: annual

Light/Soil: full sun to part shade/
consistently moist soil

Best known for the yellow color it imparts to mustard and curries, turmeric is an aromatic, slightly bitter spice from the root of *Curcuma longa*, a member of the ginger family. Its resemblance to ginger is noticeable in its growth form and habit. It reaches about three feet in height, with long, narrow leaves that look very much like a ginger plant. Its root also resembles a ginger "hand," with a fleshly rhizome from which protrude several fingers. The root of turmeric, however, is bright orange.

Turmeric has been used for centuries as a dye plant. If you have ever tried to remove a yellow mustard stain, then you are familiar with the staying qualities of the dye.

Turmeric also has many culinary uses. The root is peeled, steamed, and then dried and ground. It is an essential ingredient of curry powder and has found favor in Indian and southeast Asian dishes. Its pungent, bitter flavor is nothing like saffron, but it has been used as a saffron substitute, most likely because of its color. The results are disappointing, however, especially in baked goods.

Turmeric is a wonderful, warm spice to add to rice, chicken, chutneys, and pickles. Blend a teaspoonful into soups or stews, or whisk a little into melted butter and drizzle the mixture over vegetables.

Once ground, turmeric begins to lose its flavor, so store it in a dark place and replace it when you notice a decline in the flavor.

At the National Herb Garden, you can find this versatile herb in the Dye Garden, the Culinary Garden, and the Asian Garden.

VIOLET

Viola odorata

Family: Violaceae

Origin: Europe

Hardiness: zones 4–8

Light/Soil: sun to dappled
shade/cool, moist loam

Shyness, modesty, and devotion are the human qualities most commonly associated with sweet violets. Perhaps this is because of the way many of the flowers peek out from among their leaves, turning their faces to the earth, or because they bloom early in the spring, retreating before the profusion of spring blossoms parades forth in the garden. They certainly are not shy about reproducing, which they do prolifically. And that may be a clue to their name, which, in Greek, is "ion," which roughly translates as "to go." Affection for the little flowers grew primarily because of their indescribably sweet fragrance, which fades soon after you first notice the elusive scent. If you go back to them after a short while, your nose will again be receptive to the scent. Some unlucky souls completely lack the necessary receptors and thus never experience the enticing allure of the little violets.

Sweet violets filled the imaginations of people, who immortalized the plants in literature, art, and industry. They attracted much attention in the perfumery business and are still grown commercially for that purpose. Large violet nurseries in New York fed the demand for fresh violet bouquets in the United States from the late 1800s through the early 1900s. Few of those nurseries are left, most having closed by the early to mid-1900s, as more flashy flowers caught the public imagination. There are still those who covet violets in all their variety, searching out and growing the plants mentioned in literature and offered in old catalogs. The American Violet Society offers a forum for those interested in the flowers, providing information on violet culture as well as facts on violets in history, literature, art, and cooking.[48]

Violets have been used medicinally for thousands of years, applied for their anti-inflammatory, diuretic, and expectorant properties. Victorian ladies used a handful of violet flowers steeped in a cup of milk to moisturize and tone their skin. Just as varied is violets' history of culinary uses. They have graced tables as garnishes or flavored wines and cordials, served as the basis for hot and cold beverages, and flavored baked goods and sweets. Their leaves and flowers are used fresh in salads, and their flowers are candied as confections and as decorations for elegant desserts.

For all their versatility, violets are easy-care perennials, growing in either the sun or dappled shade, in cool, moist soils or heavy clay. They will multiply on their own, often self-pollinating, or by runners. In the fall, if you look close to the ground under violet plants, you will spot a second "flowering." These flowers have no pretty petals to catch your eye, but if you break open one of the green pods, you will find loads of tiny white seeds. The seeds drop to the ground and sprout, forming a colony of plants. Some suggest that ants pick up the seeds, carrying them to their hills as food. Some are lost along the way and sprout where they are dropped. Violets cross-pollinate freely, so if you have *V. odorata*, keep them separated from the scentless varieties to avoid ending up without any of that elusive fragrance to wake you in the spring from winter doldrums.

ZA'ATAR

A Spicy Blend

Neither a tree nor an herb, Za'atar is an Arabic word that literally means "thyme," but there is no *Thymus* species to represent it in the Arab culinary and medicinal world. Instead, Za'atar is a mixture of *Satureja, Thymbra,* or *Origanum*, depending upon where in the Mediterranean it is concocted.

The underlying selection criterion is that a plant smells right for use in the mixture. Plants that do so generally contain a large concentration of the chemical most associated with oregano, carvacrol.

If the cook lives in Crete he or she will gather the local plant *thyrba*, whose chief chemical component is carvacrol-based. In Lebanon the plant of choice is *Thymbra spicata*. In other parts of the Mediterranean it might be *T. capitata*, the "thyme of the ancients."

The plant of choice in Israel is "biblical hyssop," *Origanum syriacum*.

A traditional za'atar mixture consists of four parts za'atar *(O. syriacum)*, four parts roasted sesame seeds *(Sesamum indicum)*, one part sumach *(Rhus coriaria)*, and salt. More elaborate mixtures exist, and many families have their own recipe, in the same way that curry, kimchi, or herbes de Provence mixtures vary from family to family and region to region.

If you have bought a za'atar mixture at a Lebanese grocery store, you have tasted only one type of it, the key ingredient of which is desert or donkey hyssop *(T. spicata)*. Try making your own mixture using the "true hyssop," *O. syriacum*, and baking it on the traditional Middle Eastern bread, manaeesh, for a culinary delight of the first order.

Herbs Without Generally Recognized as Safe (GRAS) Status

In 1958, sections 201(s) and 409 of the Federal Food, Drug, and Cosmetic Act were implemented. This act declares that any substance intentionally added to food as an additive is subject to "premarket review and approval by the FDA, unless the substance is generally recognized, among qualified experts, as having been adequately shown to be safe under the conditions of its intended use." Food substances may be determined as Generally Recognized as Safe (GRAS) through "scientific procedures or, for a substance in use before 1958, through experience based on common use in food." GRAS status based on common use and experience requires a "substantial history of consumption for food use by a significant number of consumers."[1]

What this means is that you cannot necessarily rely on reported uses of a plant, historical or contemporary, to guide you in deciding what you will eat or what you will prepare to serve to others. In *The Big Book of Herbs*, Tucker and DeBaggio use the example of sassafras to illustrate the point nicely:

> An extract or oil of the root of sassafras, *Sassafras albidum* (Nutt.) Nees, contains 74 to 85 percent safrole; it also caused liver cancer in mice, rats, and dogs. Safrole is viewed as a pre-carcinogenic which is metabolized to the carcinogenic 1'-sulfoöxysafrole via 1'-hydroxysafrole (in mouse liver).
>
> Aside from safrole's ability to cause cancer, ingestion of 5 milliliters of sassafras oil by an adult or a few drops by a toddler causes death or at least induces vomiting, rapid heart beat, and muscle tremors.[2]

Banned by the FDA since 1960, sassafras is still consumed by some who either do not believe or do not care about these studies. Making such a decision for yourself is your business, but you must be especially careful about giving herbs without GRAS status to others.

There are a number of plants in the National Herb Garden, and more specifically in the Culinary Garden, that have recorded uses as culinary plants but lack GRAS status.[3] The Herb Society of America and the National Herb Garden at the U.S. National Arboretum recommend against using or consuming plants without GRAS status. Your health, and that of your family and friends, should be your first priority.

Nonetheless, the National Herb Garden continues to grow some of these plants for their history and for their attractiveness as ornamental plants. The plants from the Culinary Garden that lack GRAS status follow below.

ANISE HYSSOP

Agastache foeniculum

Family: Lamiaceae

Origin: United States

Hardiness: to at least zone 4

Light/Soil: full sun to part shade/average soil, moderately moist

A tough perennial native to North America, anise hyssop is a welcome addition to the National Herb Garden. Also known as giant hyssop, its newly expanding leaves have an attractive purple cast and unfold to a rich green. In the summer, the plant is topped with short spikes of light purple or dark blue flowers. There is a white-flowered cultivar known as 'Alabaster'.

Able to grow in almost any garden soil with full sun or just a bit of shade, anise hyssop clumps tend to get woody and are not long-lived. However, if a few flowers are left to go to seed, small plants will germinate in the garden, keeping a patch going. All aboveground parts of the plant have a unique fragrance: a light licorice scent combined with peppermint or pennyroyal. It was used as a culinary plant for many years.

Another species, closely related, is native to Asia and known as Korean mint. Its leaves and flowers are slightly larger than anise hyssop and its flowers are more violet in color.

Anise hyssop makes a wonderful addition to any herb garden. Beyond being delightfully fragrant in a gentle breeze, it is also appreciated by hummingbirds and butterflies. On a hot and sultry summer afternoon, anise hyssop is covered with many species of butterflies, as well as hummingbirds fighting for its nectar.

BEE BALM, BERGAMOT

Monarda spp.

Family: Lamiaceae

Origin: North America

Hardiness: to zone 4

Light/Soil: full sun/rich, light, moist soil

When midsummer is nigh and the magnolia is heavy with fragrant waxy white blooms, the "fireworks" plant, as some call their *Monarda didyma,* is bursting with spectacular bloom. A few magnolia blossoms, the spikes of bright blue salvia, a few blue bachelor buttons, and the brilliant scarlet *Monarda* in a basket or vase make a perfect arrangement for the Fourth of July table.

Monarda species are named to honor Nicholas Monardes, a Spanish physician who, in 1569, wrote an herbal of North American plants.[4] The fragrance of *M. didyma* reminded him of the bergamot, a small citrus fruit found growing along the Mediterranean coast, and the connection remains, though only in the common name of this plant.

Native Americans made use of *Monarda* for both culinary and medicinal purposes, most references being made to *M. fistulosa.* According to Tucker and DeBaggio, var. *fistulosa* is ordinarily found in the eastern United States, and subspecies *menthifolia* is found in the West.[5] *M. menthifolia* found favor among Pueblo Indians of the American Southwest for flavoring beans and stews. Tea was made from the dried leaves, which were also stored for winter use. The Tewa tribe near San Ildefonso in southern New Mexico carried *M. menthifolia* in small pouches around their necks and rubbed the powdered, dried leaves over their heads to relieve headaches.[6]

Flathead tribes of the Northwest gathered the fruits of the serviceberry tree both to eat fresh and to store for winter use. The dried fruits were pounded and formed into loaves, which were then sprinkled with powdered *M. menthifolia* to repel flies. The berries stored in this manner were later broken off into pieces and added to stews and pemmican recipes (pemmican is a high protein blend of meat, fat, and berries or flavorings), or mixed with flour and sweeteners to make a pudding.[7] Teton Dakota tribes brewed a tea of *M. menthifolia* leaves to soothe abdominal pains, and the plant was used by the Omaha Ponca to create a pomade for the hair.[8] The Blackfeet used the crushed leaves as a poultice for skin infections and a tea for throat gargles.[9]

Around the time of the American Revolution, *M. didyma* was adopted as an ingredient of a number of blends referred to as "Liberty Tea." Up to and following the Boston Tea Party, Americans were seeking alternatives to their favorite beverage. A number of plants were tried, among them New Jersey tea (*Ceanothus americanus*), Labrador tea (*Ledum groenlandicum*), sassafras (*Sassafras albidum*), and wintergreen (*Gaultheria procumbens*).[10] One of the most favored, for its citrus-like, minty flavor, was *M. didyma*. Colonists first learned about the plant from Oswego Indians, and they quickly adopted it to use alone or in blends.

Monarda species are hardy perennials that require full sun. Most will survive in a little shade, but they may develop problems with powdery mildew, which gives the leaves a grayish coating and causes them to curl up and die. Removing the diseased leaves will help, since the plant will replace them with fresh new leaves. *Monardas* grow to about three feet tall. They do well in moderately moist soils but will grow in most soil types. In the wild, they can be found along roadsides, in fields, and at the edges of forests.

Easy to propagate, this plant can be divided very early in the spring for best results and with no interruption in bloom. It can be moved anytime if cut back and kept in a moist, shady area until new growth forms. In summer, cuttings can be made, rooted in water, and planted in pots. Seeds can be collected when they are ripe or left to drop on the ground where the plants are to grow. Seeds, however, may not be true to the color of the parent plant.

Monardas are handsome, clump-forming plants that bloom in midsummer. If the spent flowers are removed, the plants will continue to bloom. Depending upon species, the plants may be pink, white, lavender, or red. Cultivars exist in a variety of colors, some with reported mildew resistance. Hummingbirds and bumblebees love these plants and are frequent visitors to them.

For a beautiful midsummer bloomer, plant *Monardas*. Regardless of their history, however, do not count on them for making tea.

BORAGE

....

Borago officinalis
Family: Boraginaceae
Origin: southern Europe
Hardiness: annual
Light/Soil: full sun/average soil

The pretty, clear blue flowers of borage were used for centuries to flavor cups of wine or claret, in which the star-shaped blossoms floated lightly and lent a delicate cucumber flavor to a sometimes unremarkable vintage. Such a beverage was touted by Pliny the Elder, a first-century Roman, as a means of lifting a melancholy mood. Over the years an association between the herb and the human conditions of joy and courage was established, not unlikely due as much to the wine as to the herb.

Borage grows quickly from seed in early spring. In the garden, the racemes of small five-pointed flowers face downward, supported by bristly stems reaching two feet in height. The downy buds shine in the June sun as though covered with frost and add an ethereal quality to the sometimes spindly plant. The large wrinkled leaves, covered with fine hairs, are said to have the same cucumber aroma as the flowers. Full sun, average soil, and moderately moist to dry conditions are all that is required for borage, which will occasionally re-seed in the garden.

Modern chemistry has alerted us to the presence of pyrrolizidine alkaloids, which may cause liver cancer, in the leaves, flowers, and seeds of borage.[11] All parts of the plant have been used for medicinal and culinary purposes in the past, but no parts are any longer recommended for consumption. Remember borage for its history, plant it for its beauty.

CUBAN OREGANO

Plectranthus amboinicus
Family: Lamiaceae
Origin: India
Hardiness: sensitive to frost
Light/Soil: full sun/lots of
moisture

Cuban oregano is not oregano at all, in spite of a fragrance reminiscent of both oregano and sage. Native to India, it has spread widely throughout the tropics and has a reputation as a popular flavoring in Caribbean cuisine.

Cuban oregano is an attractive plant, with large, fleshy, green leaves. *P.* 'Variegata' is edged with cream, while *P.* 'Well Sweep Wedgewood' leaves have a creamy center. The fuzzy leaves give texture to the garden, in addition to color and fragrance. The plant does well in full sun but will also grow in partial shade; it needs lots of water, though not constantly wet soil. Toward the end of the growing season, the plant puts forth spikes of small tubular flowers, generally in the lavender-blue range, that add to its appeal. It will grow to as much as thirty-six inches tall, making it a center of attraction in a small garden.

Cuban oregano will not withstand frost, but it will do well in a sunny window inside, so take cuttings and root them in water. It will remain attractive all winter and give you a good head start on your garden in the spring. It is well worth growing as an ornamental.

CULANTRO

Eryngium foetidum
Family: Apiaceae
Origin: South America
Hardiness: treat as an annual
Light/Soil: full sun/moist soil

Culantro is native to South America but has spread to tropical and subtropical areas around the world. It has been important to the cuisine of the Caribbean area, providing a distinctive flavor to soups, stews, and meat dishes. Culantro is often compared to the flavor of cilantro, but it is a bit more pungent, and the two plants are very different in appearance in spite of being in the same family. Culantro's lance-shaped leaves grow up to six inches long and have spiky, serrated edges, not easily confused with cilantro's parsley-like leaves.

Culantro grows best when shaded from hot sun and strong light, which will cause the plant quickly to flower and seed. Even so, culantro will grow in more heat than cilantro, so it is sometimes suggested that it be planted later than cilantro. Culantro seeds are slow to germinate, taking an average of two and a half weeks. Plant them in sandy loam that is kept moist but not wet. The plant will grow twelve to eighteen inches tall. Plants grown in shade are more aromatic than those grown in the sun and will provide better seed production.

One of the more popular ways to prepare culantro is in sofrito, a method of preparation with almost as many variations as there are cooks. Typically, sofrito is prepared like a pesto, and it usually contains culantro, garlic, bell peppers, onions, cilantro, and spicy peppers. Made without oil, it has a fresh and spicy flavor that makes it a natural in salsas, soups, stews, and bean and rice dishes. It is also served as a condiment with meats, and it is delicious spread lightly on a cracker. Sofrito keeps well in the refrigerator for several weeks, without the worries about spoilage associated with pesto. We recommend that you try sofrito, but that you make it with cilantro, which does have GRAS status.

EPAZOTE

....

Chenopodium ambrosioides

Family: Chenopodiaceae

Origin: southern and central
    Mexico

Hardiness: reseeding annual

Light/Soil: sun/well-drained

Epazote is included in the Culinary Garden because of its history as a flavoring herb in Central American dishes, though it is a minor herb. It achieved some status among adventurous cooks in the United States for the unique and pungent flavor it adds to soups, salads, and meat dishes. It is best known for its use in bean dishes, where it adds a flavor reminiscent of a combination of oregano, lemon, and petroleum, according to some, and a camphoraceous medicinal flavor with overtones of anise, according to others. Better choices for beans, corn, and other southwestern dishes are cilantro, chiles, and cumin.

Epazote has a reputation as a carminative (a remedy for intestinal gas), and its common name is derived from two Aztec words that roughly translate as "skunk sweat." It is known primarily for the use indicated by its botanical name, *Chenopodium,* or wormseed, a purgative for intestinal worms. The oil has been found to be deadly even at low doses.

Epazote is a native plant that reseeds freely in disturbed places and fields. It is a persistent annual, spreading by seed, and will tolerate drought. It grows to about three feet tall with deeply toothed, lance-shaped leaves and small greenish flowers in compound inflorescences that produce abundant seeds. The rough leaves, unpleasant aroma, and poisonous nature of this plant make it undesirable for the average garden and potentially dangerous in the kitchen.

MEXICAN OREGANO (1)

Lippia graveolens

Family: Verbenaceae

Origin: Mexico and Texas

Hardiness: to zone 10

Light/Soil: full sun/sandy, well-drained soil

This Mexican native is known as oregano though it is unrelated to *Origanum* spp. or to *Poliomintha bustamanta* (see next entry), both also called oregano. *Lippia graveolens* is used as an oregano substitute in Mexican cuisine and may be what you find if you purchase dried oregano in Mexico. It has some of the flavor characteristic of *Origanum* spp., with overtones of lemon and camphor, which make it so popular. The leaves are thick and roughly textured, but they are great on scent. In the drying process the leaves lose their camphor tones and become more mellow, allowing the oregano flavor to shine. Mexican oregano is traditionally used in soups, stews, corn, and pork dishes, and it is finding its way into Tex-Mex dishes in the United States.

In its native environment, Mexican oregano is a tall shrub like most of the species in the *Lippia* genus. This plant likes sandy, well-drained soil with full sun. As with most plants native to Central America, it is drought tolerant. This aromatic, tender perennial can withstand temperatures down to 20° F. If you are fortunate enough to be able to grow it outdoors, prune and shape it in late winter just prior to active growth. The tiny white flowers that bloom close to the stem add a lacy structure to the plant throughout the summer months. Whether you are growing the shrub outside in your herb garden (where it will reach heights of up to nine feet) or in a container indoors, this is a wonderful aromatic plant.

MEXICAN OREGANO (2)

Poliomintha bustamanta

Family: Lamiaceae

Origin: Mexico

Hardiness: zones 9–10

Light/Soil: full sun/well-drained, average soil

Mexican oregano is of Mexican origin, but it is not an *Origanum*. It most likely acquired its name from the slight oregano-like aroma and flavor of its leaves, and it has been used interchangeably with oregano in many dishes. It was brought into Texas from Sierra Picachos, just south of Laredo.[12] The plants are brought to market after harvesting by local people in the nearby mountains. Listed originally in the National Herb Garden as *Poliomintha longiflora*, the name has been changed to *P. bustamanta* in an effort to clear up confusion among the several species.

Mexican oregano is an attractive landscape plant, bearing one-inch-long tubular blossoms of lavender in the upper leaf axils throughout the summer growing season. The shrubby plant grows to about thirty-six inches tall, with an open, airy habit, and does best in full sun and well-drained soil. It is hardy in warm, dry climates, but it must be treated as an annual further north.

P. bustamanta is seldom found in local nurseries, so take advantage when you do come across the plant. It is worth the effort in your garden for its ornamental value.

MEXICAN TARRAGON

....

Tagetes lucida

Family: Asteraceae

Origin: Mexico

Hardiness: zone 7

Light/Soil: full sun/well-drained, moist soil

Mexican tarragon is frequently used as a substitute for French tarragon (*Artemisia dracunculus*) because they share a similar anise flavor. French tarragon has a far more subtle fragrance and a bit of spiciness to it, while Mexican tarragon, which has found favor among southern cooks because it grows reliably in warmer climates, is sweeter and has a stronger anise-like scent.

This is a hardy perennial to zone 7b, where the plant sometimes makes it through the winter. A real bonus when you grow this plant is the beautiful gold blossoms that last well into fall. All that is needed for success with Mexican tarragon is a loose, friable, but rich soil and full sun.

Mexican tarragon was used ceremonially by Aztecs and Indians of the Sierra Madre. A tea made from its leaves has been used to calm upset stomachs and to ease tension.

If you have trouble getting French tarragon to thrive in your climate because it is just too hot and humid in the summer and not cold enough in the winter, Mexican tarragon might be the solution because of its anise fragrance and attractive growth habit.

PINEAPPLE SAGE

Salvia elegans
Family: Lamiaceae
Origin: Mexico
Hardiness: to zone 6
Light/Soil: sun/rich, well-drained soil

Pineapple sage is an uncomplicated plant that wins the hearts of those who love fresh pineapple, hummingbirds, and gardens in the fall. The plant emerges from the ground in late spring, with an open-branched, airy growing habit reaching about three feet tall. In the fall it comes into its full glory and is covered with flowers that look like tiny scarlet trumpets, announcing the availability of nectar to hummingbirds that have yet to leave for their winter homes.

This plant bears little resemblance to its Mediterranean cousins in the *Salvia* (sage) genus. The egg-shaped, light green leaves, between two and four inches long and only slightly fuzzy, have a pleasant, fruity aroma similar to fresh pineapple. The plant needs full sun to produce a good show of flowers, and it does well with rich, well-drained soil. Pineapple sage is a semi-woody shrub in zones 9–11, a perennial that dies to the ground in zones 7–9, and an annual further north.

The flowers are delicate, not lasting long in a tabletop bouquet, but you can enjoy the pineapple fragrance, however short-lived.

RED VALERIAN

....

Centranthus ruber

Family: Valerianaceae

Origin: Europe and North Africa
to Asia

Hardiness: to zone 5

Light/Soil: full sun to part
shade/well-drained,
average soil

Known more for its ornamental than its culinary value, it comes as a surprise to some that red valerian has been used as a vegetable and bitter salad green. It has also been used for its sedative and antispasmodic qualities.[13]

It is an easy-care plant, with fleshy, lance-shaped, light green leaves and clusters of red, pink, or white flowers that bloom throughout the summer. It will grow in any soil, once established; it will tolerate drought and will survive winters as far north as zone 5. It grows particularly well along rock walls, perhaps because its roots are protected somewhat from temperature extremes. The mature plant reaches about two feet in height.

Red valerian, also known as Jupiter's beard, is an easy-to-overlook plant, but its attractive flowers and leaves will earn it a place of respect in your garden. Do not confuse this plant with the closely related true valerian (*Valeriana officinalis*), which is a medicinal plant.

SALAD BURNET

Sanguisorba minor

Family: Rosaceae

Origin: southern, western and
central Europe

Hardiness: to zone 5

Light/Soil: full sun to part shade/
moist, well-drained soil

With its compact, toothed leaves unfolding accordion-like at the ends of graceful arching stems, salad burnet makes an attractive edging plant for the front of an herb garden. The leaves and stems form a basal rosette reaching up to as much as eighteen inches tall. The plant's tiny green bottle-brush flowers bear bright red stamens, providing a surprise of quiet color in midsummer. William Turner's *Newe Herball*, first published in 1551, described salad burnet as looking like the wings of a bird ready to fly.[14]

Salad burnet does well in cool weather, usually surviving in the garden even though covered by snow. Though it has a delicate appearance, it starts growing again in early spring and is not particular about soil as long as the soil is well drained. It prefers lots of sun, but will grow in a little shade. Its low-growing habit makes it a good choice for containers, as the stems will hang gracefully over the edge.

Plants can be divided, but growing new ones from seed is easy. Sow seed indoors in late winter for transplanting outside in early spring. Once the plant is established, harvest the leaves as they grow. Cutting back the flowers as they develop in June and July will keep the leaves from becoming bitter, and new growth will continue to form throughout the summer.

Native originally to Mediterranean regions, this plant quickly spread throughout Europe and into the Americas. Salad burnet leaves have been used for hundreds of years in fresh green salads, with soft cheeses and herb butters, in soups, and sprinkled over vegetables. It makes an attractive garnish on serving plates. Sixteenth-century herbalist John Gerard recommended salad burnet as "pleasant to be eaten in sallads, in which it is thought to make the hart merry and glad, as also being put into wine, to which it yeeldeth a certaine grace in the drynkynge."[15] Francis Bacon favored fragrant plants, including "those which perfume the air most delightfully, not passed by as the rest, but being trodden upon and crushed, are three; that is, Burnet, Wild Thyme, and

Water-Mints; therefore you are to set whole alleys of them, to have the pleasure when you walk or tread."[16]

Such a versatile plant gets scant attention today, but is worth the little space and effort it requires to thrive as an ornamental addition to your garden.

SWEET CICELY

Myrrhis odorata

Family: Apiaceae

Origin: western Europe

Hardiness: zone 9

Light/Soil: part shade/moist soil

Growing as tall as five feet, with soft, green, fern-like leaves topped with umbels of sparkling white flowers in early summer, sweet cicely has long been a favorite of savvy gardeners for the shady nooks of their gardens. It is a lovely ornamental plant with a sweet anise-like fragrance, and it was favored by generations of western and northern European cooks, who used the leaves, unripe fruits, and roots generously in salads, fruits, and beverages.

Sweet cicely is a plant for cool temperatures; it grows quickly in early spring and into summer. In the heat and humidity of the Deep South, the plants often struggle to stay alive. The seeds may take a long time to germinate, so either sow them in the fall directly where they will grow, start them in damp peat moss in a plastic bag in your refrigerator, or simply purchase plants. If you start the seeds in the refrigerator, pot them up once they sprout, and keep them in a cool spot until you are ready to plant them outside. Once they are established and growing, trim the flowering stalks to keep the plant full and lush. Toward the end of the growing season, allow the plant to flower and set seed. Those seeds may provide you with new plants the following spring, growing alongside your parent plant.

In *A Modern Herbal* (1931), Maud Grieve wrote that the roots of sweet cicely "were supposed to be not only excellent in a salad, but when boiled and eaten with oil and vinegar, to be 'very good for old people that are dull and without courage; it rejoiceth and comforteth the heart and increaseth their lust and strength.'"[17] A glass of a lovely liqueur might accomplish the same. Despite its long history of use, however, sweet cicely should be grown only for its beauty and fragrance.

VIETNAMESE CORIANDER

Polygonum odoratum

Family: Polyganaceae

Origin: southeastern Asia

Hardiness: zone 8, otherwise treat as a tender perennial

Light/Soil: part shade/average soil, moderately moist

The weedlike little *Polygonum odoratum*, a member of the knotweed family, is commonly called Vietnamese coriander, though it neither looks nor tastes like coriander (*Coriandrum sativum*). *P. odoratum* is one of several plants that are common in southeast Asian cooking, especially in Vietnam and Malaysia, and it is a traditional herb in noodle soups called *laksa*, to which it lends a spicy, lemony fragrance. It is used with abandon in meat and seafood dishes, and it is often paired with lemongrass.

Vietnamese coriander is an easy-care plant that grows well in partial shade and moist soil. If you are in a dry region, plan on watering it regularly. It is small, reaching only about six inches in height, with light green, lance-shaped leaves that have a maroon blotch in the center of each leaf. The stems are typical of knotweeds, with many nodes. The plant seldom flowers, giving rise to the popular belief that the only way to propagate it is from cuttings. When it does flower, the inflorescence is a spike of deep pink flowers. It will sometimes form a small ground cover over the course of the summer, rooting as the plants arch over and touch the ground. For year-round use, pot a plant or two and set them in a sunny window before the first frost.

Vietnamese coriander is not recommended for consumption. If you are looking for a coriander flavor, use *Coriandrum sativum*.

Herbal Trees

What defines a tree as herbal is its use, whether culinary (for flavoring or seasoning), for medicine, dyes, or fragrance, or for cosmetic purposes. The terms *herb* and *spice* are strictly culinary terms, not scientific distinctions, and as such there are often blurry lines between the two. Occasionally a distinction will be made based on whether a plant is best when used fresh, as in the case of most herbs, or dried, as in the case of most spices. It is the leaves of bay trees (*Laurus nobilis*) that provide flavor for sweets and savories, so it is usually called an herb. Cinnamon (*Cinnamomum zeylanicum*), made from the dry inner bark of the tree, is traditionally called a spice.

Most plants used as spices appear in their dried form, including cinnamon, nutmeg (the dried "nut" or seed of the *Myristica fragrans* tree) and mace (the aril, or covering of the shell that houses the nutmeg), black pepper (the unripe dried fruits of the vining shrub *Piper nigrum*), cloves (the dried flower buds of the *Syzygium aromaticum* tree), and vanilla (the dried pods of a trailing vine, *Vanilla planifolia*).

The classification of a plant generally depends on the use to which it is being put. For example, the woody evergreen shrub or small tree *Juniperus communis* has multiple uses, including culinary (spice), medicinal (herb), and industrial. Some plants that are commonly referred to as herbs yield seeds that are considered spices: mustard, poppy, cardamom, anise, fennel, dill, cumin, caraway, and sesame, for example. The fresh leaves of some of these plants are also used, so whether you call them herbs or spices depends somewhat on what part you are using. Other plants simply defy classification. Ginger from the rhizomes of the plant, saffron from the stamens of the flower, and allspice from the unripe berries (or drupes) of the *Pimenta dioica* tree are all variously called herbs and spices.

There are twenty-five herbal trees in the National Herb Garden. Four of those are included in the Culinary Garden because they serve as flavoring agents. Several others could easily be included—such as juniper, black birch, pomegranate, and sassafras—but for reasons of space and additional uses are found elsewhere in the Garden. Still other herbal trees have no culinary merit but are included elsewhere in the Garden based on their use.

CINNAMON

....

Cinnamomum zeylanicum

Family: Lauraceae

Origin: southwest India, Sri
    Lanka

Hardiness: to zone 9, possibly 8

Light/Soil: sun or partial shade/
    moist, well-drained soil

Though it is not likely the ordinary gardener will grow a cinnamon tree to harvest the spice, you can see one in the Culinary Garden at the National Herb Garden. Grown in a large container, *C. zeylanicum* is brought into the Entrance Garden on the first of May and stays there until the last week of October. Native to Sri Lanka and southwest India, the evergreen tree grows to about thirty feet tall, with leathery green leaves, thick bark, inconspicuous yellowish flowers, and blue fruits. It is the inner bark of branches, stripped and dried, that is of interest to cooks.[1] There are several species of *Cinnamomum* available in markets, some more readily found than others.

Ceylon cinnamon (*Cinnamomum zeylanicum*)

Ceylon cinnamon, from the island of Ceylon, has a delicate, almost fruity aroma and taste, making it a good choice for dishes in which it will not have to compete with stronger flavors. It is excellent in baked goods, fruit dishes, puddings, and ice creams, and in whipped cream.

Chinese cinnamon (*Cinnamomum cassia*)

This cinnamon is native to southern China, Burma, Laos, and Vietnam, though commercial cultivation is limited to China and Vietnam. The flavor of this cinnamon is stronger and warmer than Ceylon cinnamon, holding its own against competing flavors in many baked dishes.

Indonesian cinnamon (*Cinnamomum burmannii* Blume)

This is the cinnamon you are most likely to find on grocery-store shelves. It is native to Malaysian regions and is exported in large quantities. Indonesian cinnamon is often used in commercial bakeries. It has a sharp, spicy fragrance.

Vietnamese cinnamon (*Cinnamomum loureirii* Nees)

A rich, dark cinnamon that is a favorite of many. Native to northern Vietnam, it is very similar to Chinese cinnamon, with a cassia-like flavor, but with even more depth.

It is fun to experiment with different kinds of cinnamon, and one of the easiest ways to do so is to use a plain sugar cookie recipe, dividing the dough into four separate batches and mixing in half a teaspoon or so (depending on the size of your recipe) of cinnamon in each batch. Bake as usual, and enjoy tasting the variations in flavor.

JUJUBE

Ziziphus jujuba

Family: Rhamnaceae

Origin: China

Hardiness: zone 5–9

Light/Soil: full sun/well-drained soil

One of visitors' favorite trees in the Culinary Garden is the jujube, which grows to thirty feet in height with branches that gracefully droop over the garden beds. Its name endears it to children, though it bears no resemblance to the candies once a popular snack in movie theaters. The attraction of the tree to others is its fruit—small, date-like drupes with slightly sweet flesh. Native to Asia, the trees have been a popular food source for four thousand years.

The jujube tree is now grown in northern Africa, the Middle East, and southern Europe. It was brought to the United States in 1837.[2] Jujubes are easy-care, deciduous trees, attaining their full height in many areas of the United States. To set fruit they need at least a short period of winter dormancy. They will grow in most soils, but do best in well-drained locations. They tolerate drought once established, but require moisture and lots of sunshine for good fruit production.

Tiny yellow flowers grow in the leaf axils from spring into summer, with fruits ripening over a period of several weeks from midsummer into fall. The fruits are small and oblong, usually about an inch or so wide. When ripe, the thin skins begin to take on a mahogany color, with crisp flesh that is faintly reminiscent of tart apples. As the fruits begin to dry, the skin wrinkles and they begin to resemble dates, with a drier flesh. They are best before they reach this wrinkled stage.

As with so many herbs, the fruits of the jujube tree have a history of medicinal use, primarily as a tea for sore throats.[3] Jujube fruits are prized fresh from the tree, but they can be dried or candied for use throughout the year. They must be picked when ripe, for they will not ripen once removed from the tree.[4]

MEDLAR

Mespilis germanica
Family: Rosaceae
Origin: southern Europe, Asia
Hardiness: at least to zone 5
Light/Soil: full sun/moist, not
   wet, rich soil

The medlar tree is striking in its Old World appearance, with crooked branches that bend at right angles and spread out rather than up. The leaves are almost leathery in appearance, as are the fruits, which bear some resemblance to large, maroon crabapples. The tree fits well in the Culinary Garden, being of small stature, although some cultivars do grow larger. Medlars have fallen out of favor in the modern world except with connoisseurs of unusual fruits.

Medlars are slow to germinate from seed, taking up to two years. Propagation for the trees is most often done by grafting, either onto pear, quince, hawthorn, or other medlar trees. They do well in most soils, especially if given some protection from freezing winds, and produce best in soil that tends to moist rather than dry conditions. The trees begin producing fruit in their third or fourth year.

The fruit of medlars is very hard, and to be edible it must go through a process called bletting. The fruit is harvested in the fall, while still quite hard. It is then stored in a cool room in a single layer, stem-end upright, until slightly overripe and soft to the touch. At this point the fruit is ready to eat. Properly ripened, it has a texture similar to apple butter, with a slightly sweet, tart taste. Most medlars are eaten raw, though they may be made into jelly.

In his *Complete Herbal* (1653), Nicholas Culpeper listed several remedies based on the medlar. He suggested that the powdered stones of the fruit, mixed with a little wine in which parsley root was infused, would break up kidney stones. (As with apples, pears, and apricot seeds and pits, the seeds of medlars contain a substance that converts to hydrogen cyanide when consumed. While not likely toxic in small quantities, consuming medlar seeds and pits is not recommended.[5]) Dried and powdered medlar leaves were recommended to stop bleeding, and a decoction of the fruit was useful for throat and mouth washes.

A more appetizing use of the fruit is that of Theodore Garrett, author of the 1898 *Encyclopedia of Practical Cookery*, who suggests making medlar cheeses. The recipe is quite simple, and the result is elegant. The amount of sugar called for the in recipe, however, correctly suggests that medlar fruit is not as sweet as some of the literature maintains:

> Put some medlars into an earthenware jar, stand it in a saucepan with boiling water nearly to the top and keep it boiling gently over a slow fire. When the medlars are quite soft, pass them through a fine hair sieve, and weigh the pulp, and for every pound allow one and a half breakfast cups of coarsely crushed loaf sugar and half a teaspoonful of allspice. Put all the ingredients together in the preserving pan, and stir them over the fire with a wooden spoon until thickly reduced, skimming occasionally. Turn the cheese into moulds, and keep them in a cold place. When ready to serve, turn the cheese out of the moulds on to a dish.[6]

The medlar is a tree well-suited to an herb garden. If you sip a glass of good wine while you enjoy the fruit of your tree, you will be following in a long tradition.

PAWPAW

Asimina triloba

Family: Annonaceae

Origin: North America

Hardiness: zones 5–8

Light/Soil: sun to partial shade/
rich, slightly moist soil

The children's song "Way Down Yonder in the Pawpaw Patch" is about as much as most people know about *Asimina triloba,* an indigenous American tree that produces an edible fruit. The flavor of the ripe fruit is vaguely similar to a blend of apple and mango. The four- to five-inch-long fruits have a pale yellow-green skin, several broad, flat, brown seeds, and a creamy, soft texture. Because of its appearance and texture, pawpaw fruit is commonly known as the "poor man's banana" or "custard apple."

The tree grows in abundance in sun or in open woods, with a range from Florida to Ontario; it grows naturally as far west as Nebraska and Texas. It needs a period of winter dormancy to set fruit, making the more southerly locations less desirable. The pawpaw is a small, deciduous tree, growing to about thirty feet in height, with distinctively large and drooping leaves. In early spring it produces solitary maroon flowers very close to the stems. The trees are not self-pollinated and require pollination from a genetically different tree, which means a single pawpaw tree is unlikely to produce fruit.

Pawpaws are usually understory trees found growing along stream edges in moist soil, but they are also found in dry deciduous forests with tulip poplars, maples, and sweet gum trees. Best fruit production comes from those trees getting abundant sunshine. It does not transplant easily, so in home gardens it is better planted from seed or nursery specimens.

The Pawpaw Foundation at Kentucky State University is attempting to develop a species of pawpaw tree that produces commercially viable, high-quality fruit that will withstand shipping and storage, as the soft fruit is easily bruised and keeps for only a few days after ripening.[7] The fruit is also very sweet and, according to the North Carolina State University Poisonous Plants list, can cause intestinal distress in some people.[8] The Louisiana State University Agricultural Center is also conducting variety trials on pawpaws to evaluate their ornamental use and their potential as a commercial crop.[9]

There are reports that Native Americans, who ate freely of the fruit and encouraged early colonists to partake of it, also used strips of the tree's bark to make netting. Recently, research has been conducted by Jerry McLaughlin at Purdue University to unlock the secrets of the pawpaw as a treatment for drug-resistant cancers, making pawpaw trees truly fit the definition of an herb.[10]

Pawpaw fruit is a nutritious food, with more protein, niacin, calcium, phosphorous, magnesium, iron, zinc, copper, and manganese than apples, bananas, or oranges. It is second to bananas in potassium and riboflavin, and second to apples in fiber content.[11] Peeled and seeded, it can be substituted for bananas in many recipes, but it is best eaten fresh from the tree. Pawpaws often fall from the tree before they are ripe, so if you can beat wildlife to them, ripen them until the skins turn brown and the fruits soften a bit.

Trees in the National Herb Garden at the U.S. National Arboretum

Botanical name	Common name	Garden
Aralia elata	Japanese angelica tree	Asian
Arbutus unedo	strawberry tree	Industrial
Asimina triloba	pawpaw	Culinary
Betula lenta	black birch	Native American
Citrus aurantium	sour orange	Fragrance
Corylus americana	hazelnut	Native American
Diospyros virginiana	persimmon	Native American
Eucalyptus globulus	blue gum	Medicinal
Eucommia ulmoides	hardy rubber tree	Industrial
Ficus carica	fig	Beverage
Ginkgo biloba	maidenhair tree	Medicinal
Hamamelis virginiana	witch hazel	Medicinal
Hevea brasiliensis	para rubber tree	Industrial
Juniperus communis	juniper	Colonial/Beverage
Laurus nobilis	sweet bay	Beverage
Malus 'Roxbury'	apple	Colonial

Trees in the National Herb Garden (*continued*)

Botanical name	Common name	Garden
Mespilus germanica	medlar	Culinary
Quillaja saponaria	soap-bark tree	Industrial
Pinus palustris	longleaf pine	Industrial
Poncirus trifoliata	hardy orange	Asian
Punica granatum	pomegranate	Beverage
Rhus glabra	smooth sumac	Dye
Sassafras albidum	sassafras	Native American
Vitex agnus-castus	chaste tree	Dioscorides/Fragrance
Ziziphus jujuba	jujube	Culinary

II Recipes

APPETIZERS

BIRD'S EYE BOURSIN

8 oz. cream cheese, softened

8 oz. sour cream

2 green onions, finely sliced

1 clove garlic, minced

1 tbsp. fresh thyme

1 tsp. chopped fresh rosemary

2 tsp. chopped fresh Italian parsley

2 tsp. poppy seeds

1 bird's eye pepper, seeded
    and minced

Salt to taste

In a bowl or food processor, thoroughly mix all ingredients. Refrigerate until ready to serve to increase firmness and blend the flavors. Put in a pretty crock, or shape on a platter.

Makes a good substitute for butter or mayonnaise on a sandwich and is especially good with a ripe summer tomato.

Henrietta McWillie, Member at large, Southeast District

CHEDDAR SPREAD WITH THYME AND PIMIENTOS

8 oz. cream cheese, softened

6 oz. sharp cheddar cheese, finely
    grated

2–3 tbsp. mayonnaise

1 tbsp. Dijon mustard

1/3–1/2 cup chopped pimiento;
    red bell pepper, roasted and
    peeled; or pickled peppers

1/3–1/2 cup finely diced sweet
    onion: Vidalia, Texas Sweet,
    Walla Walla, or Maui

1 1/2 tbsp. fresh minced thyme
    (or 1 1/2 tsp. dried thyme)

Soften the cream cheese in a bowl with a fork. Add the cheddar, mayonnaise, and mustard and blend well with a fork. Add the pimiento, onion, and thyme and mix thoroughly.

Cover and let the cheese mixture stand for at least 30 minutes before serving. May be prepared up to 24 hours ahead and refrigerated. Allow the spread to come to room temperature before serving.

Susan Belsinger, Potomac Unit

GEORGIA ROGER'S SPINACH BASIL SPREAD

1 pound fresh spinach, washed

1/2 cup fresh basil

1 clove garlic

3/4 cup picante sauce or salsa

1/2 cup pecans

2/3 cup grated Parmesan cheese

1/4 cup olive oil

Combine basil, garlic, picante sauce, pecans, and Parmesan cheese in a food processor. Process until well blended. Slowly add spinach and continue to process, adding olive oil as needed to maintain a spreading consistency. Serve with plain or flavored bagel chips.

Irene Davis, Member at large, South Central District

PESTO AND CREAM CHEESE ROUND

16 oz. cream cheese, softened

2 tbsp. hot water for shaping
cheese round

1 cup chopped fresh parsley

3/4 cup grated Parmesan cheese

1/4 cup chopped pine nuts

2 cloves garlic, crushed

2 tbsp. fresh basil

1/4 tsp. salt

1/8 tsp. pepper

1/3 cup olive oil

2 tbsp. butter, melted

Optional garnish:

Pimiento strips, roasted red bell
pepper strips, pine nuts, olives

Shape cream cheese into a 5 1/2-inch circle and place on serving dish. Use the hot water and a spatula to smooth cream cheese. Combine parsley, basil, Parmesan, nuts, salt, garlic, pepper, olive oil, and butter in a food processor to make pesto. Spoon pesto onto the cream cheese round. Garnish as desired. Cover and chill 2 hours.

Serve with crackers or toasted pita triangles.

Melinda Winans, Baton Rouge Unit

JULIET'S CHEESE LOG

8 oz. cream cheese
1/4 cup grated Parmesan cheese
1 tbsp. prepared horseradish
1/3 cup chopped Spanish olives
4–5 dried beef slices

In a medium bowl, thoroughly blend cream cheese, Parmesan cheese, and horseradish. Gently stir in the chopped olives. Shape the mixture into a log. Roll the cheese log in the dried beef slices until the outside is covered. Wrap in waxed paper and aluminum foil and chill.

Serve thinly sliced on assorted crackers. Also makes a good filling for cream cheese sandwiches.

Joyce Brobst, Pennsylvania Heartland Unit

ELLEN'S TORTA

8 oz. cream cheese, softened
2 tbsp. butter, softened
1/4 cup sour cream
1 or 2 garlic cloves, pressed
1/2 cup dried tomatoes packed
    in olive oil, drained and finely
    chopped
1/2 cup basil pesto

Beat cream cheese and butter together. Add sour cream and garlic; beat again. In a 4-by-8-inch clear glass oval dish (to show the layers) place in successive layers, sealing as you go:

Tomatoes
Half the cream cheese blend
Pesto
Remaining cheese blend

Cover with plastic wrap and refrigerate for at least 24 hours. Let warm slightly before serving with plain wheat crackers or thin sliced French or sourdough bread. You may wish to garnish with fresh basil sprigs. Serves about 25.

Ellen Scannell, Member at large, West District

FRESH HERB CHEESECAKE

1 tbsp. butter

1/3 cup unseasoned bread crumbs

1/4 cup freshly grated Asiago cheese

1/2 tsp. dried thyme

16 oz. cream cheese, softened

1/3 cup butter, melted

2 cloves garlic, minced

1/2 tsp. Worcestershire sauce

2 tbsp. chopped fresh parsley

1 tbsp. chopped fresh oregano

1 tbsp. chopped fresh thyme

2 tsp. chopped fresh summer savory

2 tsp. snipped fresh chives

1/4 tsp. cracked black pepper

4 large eggs, room temperature

Preheat oven to 350°F.

Using 1 tablespoon butter, grease the bottom and half-way up the sides of a 9-inch springform pan. In a small bowl, combine bread crumbs, dried thyme, and grated cheese. Press the mixture into the bottom of the greased pan. Place springform pan on a baking sheet and bake for 10 minutes. Remove the pan to a wire rack to cool.

In a quart bowl, with mixer at medium speed, beat cream cheese until fluffy. Beat in melted butter, garlic, Worcestershire sauce, and herbs until well mixed. Add eggs one at a time, beating well after each addition. Pour the filling over the baked crust. Bake for 1 hour, then turn the oven off and leave the door ajar, with the cheesecake inside. Allow cheesecake to sit in the warm oven for an additional 30 minutes, then remove to a wire rack to cool. Cover cheesecake with plastic wrap and store in refrigerator until the filling is set.

Serve in very thin slices with crackers and garnished with a few fresh thyme sprigs.

Mary Nell Jackson, North and Central Texas Unit

ROSEMARY WHITE BEAN PUREE

1 (15-ounce) can cannellini beans, drained, reserving 2 tbsp. liquid

4 (6-inch) sprigs rosemary

5 cloves roasted garlic

2 tbsp. chopped onion

1/3 cup freshly grated Parmesan cheese

2 tbsp. olive oil

1 fresh chile pepper, seeded and chopped

1/4–1/2 tsp. salt

Strip the rosemary leaves from the stems and place in a food processor. Squeeze the garlic cloves out of their skins and add to the rosemary, along with the chopped onion, Parmesan cheese, and the chile pepper. Pulse just enough to blend. Add drained cannellini beans.

Continue to blend, adding olive oil and enough reserved liquid from the beans to make a good spreading consistency.

Serve as a dip or a spread. This recipe can also be used as a layer in the preparation of a vegetable lasagna.

Vivian Utko, New York Unit

PEASANT RYE DIP

8 oz. sour cream

1 cup mayonnaise

1/3 cup chopped fresh parsley

1/4 cup finely chopped onion

3 tbsp. chopped fresh dill weed
(or 3 tsp. dried)

2 tbsp. chopped green or
black olives

1 round loaf seeded rye bread,
unsliced

In a medium bowl, blend sour cream, mayonnaise, parsley, onion, dill, and olives. Cover and refrigerate at least 2 hours or overnight.

Remove top fourth of bread, cut into chunks, and allow chunks to air-dry briefly—these chunks will be used for dipping. Scoop out the insides of the loaf, forming a bowl.

When ready to serve, put rye bowl on a serving platter and fill with the dip. Garnish with olive slices or sprigs of dill. Arrange chunks of bread around the edges.

Rose Miller, Pennsylvania Heartland Unit

GRILLED CORN DIP

1 1/2 cups corn kernels, cut from
grilled corn (4–6 ears)

3 oz. cream cheese, softened

1 tbsp. fresh lemon juice

3 tbsp. heavy cream

1 clove garlic, pressed

2 tsp. fresh oregano leaves

2 tbsp. pimiento, chopped

2 tbsp. chopped fresh chives

1 tbsp. chopped fresh parsley

1/2 tsp. salt

1 tsp. chopped fresh sage

1/4 tsp. hot pepper sauce

Tortilla chips

In a small bowl, blend together cream cheese, lemon juice, cream, garlic, oregano, pimiento, chives, parsley, and sage. Stir in corn, salt, and hot sauce to taste. Cover and refrigerate at least 2 hours.

Serve with tortilla chips.

Pat Brabazon, South Jersey Unit

LEMON VERBENA DIP

8 oz. cream cheese, softened

8 oz. lemon yogurt

1/4 cup lemon verbena leaves, very finely minced (use tender leaves)

1/4 cup sugar

1/3 cup fresh lemon juice

Mix all ingredients thoroughly. Cover and refrigerate overnight.

Serve with sliced fresh fruit or plain cookies.

Marilyn Rhinehalt, Western Reserve Unit

TARRAGON GOAT CHEESE MOUSSE

15 oz. ricotta cheese

4 oz. goat cheese

1 whole head garlic

2 tbsp. chopped fresh chives

2 (5-inch) sprigs tarragon

1 tsp. olive oil

Preheat oven to 400°F. Slice top from the head of garlic and place head on a large square of aluminum foil. Drizzle olive oil over the top and wrap. Bake for about 30 minutes—until soft and lightly browned.

Drain the ricotta cheese in a cheesecloth-lined strainer for about an hour. In a food processor, mince the herbs. Squeeze the soft garlic out of the head and into the herbs, add cheeses, salt, and pepper to taste. Process until blended. Chill.

Serve with crackers.

Linda Franzo, New Orleans Unit

HERB-ROASTED GARLIC

2 heads garlic

4 tsp. olive oil

2 tsp. honey

1 1/2 tsp. fresh basil (1/2 tsp. dried)

1 1/2 tsp. fresh rosemary (1/2 tsp. dried)

Slice the garlic heads in half horizontally. Drizzle 1 teaspoon olive oil on exposed cloves, then drizzle with 1/2 teaspoon honey. Sprinkle with herbs. Wrap garlic in aluminum foil and bake for about 45 minutes, or until soft.

Spread on whole grain crackers or pita triangles.

Ed Pierzynski, South Jersey Unit

FRESH HERBED SPRING ROLLS

1 package 8-inch round spring
   roll skins
1/2 cup finely shredded cabbage
1/3 cup finely shredded carrots
1/3 cup precooked rice vermicelli
   noodles
1/3 cup fresh mung bean sprouts
1/3 cup sliced scallions
1/3 cup finely sliced green peppers
1/3 cup finely sliced red peppers
1/4 cup small leaves of basil, sage,
   tarragon, or other favorite
   herbs
2 tbsp. nasturtium or
   calendula flowers

Finely chop all vegetables and toss lightly in a large glass bowl with noodles. Carefully wash and dry herbs and flowers, setting aside in a separate bowl.

Immerse the spring roll skins, one at a time, in a shallow bowl of warm water until softened, at least 20 seconds. Remove from water and place on a flat surface.

Place 1/3 cup prepared vegetables on a spring roll skin, leaving a 2-inch border at the bottom edge. Carefully fold bottom up over filling, fold in left and right sides, and then finish rolling the rest tightly. After a few practices, you will get good at it. It is then fun to carefully place the flowers and herbs in a decorative fashion so that they will show through the skin when the roll is finished. Try placing the decorative pieces first and then cover with the 1/3 cup of vegetables.

As completed, cover the rolls with damp paper towels and wrap tightly in plastic until ready to serve. They get tough and stick together if left dry. Refrigerate and garnish the serving dish with some of the leftover herbs and flowers.

Delicious served with a cilantro peanut sauce or a soy sauce with lime and hot pepper.

Anita Bradley, Pennsylvania Heartland Unit

CUCUMBER DILL SALSA

2 cucumbers, peeled, seeded,
   and chopped
3 plum tomatoes, chopped
1/4 cup chopped chives or
   green onions
2 tbsp. chopped garlic chives
2 tbsp. chopped, fresh dill
1 tbsp. lemon or lime juice
Pepper to taste

Combine all ingredients. Chill and serve. Makes a good dressing for hummus on a pita.

Jennifer F. Jordan, Tidewater Unit

HERBED OLIVES

2 cups unpitted ripe or green olives

1 bay leaf

2 small hot dried chiles

2 tbsp. drained capers

2 cloves garlic

12 rosemary leaves

2 tbsp. finely chopped celery leaves

1 cup olive oil (or more as needed)

Press each olive between your fingers so the marinade can penetrate the olive. Place olives in a glass jar with all ingredients except the olive oil. Pour in enough olive oil to cover the olives. Cover jar and shake well. Refrigerate for 3 or 4 days before using.

Remove garlic if olives are stored any longer than 4 days.

Marion Foster, Tidewater Unit

ROSEMARY OLIVES

1/4 cup dry white wine

3 tbsp. olive oil

1 1/2 tbsp. white wine vinegar

1 tbsp. fresh orange juice

1/4 tsp. fresh orange zest

1 1/2 tsp. minced fresh garlic

2 tsp. chopped fresh rosemary

1/2 cup finely chopped red onion

2 cups assorted brine-cured black
    and green olives

Whisk together first 7 ingredients. Stir in red onion and olives, coating all. Chill for at least 1 day, stirring several times. Drain just before serving.

Dorothy Bonitz, North Carolina Unit

INBAKAD LAX

1 skinless salmon fillet

Pie crust to fit around fillet

1/3 stick butter, melted

1 clove garlic, crushed

1 tbsp. fresh tarragon

1 tbsp. fresh chervil

Salt

1 lemon wedge

Parsley for garnish

I learned this recipe from a former student from Sweden.

Preheat oven to 400°F. Combine butter, garlic, tarragon, and chervil. Salt the salmon. Cut a slit in the salmon and pour butter mixture into the slit. Fold pie crust around the fillet. Lightly sprinkle a little water over the crust.

Bake for 20–25 minutes. Cut into hors d'oeuvre–size pieces. Serve with lemon and parsley.

Lory Doolittle, Connecticut Unit

GRANDMA ADAMS' MEAT LOAF BALLS

1 1/2 pounds lean ground beef
1/2 pound ground pork sausage
1/2 cup bread crumbs
1 medium onion, chopped
1 clove garlic, pressed
1 1/2 tsp. salt
1/2 tsp. pepper
1 rounded tsp. paprika
1/4 tsp. allspice
1 tsp. fresh summer savory
1/2 cup tomato juice

Preheat oven to 350°F. Mix all ingredients in a large bowl. Form into 2-inch balls and place on an ungreased baking sheet. Bake for 1 hour 20 minutes.

Ellen Adams, Member at large, Great Lakes District

MIXED HERB CRACKERS

1 cup all-purpose flour
1/2 tsp. salt
1/4 tsp. pepper
2 tbsp. chopped fresh chives
1 tbsp. chopped fresh thyme
1 tbsp. chopped fresh oregano
4 tbsp. cold butter
1/4 cup sour cream
Salt for sprinkling

Combine dry ingredients. Cut in the butter until crumbly. Add herbs and mix well. Stir in sour cream and mix until the dough comes together. Divide in half and roll each piece into a sheet 1/8-inch thick. Sprinkle with salt and press lightly. Cut into 2 1/2-inch squares using a fluted edge cutter.

Place on a baking sheet and pierce each cracker with a fork. Bake at 325°F until just brown and firm.

Cool on a wire rack and store in an airtight container. Yields 24 crackers.

Paula Weiss, Old Town Alabama Unit

POLENTA TRIANGLES WITH ROSEMARY AND WALNUTS

2 1/2 cups chicken broth

2/3 cup yellow cornmeal
(coarse-grain)

3/4 cup grated Gruyère cheese

3 tbsp. butter

1/3 cup walnuts, toasted and
finely chopped

1 1/2 tsp. chopped fresh rosemary

8 walnut halves

White pepper to taste

Preheat oven to 350°F. Butter a 9-inch glass pie plate. Bring broth to a boil in a medium saucepan; then gradually whisk in cornmeal. Reduce heat and whisk constantly until mixture thickens, about 10 minutes. Remove from heat.

Add cheese and 1 1/2 tablespoons butter, stirring until melted. Stir in chopped walnuts and rosemary. Season with white pepper.

Transfer polenta to a dish and spread around evenly. Cool until firm, at least 1 hour.

Cut polenta into triangles, dot with butter; place walnut half in center of each triangle and bake for 10–12 minutes, until golden brown.

Kay Wagstaff, North Carolina Unit

ROSEMARY CHEDDAR BITE-SIZED BARS

4 tbsp. butter

2 cups rolled oats

1 1/2 cups cheddar cheese, grated

1 egg, beaten

1 tbsp. fresh rosemary

Pinch of ground cayenne pepper

Preheat oven to 350°F. Grease bottom of an 8-inch square pan. Melt butter in a saucepan. Mix the remaining ingredients in a bowl, then blend in the melted butter. Press mixture into prepared pan. Bake for 35 minutes. To serve, cut into bite-sized bars.

Becky Cortino, Member at large, Mid-Atlantic District

ROSEMARY WALNUTS

2 cups walnut halves

1 tbsp. finely minced fresh rosemary

1/2 tsp. turmeric or light soy sauce

1/2 tsp. herb salt blend

1/2 tsp. Lawry's seasoned salt

Coarsely ground salt to taste

Put walnuts in a medium to large frying pan. Heat on medium until walnuts begin to release their oil, stirring frequently and watching carefully to keep them from burning. When walnuts are hot and beginning to release oils, add remaining ingredients to taste. Sprinkle with coarsely ground salt when finished.

Joan King, North Carolina Unit

WARM BRIE WITH BLUEBERRY THYME CHUTNEY

1 cup fresh blueberries (frozen
    may be substituted)

2 tbsp. finely chopped onion

1 1/2 tsp. grated fresh gingerroot

1 1/2 tsp. minced fresh lemon
    thyme

1/4 cup brown sugar, firmly packed

2 tbsp. cider vinegar

1 1/2 tsp. cornstarch

1/8 tsp. salt

1 (3-inch) cinnamon stick

1 (8- or 15-ounce) Brie

In a large saucepan, combine all chutney ingredients, mixing well. Bring to a boil over medium heat, stirring frequently. Boil 1 minute and remove the cinnamon stick. Cool slightly, then refrigerate for 30 minutes or until cooled.

Heat oven to 350°F. Place cheese on an ungreased baking sheet. Heat for 10–12 minutes, until cheese is softened.

Place cheese on a serving plate and top with chutney. Garnish with sprigs of fresh mint or thyme. Serve with crackers. Yields 10 servings.

Lola Cleavinger, Member at large, South Central District

BEVERAGES

ROSE GERANIUM TEA

2 cups sugar
1/4 cup chopped fresh rose
   geranium leaves
5 cups mineral water

Mix sugar, rose geranium leaves, and mineral water in a saucepan. Bring to a boil, reduce heat, and simmer for 5 minutes. Cool to room temperature and refrigerate overnight. Strain and discard the rose geranium leaves. Yields 3 quarts.

Pat Dennis, Northern California Unit

ROSE HIP HERBAL TEA

1 tbsp. dried rose hips
1 tsp. fennel seeds
1 tsp. freshly grated gingerroot
2 tsp. fresh lemon verbena
3 cups boiling water
3 thin slices lime
3 tbsp. rose hip liqueur

Warm a teapot by rinsing with hot water. Add all herbs to the pot, then fill the pot with freshly boiled bottled or filtered water. Cover the pot and allow the herbs to steep for 5 minutes. Strain out the herbs. Serve with a little honey and a slice of lime, or, if desired, a spoonful of rose hip liqueur. Yields 3 cups.

Katherine K. Schlosser, North Carolina Unit

SUMMER TEA

2 cups water
1 cup sugar
10 tea bags
1/2 cup packed fresh mint leaves
6 oz. frozen lemonade
6 oz. frozen limeade
Juice of 1 orange

Combine water and sugar in a saucepan and bring to a boil; reduce heat and simmer for 5 minutes. Remove sugar syrup from heat and add tea bags and mint. Allow to steep for 5 minutes, then remove tea bags. Allow mint to steep for an additional 20 minutes, then strain out the leaves. Add lemonade, limeade concentrates, and orange juice. Stir well, then add enough water to make 1 gallon. Chill until ready to serve. Can be kept in the refrigerator for several days.

Henrietta McWillie, Member at large, Southeast District

CRABAPPLE THYME LIQUEUR

1 cup water

2 cups sugar

6 (4-inch) sprigs fresh thyme

4 cups vodka

1 quart crabapples

Combine water and sugar in a small saucepan. Bring to a boil and simmer for 5 minutes. Remove from heat; add 3 thyme sprigs and allow to steep while preparing crabapples.

Wash crabapples, remove stems and seeds, and coarsely chop. If you are using small crabapples, just cut in half.

Fill a large glass jug with the crabapples; add 3 sprigs of thyme. Remove thyme from the sugar syrup, then pour the completely cooled syrup over the crabapples. Add vodka and shake well to blend; cover with a nonmetallic lid and allow to steep for 4 weeks, shaking from time to time.

At the end of 4 weeks, strain out the crabapples and thyme (use a dampened coffee filter). Pour into sterilized glass bottles and cap with nonmetallic lids.

This is great served as is; it has a lovely color and wonderful flavor. You may also use it to replace some of the liquid in your favorite pound cake or cookie recipe. Make a glaze for your cake or cookies using the liqueur as the liquid. You can also put a tablespoonful into the bottom of a wine glass, then pour in your favorite white wine. Pour a little over ice cream, or use it in a fruit marinade. Have fun with it!

Katherine K. Schlosser and **Joan Musser**, North Carolina Unit

CRANBERRY ORANGE ROSEMARY LIQUEUR

2 cups sugar
1 cup water
2 (6-inch) sprigs rosemary
1 1/2 cups vodka
1 pound cranberries
1 orange

Combine sugar and water in a small saucepan. Bring to a boil, reduce heat and simmer for 10 minutes. Remove from heat; add rosemary sprigs. Allow to cool.

Coarsely chop cranberries. Remove zest from orange, being sure to avoid the white pith.

Put cranberries and orange zest in a large glass jar. When syrup is cool, remove rosemary sprigs. Pour syrup over the cranberries and add vodka. Shake the jar to mix all ingredients. Cover with a nonmetallic lid and store in a cool, dark place for 5 weeks. Shake the jar daily.

After 5 weeks, strain the liqueur through a dampened coffee filter. Repeat this step until the liqueur is clear.

Bottle and cap with a nonmetallic lid. Keeps its color and flavor for up to a year.

Katherine K. Schlosser and **Joan Musser**, North Carolina Unit

LEMON LIQUEUR

7 lemons
1 fifth of 100-proof vodka
2 cups sugar
2 1/2 cups bottled or filtered water
1/2 cup lemon verbena leaves

Pour the vodka in a large glass jar. Carefully wash and dry the lemons, then remove the zest with a vegetable peeler or zester. Be careful not to remove any of the bitter white pith. Drop the lemon zest and lemon verbena leaves into the vodka. Cover the jar with a nonmetallic lid and let the vodka rest for 14 days in a cool, dark place. Remove lemon verbena leaves.

At the end of 2 weeks, bring sugar and water just to a boil in a small stainless steel saucepan. Allow the syrup to simmer gently for about 10 minutes. Remove from heat and allow to cool.

Uncover the vodka and add the cooled simple syrup. Cover again and age for 4 weeks, then strain out the lemon zest using a dampened coffee filter. Rebottle and store in the freezer or refrigerator.

Katherine K. Schlosser, North Carolina Unit

MINT LIQUEUR

1 1/2 cups tightly packed fresh
  mint leaves
3 cups vodka
1 cup sugar
1 cup water
1 tsp. glycerine, optional

Place mint and vodka in a quart glass jar; close tightly with a nonmetallic lid and shake well. Let steep for 10 days to 2 weeks in a cool, dark place, shaking daily. Strain and filter (use a dampened coffee filter), pressing the leaves hard to release flavor.

In a small saucepan, combine sugar and water. Bring to a boil, reduce heat, and simmer, uncovered, for 5 minutes. Cool to room temperature.

Add sugar syrup to vodka. Add glycerine to thicken slightly, if desired. Cover tightly (with nonmetallic lid), shake well, and allow to age for 4 weeks before using.

Barbara Brawley, Tidewater Unit

ROSE HIP LIQUEUR

1/4 cup water
1/2 cup sugar
1 tsp. aniseed
3 tbsp. crushed fresh rose hips
  (1 tbsp. dried)
12 oz. vodka

Put aniseed in a small glass bottle. Add vodka and allow to steep for 1 week.

Strain out the aniseed, add rosehips, and allow to steep for 4 weeks.

Combine water and sugar in a small saucepan. Bring to a boil, reduce heat, and simmer for 5 minutes. Remove from heat and allow to cool.

Filter the vodka through a dampened coffee filter. Pour into a sterilized bottle and add sugar syrup. Allow to mellow for at least 2 weeks.

Katherine K. Schlosser, North Carolina Unit

SPICE LIQUEUR

1 cup water
2 cups sugar
6 cardamom pods, seeds removed
3 tsp. aniseed
1 cinnamon stick, broken into pieces
1 whole clove
4 cups vodka

Combine water and sugar in a small saucepan. Bring to a boil and simmer for 5 minutes. Allow to cool completely.

Crush the aniseed lightly in a mortar. Put aniseed, cardamom seeds, cinnamon, and clove in a glass jar. Pour vodka over the spices, Shake well and allow to steep for 1 week.

Strain the vodka several times through a dampened coffee filter. When clear, add sugar syrup; pour into a sterilized glass bottle, cover with a nonmetallic lid, and allow to mellow for 4 weeks.

A very nice spice flavor that is good as is, drizzled over ice cream or pound cake. Put a spoonful into a steaming cup of tea!

Katherine K. Schlosser and **Joan Musser**, North Carolina Unit

MAYAN HOT CHOCOLATE

20 Sonoran chile peppers (or
   1–2 regular hot peppers)
1 pint whipping cream
1 gallon whole milk
2 vanilla beans, split lengthwise
2 oz. hazelnuts, chopped
1 tsp. Ceylon cinnamon
20 oz. semisweet chocolate
4 oz. unsweetened chocolate
2 tbsp. honey

Crush the chile peppers in a small dish; put peppers into a saucepan, and add 2 cups boiling water. Cook until liquid is reduced to approximately 1 cup. Strain water, discard peppers, and set aside.

In a large pot, combine cream, milk, vanilla beans, hazelnuts, and cinnamon. Warm over medium heat until bubbles form around edge of pot (whisking occasionally so as not to allow milk to burn on the bottom of the pan). Reduce heat to low. Add chocolate and honey. Whisk occasionally until chocolate is melted. Turn off the heat. Remove vanilla beans and strain out the hazelnuts. Add the chile-infused water a little at a time until desired level of heat is achieved (taste after each addition).

Amy Pollock, National Herb Garden Intern (2001–2002)

MAI WINE

1/2 cup sugar

1/4 cup water

12 sprigs sweet woodruff
    (include flowers)

1 orange, washed and sliced thinly

2 lemons, washed and sliced thinly

2 bottles dry white wine

1 cup brandy

Mai Wine Ice Ring (see directions
    below)

Sweet woodruff blossoms, fresh
    small whole strawberries, and
    violet blossoms for garnish

Combine sugar and water in a small saucepan. Bring rapidly to a boil, then reduce heat and simmer for 5 minutes; cool.

In a large glass container, layer sliced oranges, lemons, and sweet woodruff. Pour syrup over fruit, then add wine and brandy. Cover and steep for 24 hours.

At serving time, strain wine mixture into a punch bowl, discarding lemon, orange, and sweet woodruff. Float ice ring in center. Garnish with sweet woodruff blossoms, small strawberries, a few lemon slices, and violets.

MAI WINE ICE RING

Wash a handful of sweet woodruff blossoms and leaves, violet blossoms, and fresh strawberries with hulls and stems.

Chill a large bottle of water and a ring mold that will fit into your punch bowl and still leave room for a punch ladle. Fill the bottom fourth of the mold with the chilled water and freeze until nearly firm.

As the water begins to freeze, arrange sweet woodruff, strawberries, and violets around the ring. Make sure they stay toward the outside edges as well as in the center of the mold. Return to freezer for 30–45 minutes or until flowers are frozen in place. Slowly pour additional water around the flowers, without covering them, and taking care not to dislodge them. Return to freezer until the additional water has frozen. Add a little more water and freeze firm.

Add additional flowers, repeating the above process until the ring is full. Freeze overnight. At serving time, carefully dip mold into a large bowl of hot water, just to loosen the ice from the sides of the mold. Slip the ice ring gently into the punch bowl.

There are many variations of this recipe. You may choose edible flowers in bloom at the time you make the wine, and you may substitute champagne for one of the bottles of wine. In that case, steep the lemons, orange, and sweet woodruff in the sugar syrup, brandy, and a bottle of wine. Add a bottle of champagne just before serving.

Variations of this recipe are used by many members of the Herb Society of America.

ROSE GERANIUM CRANBERRY SORBET

24 oz. frozen cranberry juice

2 cups rose geranium tea

2 cups sparkling water

1 bottle pink champagne

Mix all ingredients and freeze until solid. Place frozen sorbet in a food processor and mix well. Refreeze until solid. Repeat this process 3 or 4 times to break down the ice crystals.

To serve, process lightly to a soft, icy consistency.

Pat Dennis, Northern California Unit

ROSEMARY FIZZ

2 tbsp. rosemary, crushed
    but not pulverized

3 tbsp. sugar

1/2 cup water

Pinch of salt

8 oz. apricot nectar

1 quart ginger ale

1/2 cup lime juice

Simmer the water, sugar, and rosemary leaves with a pinch of salt for 2 minutes. Cool and strain. In a tall chilled pitcher, mix apricot nectar with ginger ale and lime juice. Fill 8 glasses with ice and pour in the juices. Garnish with twists of lime rind.

We use dried rosemary to make this punch. The syrup can be prepared several days ahead and refrigerated. This recipe is from the Western Reserve Unit's *Savory Seasoning* cookbook, first published in 1957. The unit serves this punch for special occasions and celebrations.

Joy H. Walworth, Western Reserve Unit

BREADS

CRANBERRY ROSEMARY MUFFINS

2 cups unbleached
    all-purpose flour
3/4 tsp. salt
1 tbsp. baking powder
1 cup sugar
1 egg, beaten
1/2 cup orange juice
1/2 cup milk
1/3 cup butter, melted and cooled
2 tbsp. grated orange peel
2 tbsp. chopped fresh rosemary
1 1/2 cups cranberries, lightly
    chopped
1/2 cup chopped pecans

Preheat oven to 400°F. Lightly grease or line a 12-cup muffin tin.

Sift together the flour, baking powder, salt, and sugar.

In a separate bowl, combine the egg, orange juice, milk, and butter.

Stir the egg mixture into the dry ingredients, blending lightly. Fold in orange peel, cranberries, pecans, and rosemary.

Fill the muffin cups and bake for 20 minutes or until a toothpick inserted into the center of a muffin comes out clean.

Debra Seibert, Rocky Mountain Unit

LEMON VERBENA MUFFINS

1 cup butter, softened
2 1/2 cups confectioners' sugar
4 eggs
1 tsp. lemon zest
1 tbsp. finely chopped lemon
    verbena leaves
2 cups flour
1 tsp. baking powder

Preheat oven to 350°F. Grease muffin tin or line with paper baking cups.

Cream together the butter and sugar. Add eggs, one at a time. Beat until fluffy, then stir in lemon verbena and lemon zest.

In a separate bowl, stir together the flour and baking powder. Fold into the creamed mixture. Spoon into baking cups and bake for 20–25 minutes. Dust with additional sugar if desired.

Lorraine Kiefer, South Jersey Unit

GINGERED EARL GREY SCONES

2 1/2 cups self-rising flour

2 tbsp. sugar

2 tbsp. shortening

2 tbsp. butter

Contents of 1 Earl Grey tea bag

1 tsp. candied ginger, minced

1 egg

1/2 cup whole milk

Preheat oven to 400°F. Grease a baking sheet.

In a large chilled bowl, combine flour, sugar, shortening, butter, and tea. With your fingers, work the flour and fat together until the mixture resembles coarse meal. Stir in the candied ginger.

Beat the egg until it froths and set 1 tablespoon aside. Beat the milk into the remaining egg and pour over the flour mixture. Toss together until the dough can be gathered into a ball.

Turn dough out onto a floured surface and roll out into a 1/4-inch-thick circle. Cut the dough into wedges with a sharp knife, making about 12 scones. To reserved egg, add a teaspoon of water, then brush tops of scones with egg wash. Bake for 10 minutes or until golden brown on top.

Serve with clotted cream, strawberry jam, or lemon curd.

Barbara Blackburn, Member at large, Great Lakes District

SAVORY HERB BISCUITS

2 cups unsifted all-purpose flour

4 tsp. baking powder

1 tsp. salt

1/4 cup (1/2 stick) cold unsalted
    butter, cut in pieces

2 tbsp. chilled solid shortening

2/3 cup milk

Choice of herbs:

2 tbsp. chopped fresh basil and
    2 tbsp. toasted pine nuts; OR

1 tbsp. chopped chives and
    a few chopped flowers; OR

1 tsp. each: chopped fresh
    marjoram, thyme, and dill

Preheat oven to 425°F. In a large bowl mix the dry ingredients and toss in herbs. Using a pastry blender, cut in butter and shortening until mixture is crumbly. Slowly add milk, mixing until dough forms a ball but is not too sticky to work.

Turn dough onto a floured surface and knead a few times, then roll out to about 3/4-inch thickness. Cut with a biscuit cutter and place on an ungreased baking sheet. Bake for 12–15 minutes or until tops are golden brown.

Debby Accuardi, Member at large, West District

APPLE SAGE BREAD

1 1/2 cups unbleached
    all-purpose flour

1/2 tsp. salt

1 tsp. baking soda

1 cup sugar

1/2 tsp. cinnamon

1/2 tsp. freshly grated nutmeg

1/2 tsp. allspice

1/2 cup buttermilk

1 cup applesauce

6 tbsp. melted butter

1 cup raisins

1/2 cup chopped walnuts

2 tbsp. chopped fresh sage

Good with a cup of tea. Unusual taste sensation—there is no hint of the sage until just after eating it, then the sage note lingers. Spicy and warming!

Preheat oven to 350°F. Grease the bottom and sides of a small Bundt pan or a loaf pan.

Sift together the flour, salt, baking soda, sugar, cinnamon, nutmeg, and allspice. In a small bowl, blend the buttermilk, applesauce, and melted butter. Mix wet and dry ingredients, blending just until mixed. Fold in raisins, walnuts, and sage. Spread batter into pan and bake for 45 minutes or until a toothpick inserted in center comes out clean. Allow to cool for 10 minutes in pan, then remove and finish cooling on a wire rack.

Debra Seibert, Rocky Mountain Unit

APPLE, SAGE, AND SQUASH BREAD

1 1/4 cups salad oil

1 cup brown sugar

3/4 cup white sugar

4 eggs

1 1/4 cups pureed butternut
    squash (or pumpkin)

1 1/2 tbsp. chopped fresh sage

1 cup all-purpose flour

1 cup whole-wheat flour

2 tsp. baking soda

1 tsp. ground cinnamon

1/2 tsp. ground cloves

1/2 tsp. freshly grated nutmeg

1/2 tsp. salt

3 apples (Fuji or Gala), peeled
    and chopped

1/2 cup raisins

Preheat oven to 350°F. Grease and flour two 9-inch loaf pans.

Cream together the oil, brown and white sugar, and eggs. Blend in the squash puree. Add sage. Sift together the dry ingredients, then stir them gradually into the creamed mixture. Add apples and raisins and stir until well blended. Divide the batter between the pans and bake for 50–60 minutes. Cool on rack for 10 minutes, then turn out onto rack and cool completely.

Ed Pierzynski, South Jersey Unit

GREEN TOMATO BREAD

2 1/4 cups all-purpose flour

1 1/2 tsp. baking powder

1 tsp. baking soda

1/4 tsp. salt

1/4 tsp. freshly grated nutmeg

1 tsp. ground ginger

1 tbsp. chopped fresh oregano

1 tsp. chopped fresh basil

2 eggs

1/3 cup honey

1/3 cup unsalted butter, melted

2/3 cup unfiltered apple cider

2–3 medium green tomatoes, diced

Preheat oven to 325°F. Grease a loaf pan. Sift together dry ingredients. Add herbs.

In a separate bowl, beat the eggs; add honey and beat again. Add butter and cider and continue to beat. Stir in the tomatoes. Fold in dry ingredients until mixed. Pour batter into greased pan and bake for 1 hour or until top springs back when touched and edges begin to pull away from pan.

Cook on rack for 10 minutes, then remove from pan and cool completely on rack.

Ed Pierzynski, South Jersey Unit

HERB AND ONION BREAD

2 cups warm water

1/4 cup sugar

1 tbsp. yeast

1/2 cup nonfat dry milk

4 tbsp. melted butter

1 tbsp. salt

1 medium onion, chopped

1 tbsp. fresh dill weed

2 tbsp. fresh rosemary

1 cup medium rye flour

4 1/2–5 1/2 cups stone-ground whole-wheat flour

Preheat oven to 350°F.

Pour water into a large bowl; add yeast and sugar. Let sit for 5–10 minutes, until frothy. Add dry milk and butter. Mix in salt, onion, and herbs. Stir in flour until dough is stiff enough to knead.

Turn dough out onto a floured surface and knead for 3–4 minutes. Let rest for 5 minutes. Knead another 3–4 minutes until it feels springy (rye flour tends to be a little sticky, so don't add too much flour).

Put dough into a greased bowl and flip so that dough ball has a thin film of oil on entire surface. Cover with a damp towel or plastic wrap and let rise in a warm place until you can poke a finger into it without it springing back. Punch down and let dough rise again, or divide into 2 loaves and put them into greased 5-by-9-inch loaf pans. Let the bread rise until doubled (about 1 hour).

Bake for 40–45 minutes.

Ed Pierzynski, South Jersey Unit

SAGE CORN BREAD

2 strips bacon

3 tbsp. finely chopped fresh sage

1 tsp. baking powder

1 tsp. baking soda

1 tsp. salt

1 1/2 cups yellow cornmeal

1 egg

1 1/2 cups milk

2 tbsp. melted butter

1/2 cup corn niblets

Preheat oven to 450°F. Fry bacon in a 9-inch cast-iron skillet until crisp. Leave grease in the skillet and transfer to oven. Crumble the bacon and set aside.

Quickly mix the dry ingredients, bacon, and sage leaves in a bowl. Whisk the egg in a small bowl until frothy, then whisk in the milk. Add milk mixture and corn to the dry ingredients. Add melted butter and blend thoroughly.

When skillet is smoking hot, add batter all at once and return to oven for 20 minutes or until top is golden brown.

Eleanor Davis, Western Pennsylvania Unit

FOCACCIA WITH HERBS AND TOMATOES

Dough

1 medium potato, peeled
   and chopped

1 1/2 cups water

1 egg

4 cups unbleached flour

1 tbsp. yeast

1 tbsp. salt

2 tsp. sugar

Topping

1 tomato, sliced (may substitute
   roasted tomatoes)

2 tbsp. chopped fresh oregano

2 tsp. chopped fresh thyme

Salt

Freshly cracked black pepper

In a small saucepan, cook potato in the water until very soft. Mash the potato in water, leaving no lumps. Cool to about 115°F and set aside.

In a large bowl, add all dry ingredients. Stir in the egg and mashed potato, mixing by hand or in a mixer, until the dough forms a smooth ball.

Place dough in a well-oiled 9-by-13-inch pan. Cover with a tea towel and let rise until doubled in size, from 1/2 to 3 hours. Using your fingers, press "dimples" into the dough.

Spread tomato slices over the dough, sprinkle with herbs, salt, and pepper to taste. Bake at 425°F for 30–40 minutes. (When the bread is done, the internal temperature will be 190°F.)

Linda Franzo, New Orleans Unit

SOUPS AND SANDWICHES

CAULIFLOWER VICHYSSOISE

1/4 cup olive oil

2 leeks, chopped

4 cloves garlic, minced

8 large potatoes, peeled and diced

2 heads cauliflower, cut into small
pieces

3 1/2 quarts vegetable stock

2 large tomatoes, seeded and
chopped

4 bunches scallions, minced

1/4 cup fresh marjoram leaves,
chopped

1/4 cup chopped fresh chives for
garnish

Heat oil in a heavy stockpot over medium-high heat. Sauté leeks and garlic for 3 minutes. Add potatoes, cauliflower, and stock. Bring to a boil, reduce heat to low, and simmer for 10 minutes. Add tomato, scallions, and marjoram. Cook for another 5 minutes. Remove from heat and allow to cool slightly. Transfer to a blender and puree until smooth. Return to stockpot and heat through. Garnish with chopped chives.

Eleanor Davis, Western Pennsylvania Unit

COLD TOMATO SOUP

2 tbsp. butter

1 medium onion, chopped

28 oz. diced tomatoes

12 oz. chicken or vegetable broth

2 tbsp. basil pesto

1/2 tsp. salt

3/4 cup heavy cream

1/4 cup sour cream

1 tbsp. chopped chives

Melt butter in pot and add onions. Cover and simmer over low heat for 15 minutes or until onions are soft. Add tomatoes, broth, pesto, and salt. Simmer uncovered about 10 minutes. Puree in blender with heavy cream and sour cream. Add salt and pepper if needed. Serve chilled with chopped chives for garnish.

Anne Abbott, New Orleans Unit, North Carolina Unit, Potomac Unit

CREAM OF CHERVIL SOUP

2 cups chopped carrots, cooked

2 1/2 cups potatoes, peeled, cooked, and chopped

1 tbsp. butter

1/4 cup finely chopped scallions (or leeks)

5 cups chicken stock

1 cup half-and-half (or whipping cream)

1/2 cup chopped fresh chervil

Salt and pepper

Chervil for garnish

Melt the butter in a saucepan and gently sauté the chopped scallions for 5 minutes. Add the chicken stock, cooked carrots, and potatoes. Simmer for 10 minutes. Allow the mixture to cool slightly, then puree in a blender. Return to the saucepan and stir in cream, chervil, and seasonings. Cook until heated through. Garnish with chervil sprigs. Yields 6 servings.

Eleanor Davis, Western Pennsylvania Unit

CREOLE CRAB BISQUE

3/4 cup butter

3/4 cup flour

3 tbsp. tomato paste

1 1/2 cups chopped onion

1 cup chopped celery

1/2 cup chopped scallions

4 cloves garlic, pressed

2/3 cup chopped green pepper

3 tbsp. chopped fresh parsley

2 quarts chicken stock

1 tbsp. Worcestershire sauce

1 bay leaf

1 tbsp. fresh thyme

1 tsp. salt

1/8 tsp. white pepper

1/8 tsp. cayenne pepper

1/2 tsp. catsup

1 pound fresh lump crabmeat

In a large pot, melt the butter and gradually add flour, stirring constantly until roux is golden brown (20–30 minutes).

Add tomato paste, onions, celery, green pepper, scallions, and garlic. Cook until tender; add parsley.

Slowly stir in stock. Add Worcestershire sauce, bay leaf, thyme, salt, peppers, and catsup. Stir in crabmeat.

Cover and simmer for 40 minutes, stirring occasionally.

Terri Reiman, Roanoke Valley Unit

FRESH VEGETARIAN TOMATO SOUP WITH BASIL

2 tbsp. butter

1 medium onion, peeled and
    chopped

4 medium tomatoes, peeled,
    seeded, and chopped

4 cups bottled or filtered water

1 vegetable bouillon cube

1/4 cup tightly packed, chopped
    fresh basil

Sauté onions in the butter in a large saucepan until translucent and beginning to lightly brown. Chop tomatoes and add to the sautéed onions. Add water and vegetable bouillon. Bring just under the boiling point, then allow to simmer, covered, for 45 minutes.

Remove from heat and allow to cool enough to puree. Then pour soup into a blender and puree until smooth. Return to saucepan and heat through, stirring in fresh basil.

Serve with a garnish of basil leaves, a sprinkle of freshly grated Parmesan, or a swirl of cream.

Katherine K. Schlosser, North Carolina Unit

GINGERED BUTTERNUT SQUASH SOUP

2 tbsp. olive oil

2 tbsp. vegetable oil

1 medium onion, chopped

2 medium carrots, sliced

2 pounds butternut squash, peeled
    and cut in small chunks

6 cups vegetable stock

2 whole bay leaves

4 tsp. fresh thyme

1 (2-inch) piece fresh gingerroot,
    grated

1 tsp. salt

2 tbsp. butter

Toasted pumpkin seeds for garnish

Heat olive and vegetable oils in a heavy 3-quart saucepan. Add onions and carrots; cook until onions are translucent. Add squash, vegetable stock, and bay leaves. Cover and simmer for 15 minutes. Add grated ginger and continue cooking until squash is tender, about 15 minutes. Allow soup to cool slightly, then remove bay leaves. Pour soup into a food processor and blend until smooth. Return soup to saucepan and add thyme and salt.

Cook over low heat until hot but not boiling. Stir in the butter. Garnish with toasted pumpkin seeds.

Katherine K. Schlosser, North Carolina Unit

HERBAL GARLIC SOUP

1/4 cup chopped fresh garlic

1/4 cup chopped celery or lovage leaves

2 tbsp. olive oil

1 tsp. honey

1/2 tsp. grated lemon peel

6 cups chicken or vegetable stock

1/2 cup cooked, shredded chicken, if desired

1/2 cup chopped greens (spinach, dandelion, sorrel, or Swiss chard)

1 tsp. chopped fresh thyme (lemon thyme is good)

1 tbsp. chopped fresh lemon balm

1 egg white

2 tbsp. freshly grated Parmesan

1 tsp. calendula petals (seasonal)

Lightly sauté garlic and celery or lovage in olive oil, honey, and lemon until tender. Add chicken or vegetable stock and greens (also add chicken if desired). Simmer for 15 minutes or until greens are soft. Add herbs and simmer an additional 5 minutes. Whisk in the egg white and remove from heat. Sprinkle with grated cheese and calendula leaves to serve. Yields 4 servings.

Ed Pierzynski, South Jersey Unit

HERBED YOGURT SOUP

4 cups plain yogurt

3 cups chicken or vegetable stock

1 egg

2 tbsp. cornstarch

1 1/2 cups cooked brown rice

1 1/2 cups chopped cooked meat or vegetables

3 cloves garlic, minced

4 tbsp. spearmint or peppermint leaves, crushed

Salt and pepper to taste

I learned to make this soup while living in the Middle East, where every family has their own variation. The most important thing, I was told, was that you must never cover the pot and the soup must always be stirred in the same direction until it reaches the boiling point. These recipes have been handed down for hundreds of years, so I'm not going to go against their collective wisdom!

Combine yogurt, stock, egg, and cornstarch in a blender. Pour into a heavy saucepan and cook over medium heat just until the mixture begins to boil. Lower the heat.

Sauté garlic in a small pan in a little oil just until cooked and fragrant. Do not overcook.

Add garlic, cooked rice, and meat or vegetables to the soup. Stir in crushed mint, salt, and pepper to taste. Continue cooking over low heat until all ingredients are heated and flavors have blended. Yields about 2 quarts.

Rita Salman, Baton Rouge Unit

LORRAINE'S CHICKEN SOUP WITH DANDELION AND VIOLETS

1 chicken, cut into pieces

8 cups fresh spring water

2 onions, sliced

6 stalks celery

2 cups barley

6 carrots, sliced

3/4 cup chopped parsley

3 cups dandelion leaves

2 cups violet leaves

1 tsp. sea salt

1/2 tsp. freshly cracked black pepper

1/2 cup freshly grated cheddar
    cheese

Place chicken pieces in a stock pot. Add water, onion, and the chopped tops of the celery stalks (reserve remaining celery for later in the cooking process). Simmer for 2 hours.

Remove the chicken from the stock and take the meat from the bones. Return the meat to the stock, then add the remaining celery, which has been sliced. Add barley, carrots, and 1/2 cup parsley. Simmer for 30 minutes, adding more water if soup thickens too much.

While soup is simmering, carefully wash and chop 3 cups dandelion leaves and 2 cups violet leaves. Add the leaves to the soup about 10 minutes before serving. Add salt and black pepper, using more or less to taste.

Serve in bowls garnished with the remaining parsley and a spoonful of grated cheese.

Lorraine Kiefer, South Jersey Unit

RED LENTIL SOUP WITH CILANTRO AND CUMIN

2 1/2 cups red lentils, rinsed
and stones removed

8 cups vegetable broth

1/2 tsp. ground turmeric

3 medium potatoes, peeled
and cubed

2 bay leaves

2 stalks celery, sliced thinly

2 tbsp. olive oil

1 red onion, peeled and chopped

1 tsp. ground cumin

2 tomatoes, seeded and chopped

1 (1-inch) piece gingerroot, peeled
and grated

4 tbsp. chopped fresh cilantro
(or parsley, if you prefer)

Freshly ground black pepper and
salt to taste

Place lentils, vegetable broth, turmeric, potatoes, bay leaves, and celery in a large stainless steel pot. Bring to a boil, reduce heat, and simmer for about 20 minutes, or until lentils and potatoes are soft.

While lentils are cooking, heat olive oil in a sauté pan, then add onions. Cook over medium heat until soft and well browned, about 10–15 minutes, stirring frequently. Remove from heat and stir in the cumin.

Add onions, chopped tomatoes, and grated ginger to the soup. Cook over low heat for 15 minutes.

Remove bay leaves and stir in cilantro (or parsley) just before serving. Season with freshly ground black pepper, salt, and a little chopped cilantro (or parsley).

Katherine K. Schlosser, North Carolina Unit

ROASTED RED PEPPER SOUP WITH BASIL

6 medium red peppers

2 small red serrano peppers

6 cloves garlic

1 tbsp. olive oil

1 (14.5-ounce) can chicken broth

1 bay leaf

1/2 cup heavy cream

1/2 cup loosely packed, chopped
   fresh basil

Additional peppers and basil for
   garnish

Preheat oven to 425°F.

Halve peppers, removing stems, membranes, and seeds. Place peppers, cut side down, on a foil-lined baking sheet. Add garlic. Brush peppers and garlic with oil and bake for 20–25 minutes or until skins are bubbly. Wrap peppers in foil; let stand 20–30 minutes. Using a paring knife, pull the skins off the peppers.

In a saucepan, combine red peppers, garlic, bay leaf, and broth. Bring to a boil, reduce heat, and simmer uncovered for 10 minutes. Remove bay leaf.

With immersion blender, blend until peppers are reduced to small chunks (or pour into a blender and process lightly). Add cream and blend again to mix thoroughly. Season with salt and pepper. Cook, stirring, until heated through.

Garnish with chopped peppers and basil.

Laurel Keser, South Jersey Unit

SAFFRON SOUP

4 large turnips, peeled and
   thinly sliced
2 large parsnips, peeled and
   thinly sliced
3/4 cup chopped onion
3/4 cup chopped leek (white
   part only)
1/2 cup finely chopped celery
4 tbsp. butter
1 bay leaf
2 tsp. thyme
10 fresh parsley stems
5 cups chicken or vegetable stock
3/4 cup water
1/2 cup heavy cream
1/4 tsp. crumbled saffron threads
Salt and pepper to taste

In a covered heavy saucepan, lightly sauté the turnips, parsnips, leeks, onion, and celery in the butter over low heat for about 10 minutes, or until vegetables are soft. Season with salt and pepper. Add stock, 3/4 cup water, bay leaf, parsley stems, and thyme. Simmer, covered, for 30 minutes. Discard bay leaf and parsley stems.

Puree the soup in small batches in a blender, then return to a clean saucepan. Stir in the saffron, allow the soup to stand for 10 minutes, then stir in the cream. Yields 6 servings.

Eleanor Davis, Western Pennsylvania Unit

SOUPE VERTE

2 tbsp. butter
1/3 cup green onions, chopped
2 tbsp. minced parsley
1 tbsp. chopped fresh basil
1/2 tsp. chopped purslane leaves
3/4 cup shredded lettuce
3/4 cup shredded watercress
1/4 cup spinach, shredded
6 1/2 cups chicken stock
1/2 tsp. salt
1/8 tsp. pepper
1/3 cup sweet cream
2 tbsp. chopped chives, nasturtium
   blossoms for garnish

This recipe was translated from my Belgian "mother" when I was an exchange student in the 1960s.

Melt butter in a skillet and simmer the vegetables and herbs. Keep covered but stir occasionally. Cook for 10 minutes. Add stock and seasoning. Cook slowly for about 30 minutes so the greens will flavor the soup. Add cream, and sprinkle chives on top of each serving. A nasturtium makes a nice garnish. Yields 6 servings.

Barbara Blackburn, Member at large, Great Lakes District

TUSCAN STEW

3 cups uncooked whole-wheat
    penne pasta
2 tbsp. olive oil
2 cups minced onion
1 tbsp. minced garlic
1 tbsp. fresh thyme
1 tbsp. chopped fresh sage
3 tbsp. chopped fresh basil
2 pounds fresh spinach, cleaned
    and chopped
2 (14.5-ounce) cans diced tomatoes
2 (15-ounce) cans cannellini beans,
    rinsed and drained
Freshly ground black pepper to taste
3 tbsp. fresh grated Parmesan
2 tsp. red wine vinegar

Heat a pot of salted water for the pasta. When it boils rapidly, add the pasta, give it a stir, and cook until tender, according to package directions. Drain pasta and set aside. Heat the oil in a large deep saucepan. Add the onion and half the prepared garlic and sauté for 5 minutes over medium heat, stirring often.

Add spinach, tomatoes, remaining garlic, and salt. Stir, cover, and let simmer over medium heat for 10 minutes. Add beans, cooked pasta, and herbs. When heated through, stir in a generous amount of black pepper, the grated Parmesan, and vinegar. Serve in bowls with extra cheese and a cruet of additional vinegar.

Dorothy Spencer, North Carolina Unit

ZUCCHINI SAGA SOUP

1 1/2 pounds zucchini
3 slices bacon, cut into 1/4-inch
    pieces
1 onion, chopped
3 1/4 cups chicken broth
1 tsp. fresh thyme
1 1/2 tsp. fresh summer savory
4 oz. Danish Saga Blue Cheese

In a large saucepan fry bacon until crisp. Discard fat. Add chopped zucchini, onion, 1 cup chicken broth, and herbs to pan with bacon and simmer until zucchini and onions are soft, about 15 minutes.

Add remaining chicken broth and cheese. Puree in blender in small batches. Return to pan and keep warm over low heat until ready to serve. Ladle into bowls, garnish with thyme sprigs, and serve.

Submitted by Western Reserve Unit

GRILLED VEGETABLE SANDWICH WITH RED ONION MARMALADE

Red Onion Marmalade

1 red onion

2 tbsp. olive oil

1/2 tsp. brown sugar

1 tbsp. balsamic vinegar

Salt and pepper to taste

Grilled Vegetables

1 zucchini, sliced into 1/4-inch-thick
    lengthwise slices

1 yellow squash, sliced into 1/4-
    inch-thick lengthwise slices

1 red bell pepper, cut into rings

1 tbsp. olive oil

1 tsp. chopped fresh thyme (or
    1/3 tsp. dried thyme)

1 tsp. chopped fresh basil (or
    1/3 tsp. dried basil)

1 tsp. chopped fresh oregano (or
    1/3 tsp. dried oregano)

Additional Ingredients

3 oz. feta cheese, crumbled

Mayonnaise (herbed, if you like)

4 good sandwich rolls (panne or
    ciabatta)

RED ONION MARMALADE

Slice onions thinly and sauté over medium heat until they start to brown, about 10 minutes. Stir in the brown sugar, salt, and pepper. Add balsamic vinegar and stir until the vinegar is reduced. Remove from pan and keep warm until needed.

GRILLED VEGETABLES

Brush vegetable slices with olive oil, sprinkle with dried herbs, and grill until beginning to brown. Or heat olive oil in a pan, add vegetable slices, and sprinkle with herbs. Cook over medium-high heat until just tender and beginning to brown. Turn and brown other side.

ASSEMBLY

Heat the rolls and slice in half. Spread rolls with mayonnaise; add hot grilled vegetables; sprinkle with feta cheese. Put onions in a pan to reheat quickly, then place on top of the feta cheese. Top with the other half of the roll and serve warm.

Katherine K. Schlosser, North Carolina Unit

tester's note: *This is a delicious surprise. Could also be served open face on Italian bread, much like a bruschetta.*

FRESH TUNA SALAD PITA

8-ounce tuna fillet, cooked
    and chopped

2 tbsp. mayonnaise

2 tbsp. light yogurt

1 tsp. fresh lemon juice

1 tsp. minced onion

1 tsp. capers

2 tsp. toasted pine nuts, chopped

1/4 cup chopped cucumber

2 tbsp. minced celery

2 tsp. chopped fresh dill

1 tsp. chopped fresh lemon thyme

4 whole-grain pitas

Blend all ingredients together. Serve on a warmed whole-grain pita with green-leaf lettuce and thinly sliced tomatoes.

Katherine K. Schlosser, North Carolina Unit

TURKEY FINGER SANDWICHES

1 pound cooked turkey breast,
    cut up into small pieces

1/4 cup minced sweet onion

1/4 cup finely chopped rosemary

Salt and pepper to taste

2 tsp. curry powder

2 tbsp. half-and-half

3 heaping tbsp. mayonnaise

Thoroughly mix all ingredients and refrigerate overnight.

Cut crusts off whole-grain bread. Spread softened butter on each slice, then top with a spoonful of turkey salad. Top with another slice of bread. Cut each sandwich into 4 "fingers."

Submitted by Western Reserve Unit

SALADS AND
SALAD DRESSINGS

ARUGULA, SPINACH, DANDELION, AND FETA SALAD

Savory Dressing

1/2 cup olive oil

1/4 cup white wine vinegar

3 tbsp. fresh orange juice

1/2 tsp. salt

2 tsp. chopped fresh basil

2 tsp. chopped mint leaves

2 tsp. chopped summer savory

1/4 tsp. freshly ground black pepper

Salad

1 cup arugula leaves

1 cup baby spinach leaves

2 cups torn red-leaf Boston lettuce

1 cup dandelion leaves, torn

1 orange, peeled, seeded, and
    cut into sections

1/2 cup chopped pecans

3/4 cup crumbled feta cheese

SAVORY DRESSING

Whisk together the olive oil, vinegar, orange juice, salt, and pepper. Add herbs and stir thoroughly. Keep in a covered jar in refrigerator, allowing flavors to blend for at least 2 hours. Shake well before using.

SALAD

Toss all ingredients and serve, chilled, with Savory Dressing.

Katherine K. Schlosser, North Carolina Unit

AUGUST CHICKEN SALAD

4 boneless chicken breasts

3 ripe peaches

3 ripe tomatoes

2 cucumbers

4 tbsp. olive oil

3 tbsp. white wine vinegar

4 tbsp. Dijon honey mustard

1 tbsp. fresh thyme leaves

3 peppermint leaves, chopped

Baby spinach, as a bed

1/4 tsp. sea salt

Cracked black pepper to taste

Coat chicken breasts with half the thyme leaves and grill until cooked through, about 20–25 minutes. Remove to a cutting board to cool. When cool, cut into ¾-inch chunks.

While the chicken is cooking, clean and chop the peaches, tomatoes, and cucumbers. Put into a large bowl for mixing.

In a small bowl, combine olive oil, vinegar, and mustard. When fully blended, add the remaining thyme and the peppermint. Stir until uniform. Retain 2 tablespoons for later use. Add chicken to the fruit mixture, sprinkle with the remaining dressing and gently toss until mixture is evenly coated. Refrigerate 1 hour, or overnight.

Form a bed of cleaned baby spinach leaves in a serving bowl; add the salad mixture, season with cracked black pepper and sea salt, and drizzle with the reserved 2 tablespoons of dressing. Garnish with pansies or nasturtiums.

Joe Money, South Jersey Unit

CARROT SALAD WITH HYSSOP

1 pound carrots, shredded (about 2 1/2 cups)

1/2 cup pitted black olives, chopped

1 1/2 tbsp. extra virgin olive oil

3 tbsp. minced fresh hyssop leaves

1 tbsp. balsamic vinegar

1 tbsp. white wine vinegar

1/4 tsp. freshly ground black pepper

Combine all ingredients in a bowl. Cover and refrigerate for at least 2 hours to allow flavors to blend. Garnish with fresh hyssop blossoms. Yields 4 servings.

Eleanor Davis, Western Pennsylvania Unit

CILANTRO TOMATO PASTA SALAD

1 large cucumber

1 cup chopped red tomatoes

1/2 cup chopped red onion

2 tbsp. fresh lime juice

1 tbsp. chopped cilantro

1 tsp. sugar

1/4 tsp. salt

1/4 tsp. black pepper

1 cup dry small shell pasta, cooked
and drained

Bring a saucepan of water to a boil and cook pasta according to package directions. Drain and set aside to cool.

Peel the cucumber and cut in half lengthwise. Use a spoon to scrape away the seeds. Chop the cucumber into a large bowl with remaining ingredients, except pasta. Add cooked pasta and toss until mixture is well blended. Chill for about an hour before serving.

Debra Seibert, Rocky Mountain Unit

tester's note: *This is a nice crisp salad that goes great with BBQ or hamburgers on a hot summer night.*

DANDELION SALAD WITH CITRUS DRESSING

Citrus Dressing

1/2 cup fresh orange juice

2 tbsp. fresh lemon juice

2 tbsp. fresh lemon thyme

2 tbsp. chopped fresh lemon balm

2 tbsp. chopped fresh chives

2/3 cup olive oil

Salad

2 cups dandelion leaves, washed
and patted dry

2 cups fresh spinach, washed
and patted dry

1 cup leeks, sliced

1/2 cup alfalfa sprouts

1/4 cup minced fresh parsley

1/4 cup dandelion or calendula
petals

3 tbsp. raisins

2 tbsp. chopped almonds

CITRUS DRESSING

Whisk all ingredients together and set aside for flavors to blend.

SALAD

In a large bowl, combine dandelion leaves, spinach, leeks, alfalfa sprouts, parsley, and flower petals. Drizzle with enough dressing to coat leaves and toss well. Sprinkle each serving with raisins and almonds.

Be absolutely certain that the dandelion you collect has never been sprayed with herbicides or pesticides and that it comes from an area away from automobile exhaust fumes.

Pat Crocker, Member at large, Great Lakes District

FALL GARDEN SALAD

Fall Garden Dressing

1/2 cup olive oil

1/3 cup red wine balsamic vinegar

1 tbsp. fresh thyme leaves

1 tsp. chopped fresh rosemary

1 tbsp. chopped Greek oregano

1/2 tsp. salt

Freshly ground black pepper to taste

Salad

1 fennel bulb, sliced thinly

1 cup red leaf lettuce

1 cup green leaf lettuce

1 cup spinach

1/4 cup lovage leaves

2 tbsp. fresh sage leaves, cut
    into thin strips

1/2 red onion, thinly sliced

1/2 cup pine nuts, toasted

1/2 cup fresh Parmesan or fontina
    cheese, grated

FALL GARDEN DRESSING

Whisk all ingredients together. Allow to sit in refrigerator for 2 hours.

SALAD

Wash all greens and herbs. Tear lettuce and spinach leaves into bite-sized pieces. Toss together all ingredients except pine nuts and grated cheese.

Divide salad among 6 plates and sprinkle each with pine nuts and grated cheese. Drizzle Fall Garden Dressing over each.

Katherine K. Schlosser, North Carolina Unit

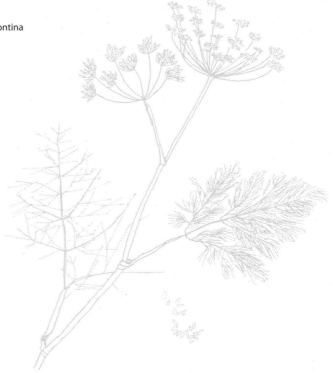

FIVE-HERB PASTA SALAD

1 cup fresh herbs (any combination
  of basil, sage, oregano, thyme,
  marjoram, parsley, or others)
2 cloves garlic, sliced
1/4 cup olive oil
1 pound spaghetti, broken into
  small pieces and cooked
1/2 cup sliced black olives
12 cherry or grape tomatoes, halved
1/2 cup freshly grated Parmesan
  cheese

Wash and dry herbs. Chop all herbs and garlic in a food processor, slowly adding oil. Allow pesto to sit in the refrigerator for at least an hour for flavors to blend.

Cook spaghetti and cool. Toss with pesto, olives, and tomatoes. Serve cold, sprinkled with Parmesan cheese.

Barbara Brouse, Colonial Triangle of Virginia Unit

GREEK PASTA SALAD

8 oz. penne pasta
2 tbsp. extra virgin olive oil
1/2 tsp. fresh lemon juice
1 tsp. red wine vinegar
2 tsp. chopped fresh basil
2 tsp. chopped fresh oregano
2 tsp. chopped fresh Italian parsley
1/2 tsp. freshly grated black pepper
1 clove garlic, finely minced
l large tomato, seeded and diced
1 red, green or yellow sweet
  pepper, seeded and diced
1/2 onion, chopped
1 cucumber, seeded and coarsely
  chopped
1/2 cup black olives, sliced
4 oz. feta cheese, crumbled

Cook pasta in boiling water according to package directions, until al dente. Rinse in cold water and drain. In a small bowl, whisk together the olive oil, lemon juice, vinegar, basil, oregano, parsley, pepper, and garlic.

In a large bowl, combine cooled pasta, tomatoes, sweet pepper, onion, cucumber, black olives, and feta cheese. Add dressing and toss to coat. Cover and chill in refrigerator at least 1 hour. Yields 6 servings.

Ellen Adams, Member at large, Great Lakes District

NANNETTE'S ORZO SALAD

1/2 pound orzo pasta, cooked
and drained

3 tbsp. olive oil

2 tbsp. red wine vinegar

1 tsp. Dijon mustard

1 tsp. chopped fresh Greek oregano

1 tsp. fresh thyme

1 tsp. chopped fresh chives

1/2 tsp. salt

1/2 cup seeded and diced orange
bell pepper

1/2 cup finely chopped onion

4 tbsp. crumbled feta cheese

12 Kalamata olives

2 tbsp. minced fresh parsley

4 tbsp. chopped fresh Greek
oregano

1/2 cup chopped Roma tomatoes

Salt and pepper to taste

Cook pasta in boiling water for about 8 minutes; drain.
Combine olive oil, vinegar, mustard, 1 teaspoon Greek
oregano, 1 teaspoon thyme, 1 teaspoon chives, and 1/2 teaspoon salt. Blend thoroughly and pour over pasta. Mix
well and allow to chill in refrigerator for about 1 hour.

Stir in chopped vegetables, cheese, olives, and additional herbs. Add salt and pepper to taste. Serve chilled
or at room temperature. Yields 8–10 servings.

Nannette Wilson, North Carolina Unit

TURKEY PASTA SALAD

12 oz. bow-tie pasta, cooked
    according to directions
    and cooled

Vinaigrette Dressing

1/2 cup olive oil

1/4 cup white wine vinegar

1/4 cup water

1 tsp. black pepper

1 1/2 tsp. salt

1 clove garlic, pressed

Salad

1 pound broccoli, cooked, cooled,
    and cut into 1-inch pieces

10 oz. fresh spinach, cleaned and
    chopped

1/4 cup shredded carrots

1 pint cherry tomatoes, halved

1/4 cup fresh parsley, chopped

1/2 cup chopped fresh basil

1/3 cup slivered almonds, toasted

1/4 cup sliced red onion

1 pound smoked sliced turkey
    breast, cut into strips

Combine dressing ingredients, toss with pasta, and chill for 2 hours.

Combine all salad ingredients with the pasta, tossing to coat. Chill and serve.

Lori Schaeffer, Pennsylvania Heartland Unit

MINTED GRAIN SALAD

1 1/2 cups cooked brown rice

1/2 cup sliced green onions

2 ripe tomatoes, seeded and diced

1/2 cup diced cucumber

1 cup canned black beans, rinsed
   and drained

2 tbsp. chopped fresh parsley

2 tbsp. chopped fresh mint

3 tbsp. fresh lemon juice

1 tbsp. extra virgin olive oil

Freshly ground black pepper

Mix all ingredients together in a large mixing bowl. Cover and chill for 2 hours or more. Serve on a bed of dark green lettuce.

Jennifer F. Jordan, Tidewater Unit

tester's note: *Proportion of beans to rice and tomatoes was good. Tastes like tabouli—Yum!*

CALICO HERB RICE SALAD

1/2 cup chopped onion

1/4 cup chopped green pepper

1/4 cup thinly sliced celery

1/3 cup mayonnaise

1/2 clove garlic, minced

2 tbsp. Parmesan cheese

2 tbsp. prepared mustard

1/4 cup herbed vinegar

1 tsp. salt

1/2 tsp. pepper

3/4 cup extra virgin olive oil

2 tsp. chopped fresh tarragon

2 tsp. chopped fresh basil

3 cups cooked rice

1/2 cup sliced mushrooms

1/2 cup raisins or dried cranberries

1/2 cup diced green, red, or orange
   sweet pepper

In a blender, mix the onion, ¼ cup green pepper, celery, mayonnaise, garlic, Parmesan, mustard, herbed vinegar, salt, pepper, and olive oil. When well blended, toss in tarragon and basil and mix lightly.

Pour the mixture over cooled rice, toss in the mushrooms, raisins, and sweet pepper. Mix lightly. Cover and chill until ready to serve. Yields 5 cups.

Virginia Chaney, Central Ohio Unit

WARM WILD RICE AND BARLEY SALAD

Salad Base

3/4 cup wild rice, rinsed

3/4 cup pearl barley, rinsed

2 tsp. olive oil

3 tbsp. unsalted butter

2 ripe tomatoes, seeded and
chopped

2 tbsp. chopped fresh flat-leaf
parsley

2 tbsp. chopped fresh lovage

2 tbsp. chopped fresh basil

1 tbsp. chopped fresh chives

Salt and pepper

1/2 cup freshly grated Parmigiano-
Reggiano cheese

Vegetable additions, choose one:

1 pound asparagus, cooked and cut
into pieces

1 pound fresh spinach, chopped
and sautéed with a little garlic

4 fresh artichokes, prepared

2 cups broccoli florets, cooked just
until tender

4 Portobello mushrooms plus one
of the above green vegetables

Put the wild rice and barley in separate saucepans with water to cover, 1 teaspoon salt and 1 teaspoon olive oil each. Cook at a gentle boil until the grains are tender but still firm. You may need to add more water—there should always be at least some liquid in the pots. The rice will take about 1 hour; the barley, about 30 minutes. When done, drain off excess liquid and place grains together in a large bowl; stir in butter. Cover with aluminum foil to keep warm.

Prepare selected vegetable. Stir tomatoes, chopped herbs, and vegetable into the grains. Add fresh pepper and additional salt to taste, then stir in cheese.

Serve warm.

Betty Muench, courtesy of **Bethany Hoffman**,
North Carolina Unit

FRESH GREEN BEAN SALAD

1 quart fresh green beans, julienned

1 tbsp. mayonnaise

1 tbsp. lemon juice

1 tbsp. extra virgin olive oil

2 tbsp. chopped fresh basil

2 tbsp. chopped Italian parsley

1/4 cup pine nuts

Salt and freshly ground pepper
   to taste

Steam the julienned green beans just until tender, taking care not to overcook. They should still have a bit of crunch. As soon as removed from the steamer, run under cold water to cool.

Place pine nuts in a heated sauté pan over medium heat. Stir constantly to keep nuts from burning, and cook until light golden brown. Remove from heat and transfer to a plate lined with paper towels; allow to cool.

Blend mayonnaise, lemon juice, olive oil, basil, parsley, salt, and pepper. Pour dressing over the prepared green beans and toss lightly. Just before serving, stir in the pine nuts. Yields 3 cups (6 servings).

Kitchen shops offer a small, inexpensive tool for cutting beans French style. It is a plastic tool with several small metal blades that the beans are pushed and pulled through. Easy and fun!

Kay Wagstaff, North Carolina Unit

POTATO SALAD WITH HORSERADISH

5 pounds red potatoes

2 cups mayonnaise

2 cups sour cream

1/4 cup wine vinegar

1/4 cup sugar

1/4 cup freshly grated horseradish

3 tbsp. chopped fresh parsley

2 tbsp. fresh dill

Scrub potatoes and cut into bite-sized pieces. Boil in salted water until tender. Drain and toss with remaining ingredients while still warm, but not hot.

Lorraine Kiefer, South Jersey Unit

POTATO SALAD WITH LOVAGE

2 pounds small red potatoes

1/2 cup chopped chives (use
    blossoms too if available)

1 green pepper, chopped finely

2 celery stalks, chopped finely

1/4 cup chopped fresh lovage

1/4 cup dry white wine

1/8 cup tarragon vinegar

1/2 cup salad oil

Wash and cut potatoes into bite-sized pieces. Cover potatoes with water and cook until tender. Drain potatoes and pour wine over them while still warm. Add green pepper, chives, celery, and lovage, tossing lightly. In a small bowl, whisk together oil and vinegar. Pour over the potato mixture and toss.

I use this recipe for picnics in very warm weather as it can stand the heat.

Jo Sellers, Potomac Unit

TARRAGON MINT POTATO SALAD

3 pounds red potatoes

1 cup diced celery

1/2 cup diced green pepper

1/4 cup diced cucumber (seeds
    removed)

1/4 cup diced onion

1 tbsp. chopped fresh mint

1 tbsp. chopped fresh tarragon

2 tbsp. chopped fresh parsley

1/2 cup mayonnaise

3 tsp. honey mustard

1 tbsp. sweet pickle juice

1/2 tsp. salt

1/4 tsp. pepper

Wash potatoes and cook, unpeeled, in boiling water until tender. Drain and cool slightly. Peel and dice the potatoes and mix with celery, green pepper, cucumber, onion, mint, tarragon, and parsley. Blend the mayonnaise with the mustard, pickle juice, salt, and pepper and mix gently with the potato mixture. Chill in the refrigerator until ready to serve.

This is better if prepared the day before you are going to eat it.

Mary E. Leslie, Member at large, Northeast District

ROSEMARY FRUIT

1 cup sugar

1/2 cup water

3 sticks cinnamon

5 whole cloves

3 whole juniper berries

3 sprigs fresh rosemary

2 tbsp. fresh lemon juice

3 cups fresh fruit

In a small saucepan, combine all ingredients except the fruit. Simmer, stirring frequently, for 3 minutes or until the sugar is dissolved. Remove from heat and cool. When cool, pour over prepared fruit in a deep bowl, stirring gently to coat. Cover and marinate overnight in the refrigerator. Before serving, remove the cinnamon sticks, cloves, juniper berries, and rosemary. Garnish with fresh rosemary sprigs. Yields 6 servings.

A combination of sectioned oranges, fresh pineapple chunks, unpeeled apple slices, pears, and pomegranate seeds works well for the fresh fruit.

Alma de la Guardia, Nashville Unit

CILANTRO SALAD DRESSING

1 tbsp. chopped red onion

1 tbsp. balsamic vinegar

3 tbsp. red wine vinegar

1/3 cup olive oil

2 tsp. chopped fresh oregano

1 tbsp. lime juice

1/2 cup lightly packed cilantro
    leaves, chopped

2 tbsp. chopped fresh dill weed

1/4 tsp. freshly ground black pepper

3/4 cup black olives, pitted and
    chopped

1/8 tsp. crushed red pepper

Whisk all ingredients together until well blended. Store in the refrigerator. Yields 1 1/2 cups dressing.

Eleanor Davis, Western Pennsylvania Unit

CREAMY VINAIGRETTE

1 ounce olive oil

2 oz. apple cider vinegar

4 oz. plain nonfat yogurt

1/2 tsp. Dijon mustard

1 tsp. maple syrup

1/8 tsp. sea salt

1/8 tsp. black pepper

1/2 tsp. chopped fresh basil

1/2 tsp. chopped fresh tarragon

Mix all ingredients thoroughly. Store in refrigerator.

Barbara Brouse, Colonial Triangle of Virginia Unit

PARSLEY SALAD DRESSING

1 bunch fresh parsley (standard grocery-store bunch)

3 tbsp. chopped chives

1 tbsp. sugar

1/2 cup lemon juice

1 clove garlic, minced

1 tbsp. chopped scallions

1 cup olive oil

1 tsp. salt

Freshly ground black pepper to taste

Place all ingredients in a blender and process until mixed.

Eleanor Davis, Western Pennsylvania Unit

tester's note: *Nice, green, fresh salad dressing. I really liked the taste of this one!*

ZESTY SPRING DRESSING

1/2 cup olive oil

1/4 cup champagne vinegar

2 tbsp. fresh lemon juice

Zest of 1 lemon

1/4 tsp. salt

2 tsp. fresh dill

2 tsp. chopped parsley

1 tbsp. chopped chervil

Whisk together the olive oil, vinegar, lemon juice, and salt. Add lemon zest and herbs, stirring thoroughly. Keep in a covered jar in refrigerator, allowing flavors to blend for at least 2 hours.

Katherine K. Schlosser, North Carolina Unit

MAIN DISHES

BEEF TENDERLOIN TIPS WITH CARAWAY AND MARJORAM

1 1/2 pounds beef tips
3/4 cup chopped onion
1/4 cup butter
1 1/2 tsp. caraway seed
1 tbsp. fresh marjoram
2 cloves garlic, minced
2 cups water
3 tbsp. paprika
4 tbsp. catsup
1 1/4 tsp. salt
6 hot boiled potatoes
3 hard-boiled eggs, sliced
Fresh parsley for garnish

Sauté onion in butter; add beef, caraway, marjoram, garlic, salt, and 2 cups water. Bring to a boil, cover, and simmer 1 hour or until meat is tender. Combine paprika, catsup, and 2 tablespoons water. Add to meat and simmer another 10 minutes. Serve in a casserole with whole boiled potatoes and egg slices, garnished with chopped fresh parsley.

Virginia Chaney, Central Ohio Unit

PORT ORANGE BEEF STEW

2 pounds round steak
1/2 tsp. black pepper
1 tsp. paprika
1/4 tsp. garlic powder
2/3 cup all-purpose flour
3 tbsp. cooking oil
1 large onion, coarsely chopped
2 carrots, diced
1/3 cup tawny port wine
1 cup beef broth, divided
1/4 cup tomato juice
1/4 tsp. ground allspice
1 1/2 tsp. fresh lemon thyme
1 1/2 tsp. fresh rosemary
1 large navel orange
1/3 cup toasted chopped walnuts
    for garnish
Fresh parsley or chives for garnish

Cut round steak into bite-sized pieces, trimming excess fat. Combine pepper, paprika, garlic powder, and flour. Coat beef pieces in seasoned flour. Shake off excess flour.

Heat oil in a 4-quart Dutch oven over medium-high heat. Add meat pieces, a few at a time, and brown on all sides. As meat browns, transfer to a plate.

Add 1/4 cup of beef broth to the pan. Stir to incorporate any browned bits in the pan. Add chopped onion and carrots; cook until softened, about 5 minutes, stirring occasionally. Add remaining beef broth, wine, tomato juice, allspice, and herbs. Return browned meat to pan.

Preheat oven to 350°F.

In order to save all of the orange juice, use a shallow bowl in which to cut unpeeled orange into small pieces (remove the white pith in center). Add orange pieces and juice to the pan. Bake uncovered for another 30 minutes.

Add garnish and serve. Yields 4–6 servings.

Submitted by Western Reserve Unit

STUFFED CABBAGE

1 large head cabbage

1 cup raw rice

1–2 pounds ground beef, pork,
    veal combination

1 medium onion, chopped

1 tbsp. fresh dill

1/4 cup parsley, chopped

1 egg

1/4 cup sour cream

3 tbsp. soy sauce

5–6 dashes Worcestershire sauce

1/2 tsp. salt

1/4 tsp. pepper

Red Sauce

28 oz. stewed tomatoes

1/2 cup catsup

1 tsp. sugar

1/2 tsp. salt

Parboil cabbage for 10 minutes. Cook rice in 2 cups water, ½ teaspoon salt, and 1 tablespoon butter.

Preheat oven to 375°F.

Combine rice, ground meat, onion, dill, parsley, egg, sour cream, soy sauce, Worcestershire sauce, salt, and pepper. Peel off individual cabbage leaves and wrap each around 2 tablespoons of the meat mixture. Place in layers in deep casserole dish. Add 1/2 cup water, cover tightly with lid or foil, and bake for 1 hour 20 minutes. Remove cover, drain liquid, and pour Red Sauce (see below) over top. Cover casserole tightly and continue to bake an additional 1 1/2 hours.

RED SAUCE

Combine sauce ingredients and stir thoroughly.

Lorraine Kiefer, South Jersey Unit

STUFFED EGGPLANT

1 eggplant (select the smallest and
   lightest available)

2 tbsp. olive oil, divided

1/2 pound ground lamb

1/2 pound ground round steak

1 tbsp. butter

1 small onion, finely chopped

Salt to taste

1/3 tsp. cinnamon

1/3 tsp. black pepper

1/3 tsp. allspice

2 tbsp. chopped fresh Italian parsley

1/4 cup toasted pine nuts, chopped

16 oz. canned whole tomatoes,
   chopped fine

Preheat oven to 400°F.

Peel the eggplant and cut in half lengthwise, then cut in half lengthwise again, creating 4 "boats." Scoop out part of the center, like cutting a piece of cantaloupe. This leaves a flat area for the filling.

Rub a pan with olive oil and rub oil on the eggplant sections. Bake for 10–15 minutes or until they separate a bit where they were cut. Set aside.

Heat 1 tablespoon olive oil and 1 tablespoon butter in a sauté pan. Add meats and cook until brown. Add salt, cinnamon, black pepper, allspice, and parsley and mix. Remove from heat.

Fill eggplant boats with filling, placing them in an oiled baking dish. Press 1 tablespoon pine nuts on top of each boat. Pour finely chopped tomatoes over the eggplant. Bake for 10 minutes or until tomatoes are bubbly.

Sue Rountree, Virginia Commonwealth Unit

tester's note: *This was easy and good. Serve it with rice or couscous and a salad.*

ZUCCHINI-PESTO LASAGNE

8 oz. lean ground beef

8 oz. tomato sauce

2 cloves garlic, pressed

1 tbsp. chopped fresh basil

1 tbsp. chopped oregano

8 oz. mushrooms, sliced and drained

1/2 cup basil pesto (see Simple
    Ideas section)

1 cup cottage cheese

1/4 cup grated Romano cheese

1 egg, slightly beaten

2 tbsp. flour

2–3 zucchini, sliced horizontally
    1/4-inch thick

4 oz. mozzarella cheese,
    sliced thin

3 tbsp. grated Romano cheese

Salt zucchini slices lightly and let drain. When ready to use, do not rinse, but pat dry.

Brown beef and drain the fat. Add mushrooms, tomato sauce, and garlic. Simmer, uncovered, until thick, about 30 minutes. Remove from heat and stir in basil and oregano.

Preheat oven to 350°F. In a separate bowl, stir together the cottage cheese, Romano cheese, egg, and flour. Set aside.

Spray a 9-inch square baking dish with cooking spray. Put a thin layer of meat on the bottom. Add a layer of zucchini, a layer of cottage cheese mixture, and a layer of pesto (use all of the pesto). Repeat. On second layer, place zucchini slices in opposite direction from the first row. Top with a layer of mozzarella cheese and Romano cheese.

Cover lasagna with aluminum foil and bake for 30 minutes. Uncover and bake for an additional 10 minutes. Let stand for 10 minutes before serving. Yields 4 servings.

To cook in the microwave, cover with plastic wrap, leaving a vent hole. Microwave on high for 10 minutes. Uncover and microwave on high for 5 minutes. Let stand for 10 minutes before serving.

Mary Swain, Tidewater Unit

BUTTERFLIED LAMB BEAUJOLAIS

1 cup Beaujolais wine

Juice and grated rind of 1 orange

1/4 cup thyme

2 cloves garlic, minced

1/4 cup olive oil

1/2 tsp. salt

1 leg of lamb, butterflied

1–2 sprigs (4–6 inches) of
    rosemary or thyme

Whisk together the wine, orange juice, zest, thyme, garlic, olive oil, and salt. Place lamb in glass container and pour marinade over making sure it is evenly distributed. Cover tightly and refrigerate at least 6 hours, preferably overnight.

Remove lamb from marinade and grill over hot coals for about 3 minutes each side to sear meat.

Strain the remaining marinade and heat in a saucepan until it is reduced and thickened.

Cover and grill 25–30 minutes for medium rare, turning once. Allow the lamb to rest for 10 minutes. Slice against the grain and serve garnished with a sprig of rosemary or thyme. Serve reduced marinade alongside the lamb.

Barbara Brouse, Colonial Triangle of Virginia Unit

tester's note: *I served this to four people, with roasted new potatoes and shallots, steamed asparagus, and a fresh fruit salad. All agreed it was exceptional and a delicious change from steak.*

LAMB WITH TOMATOES AND MARJORAM

8 (6-ounce) lamb shoulder chops,
 1 1/2 inches thick
6 cloves garlic, minced
2 cups dry white wine or chicken
 stock
5 pounds canned plum tomatoes,
 chopped
1/4 tsp. red pepper flakes
1/4 cup plus 2 tbsp. fresh
 marjoram, minced

Season the lamb chops with salt and pepper to taste. Spray a heavy nonstick skillet with oil and heat over medium-high heat. Sauté lamb 2 minutes per side until browned. Transfer lamb chops to a platter. Reduce heat to medium.

Sauté garlic for 1 minute. Add wine, stirring with wooden spoon to deglaze. Stir in remaining ingredients. Return lamb chops to the skillet. Reduce heat to low, cover, and simmer for 30 minutes, turning occasionally, until lamb is tender.

Transfer lamb to a platter and keep warm. Simmer tomato sauce an additional 10 minutes or until slightly thickened, adding any accumulated juices from platter.

Salt and pepper to taste. Serve sauce over the lamb chops. Yields 8 servings.

Eleanor Davis, Western Pennsylvania Unit

CHICKEN LINGUINE WITH FENNEL AND TARRAGON

3 tbsp. olive oil
2 fennel bulbs, chopped, with
 tops reserved
1 pound boneless, skinless
 chicken breasts
1/2 tsp. salt
1/4 tsp. black pepper
3/4 cup chicken stock
1/4 cup dry white wine
3 tbsp. fresh tarragon
3 tbsp. fresh parsley
2 tbsp. butter
3/4 pound linguine

In a large frying pan, heat the oil over moderate heat. Add the fennel bulbs with salt and pepper. Cook fennel until it is golden brown, about 10 minutes.

In a medium frying pan, heat remaining oil. Cook the chicken until brown, about 5 minutes per side. Cover the pan and cook chicken over moderate heat 5 minutes longer. Remove chicken, let cool, and tear into large shreds.

Add stock and wine with tarragon to the pan. Boil, scraping pan of any browned bits. Reduce to 1/2 cup. Remove from heat and whisk in butter. Add the fennel and chicken to the sauce.

Cook pasta according to package directions. Drain the pasta and toss with the chicken mixture. Top with parsley and fennel sprigs.

Pat Sagert, Member at large, Great Lakes District

CHICKEN FETTUCCINI IVERSON

2 whole chicken breasts, cut into
    1-inch cubes
16 oz. fettuccini
4 cups fresh mushrooms, cut in half
2 cups chopped white onions
3 cloves garlic, minced
2 tbsp. olive oil
1/2 dry white wine
1 tbsp. instant chicken
    bouillon granules
2 tbsp. fresh basil
3 tbsp. fresh oregano
2 tsp. cornstarch
1/4 tsp. pepper
4 medium tomatoes, peeled,
    seeded, and chopped
1 cup fresh snow peas
1/2 cup freshly grated Parmesan
    cheese
1/4 cup chopped fresh parsley

Cook fettuccini and drain—set aside covered so it will not dry out.

Brown chicken in oil in a large skillet and then remove from the pan, leaving the oil behind.

Cook mushrooms, onions, and garlic in the oil until the onion is tender but not brown. Combine wine, bouillon, basil, oregano, cornstarch, and pepper. Add to the saucepan, cooking until just beginning to boil. Add cooked chicken and simmer for 2–5 minutes. Stir in tomatoes and snow peas and continue heating.

Add fettuccini, cheese, and parsley. Toss together, coating the cooked pasta. Yields 6–8 servings.

Rosalinda R. Madara, Philadelphia Unit

CHICKEN PIEDMONTE

1 (7-pound) roaster chicken
20 garlic cloves
3 lemons, cut into wedges
1/2 cup dry white wine
2 tbsp. olive oil
8 (6-inch) fresh rosemary stalks
Salt and pepper

Preheat oven to 375°F.

Wash chicken and pat dry. Fill cavity with 15 garlic cloves, 6 lemon wedges, and 4 rosemary sprigs. Place in a large baking dish and rub the outside of the chicken with 1 tablespoon olive oil, sprinkle with salt and pepper. Scatter remaining garlic, lemon, and rosemary on the chicken. Add white wine and remaining olive oil. Cover and bake for 2 hours, basting every 30 minutes.

Serve with roasted potatoes or rice.

Dorothy Bonitz, North Carolina Unit

tester's note: *Outstanding!*

CHICKEN WITH LIME AND SPICES

4 boneless chicken breasts

2 tbsp. olive oil

Marinade

3 tbsp. fresh lime juice

1 tsp. ground coriander

1 tsp. ground cumin

1/2 tsp. turmeric

1 tbsp. chopped fresh mint

Combine all marinade ingredients in a bowl. Cut chicken breasts into 5/8-inch strips. Add chicken strips to marinade, cover, and allow to marinate several hours or overnight in the refrigerator. Drain chicken.

Heat olive oil in a medium pan, add chicken. Cook over medium-high heat for 5–10 minutes, until lightly browned and tender.

Mark Ragland and **Scott Norton**, Virginia Commonwealth Unit

COQ AU VIN

8 chicken breasts (boneless and
    skinless if desired)

1/2 cup butter

Salt and pepper

1 1/2 cups flour

6 slices bacon, cooked and chopped

1/2 pound whole small onions, boiled

1/2 pound mushrooms, sliced and
    sautéed in 3 tbsp. butter

1/2 cup brandy, warmed

1 1/2 cups red wine

2 cups beef stock

1 tsp. fresh thyme

2 cloves garlic, crushed

1 tbsp. tomato paste

2 bay leaves

3 tbsp. butter

3 tbsp. flour

Lightly season chicken with salt and pepper and dredge in flour. Melt 1/2 cup butter in a Dutch oven, add cooked bacon, and brown chicken. When chicken is brown, cover and cook for 15 minutes over low heat. Add cooked onions and sautéed mushrooms. Pour warm brandy over chicken and vegetables and ignite. Add wine, beef stock, thyme, garlic, tomato paste, and bay leaves. Cook uncovered until tender (about 30–45 minutes).

Remove chicken and vegetables and arrange in a casserole dish. There should be about 1 ½ cups liquid in the pan. In another pan, make a roux by browning 3 tablespoons flour in 3 tablespoons butter; add liquid. Cook until thickened. Pour over the chicken and vegetables. Dish may be refrigerated at this point.

Warm for 30–40 minutes in a 350°F oven before serving. Yields 6–8 servings.

Anne Abbott, New Orleans Unit, North Carolina Unit, Potomac Unit

tester's note: *I made this the night before serving, and it was great!*

HERBAL ASIAN CHICKEN SALAD WITH NOODLES AND PEANUT DRESSING

1 pound boneless chicken breasts

2 bay leaves

1/3 cup chicken stock

10 oz. noodles (Chinese egg, cellophane, or angel-hair pasta)

2 tsp. sesame oil

2 tsp. orange juice

1 cup bean sprouts

1/2 head iceberg lettuce

1 cucumber, sliced

1 carrot, sliced

1 red pepper, seeded and sliced

2 scallions, sliced

1/2 cup cilantro, chopped

Peanut Dressing

10 Thai basil leaves

1/2 cup peanut butter

1/3 cup reserved stock

1/4 cup light soy sauce

4 tbsp. sesame oil

2 tbsp. minced gingerroot

2 tbsp. minced garlic

2 tbsp. sugar

2 tbsp. rice wine vinegar

2 tsp. hot chili oil

1/4 cup heavy cream

Poach chicken breasts in stock with bay leaves. Reserve stock after cooking. Slice chicken.

Boil noodles. Rinse under cold water and toss with sesame oil, orange juice, and bean sprouts.

Slice iceberg lettuce. Arrange on 6 individual plates. Top with noodles and chicken. Garnish with cucumbers, carrots, red pepper, scallions, and cilantro. Serve with Peanut Dressing. Yields 6 servings.

PEANUT DRESSING

Blend all ingredients except cream in a food processor. When well blended, stir in cream.

Hope Riley, Philadelphia Unit

GRACIE'S BAKED CHICKEN BREAST WITH TARRAGON

1 large chicken breast, boned,
  skinned, cut in half and
  flattened
1 onion, thinly sliced
1 tsp. chopped fresh tarragon
  leaves
3 tbsp. sour cream
Pinch of paprika

Preheat oven to 350°F. Place chicken on a foil-lined baking dish. Cover with thinly sliced onions. Spread tarragon over the chicken, then cover with sour cream and sprinkle with a little paprika. Bake for 20 minutes. Yields 2 servings.

This recipe can be increased for any number of people, using the same formula.

Grace L. Madeira, Philadelphia Unit

LIME CHICKEN WITH THYME

4 boneless, skinless chicken
  breast halves
3 tbsp. flour
1/2 tsp. salt
1/4 tsp. pepper
3 tbsp. oil
1 large onion, chopped
1 tbsp. butter
1 cup chicken broth
3 tbsp. fresh lime juice
1 tbsp. fresh lemon thyme
1/4 cup red wine
1 package (16 oz.) angel-hair
  pasta, cooked

Combine flour, salt, and pepper and dredge chicken in the seasoned flour. Reserve remaining flour.

Heat olive oil in a large skillet and brown the chicken till golden (about 5 minutes per side). Remove chicken and set aside. Add butter to the skillet and sauté onion until soft and transparent. Stir in reserved flour until well blended.

Add chicken broth, lime juice, thyme, and wine. Heat to boiling, stirring constantly. Return chicken to skillet, cover, and reduce heat to medium-low. Cook chicken until done.

Serve over angel-hair pasta, spooning sauce over the chicken and noodles.

Gladys Denham, North and Central Texas Unit

ROASTED GREEK CHICKEN

....

5 pounds chicken quarters (leg
    and thigh together)

2/3 cup minced garlic (about 3 heads)

1/2 cup lemon juice

1/4 cup olive oil

6 tbsp. chopped fresh oregano

2 tbsp. black pepper

2 tsp. salt

1/4 cup chopped fresh parsley

Preheat oven to 375°F. Rinse chicken, pat dry, and remove any visible fat. Place the quarters in a large pan.

In a bowl, mix the minced garlic, lemon juice, olive oil, oregano, pepper, and salt. Smear the garlic mixture evenly over the chicken, then arrange chicken in a single layer. Bake about 1 1/2 hours (until skin is well browned). After 45 minutes, baste the chicken with pan juices about every 15 minutes.

When done, transfer chicken to a warm platter. Skim the fat off of the juices and discard. Add 1/2 cup boiling water to the pan, stirring to loosen browned bits, while heating on a medium burner. Boil for a minute or so, and transfer to a bowl or gravy server.

Sprinkle the chopped parsley over the chicken and serve with the sauce. Yields 8 servings.

Debra Seibert, Rocky Mountain Unit

ROSEMARY CHICKEN

....

4 large chicken breasts, skinned

1/4 cup fresh lemon juice

1/4 cup olive oil

2 cloves garlic, minced

1 1/2 tsp. fresh thyme

1 bay leaf

1 1/2 tbsp. fresh rosemary,
    chopped

1/2 tsp. salt

Mix lemon juice, olive oil, garlic, thyme, bay leaf, rosemary, and salt. Place chicken breasts in a large plastic bag and pour in the marinade. Seal and refrigerate overnight, with an occasional shaking. Remove chicken breasts and grill under a broiler on high for about 15 minutes, or until done, basting with the marinade and turning halfway through the cooking period. Dispose of unused marinade.

May also be grilled over coals or a gas grill.

Jane Thomson, Sangre de Cristo Unit

OUR FAVORITE ROSEMARY CHICKEN

1 fryer-broiler (2 1/2–3 pounds), or
    favorite chicken parts

2 tbsp. olive oil

1 cup sliced green onions, or 1
    small yellow onion, chopped

1 cup sliced celery

1 large clove garlic, mashed

1/2 cup dry white wine

1/4–1/2 cup chicken broth (re-
    served from deglazing pan)

1 tbsp. chopped fresh rosemary

1/2 tsp. salt

1/8 tsp. freshly ground black pepper

1 1/2 tbsp. chopped fresh basil

Chopped fresh parsley for garnish

This is an excellent method to use when preparing chicken for a very large crowd.

Preheat oven to 450°F. Cut fryer into serving pieces. Place chicken on a flat baking pan (with 1-inch sides) and brown in hot oven until lightly colored. Remove from oven and carefully add about 1/2 cup water to deglaze pan, or just enough to cover bottom. Let stand 5 minutes to cool slightly, then skim any fat which rises to the top.

While chicken is browning, heat olive oil in a large skillet fitted with a lid. Add green onion, celery, and garlic, stirring often; cook until vegetables are softened and wilted, but do not brown. Remove pan from heat until chicken is browned and pan deglazed.

Using a meat fork or tongs, carefully place chicken pieces on top of softened vegetables in skillet. Sprinkle rosemary, salt, and pepper evenly over chicken; pour in wine and broth from deglazing pan. Scrape pan with a rubber spatula to release all browned bits. Return to heat and bring to a boil; reduce heat and cover pan. Cook over low heat for 25 minutes until chicken juices run clear; baste with liquids in pan every 10 minutes. Add more broth or water to keep liquid from evaporating. Do not add more wine. When chicken is tender and no trace of pink remains near bone, add chopped fresh basil, stirring to combine completely. Sprinkle with chopped parsley to garnish before serving. Delicious with fluffy rice, noodles, or new potatoes. Yields 4–5 servings.

This was inspired by an old James Beard recipe adapted to fresh herbs. Chicken may be finished in oven. Wilt chopped vegetables as directed above, then place in a 2-inch deep baking pan, along with browned chicken. Add seasonings and liquids on top to keep moist. Cover tightly with a lid or aluminum foil and cook at 350°F for about 30 minutes. Reduce heat to 300°F and continue cooking until no trace of pink near bone is visible, 45 minutes to 1 hour, basting several times. Remove cover, and increase heat during last 10 minutes to brown meat.

Madalene Hill and **Gwen Barclay**, The Flavour Connection, Pioneer Unit

SAVORY CHICKEN AND HAM BAKE

6 chicken breast halves

6 slices ham (very thin)

1/2 cup all-purpose flour

1/2 tsp. salt

1/4 tsp. black pepper

4 tbsp. vegetable oil

12 small fresh mushrooms

1 head Belgian endive or hearts
   of celery

2 small onions, chopped

1 cup chicken broth

1 tsp. chopped fresh savory

1/2 tsp. minced garlic

1 tsp. chopped fresh parsley

1/2 cup orange juice

2 tsp. brown sugar

Place flour, salt, and pepper in a paper bag. Drop chicken breasts, one at a time, in bag and shake to coat. Heat 3 tablespoons cooking oil in a large frying pan over medium-high heat. Add chicken breasts and brown on both sides. Drain on paper towels, then place in a large rectangular baking dish.

Roll up ham slices and arrange around chicken breasts. Tuck the mushrooms and either Belgian endive or hearts of celery around the chicken and ham.

In 1 tablespoon of oil, sauté onions until beginning to brown. Then add chicken broth, savory, garlic, and parsley and simmer for 2 minutes. Add brown sugar and orange juice. Simmer for 1 minute and pour mixture over chicken, ham, mushrooms, and greens.

Cover with foil and bake at 350°F for 1 hour 15 minutes.

Gail Seeley, Pennsylvania Heartland Unit

STUFFED CHICKEN CASSEROLE

6 skinless, boneless chicken
   breast halves

7 oz. diced chiles

4 oz. Monterey Jack cheese,
   cut into strips

1/2 cup bread crumbs

1/2 cup Parmesan cheese

1 tbsp. chili powder

1/2 tsp. salt

1/4 tsp. ground cumin

1/4 tsp. black pepper

6 tbsp. butter, melted

2 cups canned enchilada sauce

Preheat oven to 400°F. Combine bread crumbs, Parmesan, chili powder, salt, cumin, and pepper. Set aside.

Pound chicken to 1/4-inch thin. Place 2 tablespoons chiles and 1 strip of cheese in center of each chicken breast. Roll the chicken up and dip into melted butter, then roll in crumb mixture. Place each roll in a baking dish, seam side down, and drizzle with remaining butter.

Bake for 30 minutes. To serve, heat the enchilada sauce and spoon a little over each chicken roll. You may also top with extra cheese, a little sour cream, and some sliced green onions.

Debra Seibert, Rocky Mountain Unit

TARRAGON CHICKEN

1 1/2 cups mayonnaise

1 cup chopped fresh parsley

1/4 cup fresh lemon juice

1/4 cup fresh tarragon (or
2 tbsp. dried)

1/8 tsp. freshly ground black pepper

1 tbsp. chopped fresh scallions

2 cloves garlic, minced

1 (16-ounce) package phyllo dough

12 chicken breast halves

1 1/3 cups butter, melted

1/2 cup grated fresh Parmesan
cheese

Preheat oven to 375°F.

Combine the first 7 ingredients to make a sauce. Lay down 1 sheet of phyllo dough and brush with melted butter. Put another sheet on top and brush again with melted butter. Put 1 1/2 tablespoons of the sauce on the corner of the dough. Put a chicken breast on the sauce and top it with another tablespoon of the sauce. Fold the dough into an envelope, enclosing the chicken, and brush the top with melted butter. Sprinkle with Parmesan cheese.

Repeat with remaining chicken breasts. (If desired, chicken may be frozen at this point and baked later.) Bake for 25 minutes or until dough is golden brown.

Billie Beadle, Pennsylvania Heartland Unit

WALNUT-STUFFED CHICKEN BREASTS

1/2 cup shredded white cheddar
cheese

1/4 cup soft whole-wheat bread
crumbs

1/4 cup chopped walnuts

1 tbsp. minced onion

1/4 tsp. salt

1/8 tsp. ground black pepper

1 tbsp. chopped fresh sage

2 tbsp. butter, melted

1/4 cup all-purpose flour

1/2 cup chicken broth

1/4 cup dry white wine

6 chicken breasts, boned, skinned,
and halved

1 tbsp. chopped fresh parsley

Combine cheese, bread crumbs, walnuts, onion, salt, pepper, and sage. Mix well and set aside.

Place each chicken breast between 2 pieces of waxed paper and flatten to about 1/4-inch thickness. Place a heaping tablespoon of cheese mixture in middle of each breast and roll up jelly-roll style, using a toothpick if necessary to hold together. Roll breasts in flour and let stand 10 minutes.

Sauté chicken in butter in a skillet over medium heat, turning to lightly brown all sides. Add chicken broth and wine. Cover, reduce heat to low, and simmer 10 minutes. Remove to warm platter.

Bring broth mixture to boil several minutes or until sauce thickens. Pour over chicken and sprinkle with parsley.

Barbara Brouse, Colonial Triangle Unit

tester's note: *This was a surprise! It is truly delicious and rather nice for party food.*

TURKEY TENDERLOINS WITH LINGONBERRY ROSEMARY SAUCE

1 tbsp. butter or margarine
3 (8-ounce) turkey tenderloins
1/4 tsp. salt
1/4 tsp. pepper

Lingonberry Rosemary Sauce
1–2 shallots
1/2 cup dry red wine
3/4 cup fat-free beef broth
2/3 cup lingonberry preserves
1/4 tsp. salt
1/4 tsp. pepper
1/4–1/2 cup chopped fresh rosemary
1/4 cup chopped fresh parsley

Melt butter in large skillet over medium-high heat (do not brown). Reduce heat to medium. Add tenderloins and cook 7–9 minutes on each side or until done. Sprinkle with 1/4 teaspoon salt and pepper. Transfer to serving dish, reserving drippings in skillet. Keep tenderloins warm.

LINGONBERRY ROSEMARY SAUCE

Add shallots to skillet and sauté until crisp tender. Add wine. Bring to boil. Boil stirring constantly until thickened. Stir in broth, rosemary, preserves, salt, and pepper. Continue cooking until heated through. Remove rosemary sprig before serving.

Serve sauce over tenderloins, and sprinkle with fresh chopped parsley.

Barbara Brouse, Colonial Triangle of Virginia Unit

GRILLED PORK BACK RIBS WITH ASIAN GREMOLATA

3 full racks of back ribs
1 (hand-size) piece fresh ginger, peeled and sliced
Your favorite barbecue sauce
Gremolata (see below)

Asian Gremolata
2 (2-inch) pieces fresh ginger, peeled and cut into small pieces
1/2 cup packed cilantro leaves
1 bunch scallions, cleaned and cut into pieces

Cut racks into 4–6 rib pieces and layer in a large stock pot with the sliced ginger. Cover with water, bring to a boil, and boil for 10 minutes. Turn off the heat and let stand until cool. Place in the refrigerator.

When cold, remove the rendered fat. Place the ribs in a big plastic bag and marinate in your favorite barbecue sauce for 1 hour.

Grill ribs briefly over high heat. Sprinkle with Gremolata and serve. Yields 8–10 servings.

ASIAN GREMOLATA

Place Gremolata ingredients in a food processor and chop lightly.

Hope Riley, Philadelphia Unit

CRAB CASSEROLE

1 pound white crabmeat

2 tbsp. lemon juice

1/2 stick butter

1/2 bunch green onions, chopped

1 1/2 cups fresh bread crumbs
   (about 3 slices French bread
   processed to crumbs)

3 cloves garlic, crushed

1/4 tsp. cayenne pepper

1 tbsp. chopped fresh flat-leaf
   parsley

1 tbsp. chopped fresh chives

1 tbsp. finely chopped fresh
   lemon thyme

1 tbsp. chopped fresh basil

1 1/2 cups half-and-half

Preheat oven to 350°F. Rinse and lightly season crabmeat with salt, cayenne, and lemon juice. Set aside.

Melt butter in a skillet; sprinkle with salt, cayenne, and garlic. Toss crumbs in butter mixture until lightly browned. Stir in fresh herbs and set aside.

Lightly butter a 1 1/2-quart casserole. Using half of each, layer crabmeat, green onion, and crumb mixture. Repeat layers. Gently pour half-and-half over top.

Bake until golden brown, approximately 45 minutes.

Sarah Liberta, Baton Rouge Unit

GRILLED TUNA WITH MANGO-LEMON-BASIL COULIS

1 pound tuna steak

2 tbsp. balsamic vinegar

1/2 tsp. salt

1/4 tsp. black pepper

Mango-Lemon-Basil Coulis

1 mango, peeled and diced

1/2 cup lemon basil leaves

2 dashes white truffle oil

Lightly brush the tuna with balsamic vinegar and season with salt and pepper. Cover and put in refrigerator for 1–2 hours.

At serving time, place mango and lemon basil leaves in a food processor and process until finely chopped. Drop in truffle oil at the end of processing.

Grill the tuna over hot coals until medium-rare, about 4 minutes per side or until the tuna reaches desired degree of firmness. Top each serving with half the mango mixture. Yields 2 servings.

note: *Coulis (koo-LEE) refers to a thick puree or sauce.*

Laurel Keser, South Jersey Unit

MARTHA'S SHRIMP

1/4 pound butter, melted

6 tbsp. chopped fresh parsley

1 tbsp. chopped fresh chervil

2 tbsp. finely chopped onion

1 tbsp. chopped fresh tarragon

1 tsp. salt

1/2 tsp. black pepper

1/2 tsp. mace

1/2 tsp. freshly grated nutmeg

2 garlic cloves, pressed

2 pounds fresh shrimp, cleaned

3/4 cup dried bread crumbs

1/2 cup sherry

Cook all ingredients except shrimp, bread crumbs, and sherry in a large frying pan until garlic is tender, about 5 minutes.

Add shrimp and cook until pink. Add bread crumbs and sherry. Simmer for 5 minutes.

June Vercellotti, Member at large, Southeast District

OYSTERS LARA

2 pints oysters, cleaned oyster shells and oyster liquid reserved

2 small onions

2 cloves garlic

1 bay leaf

6 pieces celery

1 tsp. fresh thyme

3 tbsp. butter

3/4 cup bread crumbs (1/2 cup plus 1/4 cup)

4 tbsp. butter, divided

6 strips bacon, fried crisp and crumbled

1/2 cup chopped fresh parsley

Dry straight sherry

Lemon wedges

Rock salt

Chop oysters and drain, reserving liquid. Mince onions, garlic, celery, and thyme. Melt butter in an iron skillet and cook onion mixture until browned. Add chopped oyster and bay leaf and stir to blend. Moisten 1/2 cup bread crumbs with oyster liquid and add to mixture in skillet. Simmer for about 20 minutes, or until oysters have stopped drawing water.

Remove bay leaf. Add 2 tablespoons butter and cook until butter is melted.

Preheat oven to 375°F.

Boil and scrub oyster shells and fill each with oyster mixture. Sprinkle with 1/4 cup bread crumbs, parsley, sherry, bacon, and 2 tablespoons butter. Place filled oyster shells on a bed of rock salt in pie pans. Bake for 6 minutes or until thoroughly heated.

Serve with lemon wedges. Yields 30–36 oysters, depending on size of shells.

Melinda Winans, Baton Rouge Unit

RICE PAPER SALMON WITH FRESH HERBS

6 (3-ounce) salmon fillets

6 pieces of rice paper

2 tbsp. each chopped fresh mint, basil, and cilantro

Finely shredded vegetables of your choice (cabbage, carrots, red and green pepper, green onion, pickled ginger, jalapeños)

Optional:

6–12 small cooked shrimp; ginger sauce

Preheat oven to 400°F.

Immerse the rice paper 1 sheet at a time in warm water for 15 seconds. Remove, lay on a clean, flat surface. Sprinkle with herbs. Place a salmon filet in the center. Fold the bottom part of the rice paper over the fish. Fold in the sides and continue to roll up. You want it to look pretty, with the pink salmon peeking out from the rice paper.

Place folded side down on a baking sheet sprayed with oil. Bake for 15 minutes. Remove fish to a plate and top with a selection of finely shredded vegetables.

Arrange the vegetables to suit and to make an attractive presentation. If desired, you may also place a small cooked shrimp on top of the vegetables, and you may top all with a spoonful of purchased ginger sauce.

Joan Jordan, South Texas Unit

SHRIMP AND CHEESE CASSEROLE

6 slices French bread

1 pound fresh shrimp, cleaned

1/2 pound mixed cheese (cheddar, Swiss, or whatever you have on hand)

1/4 cup butter, melted

1 tsp. Dijon mustard

3 eggs, lightly beaten

2 cups milk

1 clove garlic, minced

1/4 tsp. freshly grated nutmeg

2 tsp. chopped fresh rosemary

This is a great dish for New Year's or Christmas Eve supper.

Sauté cleaned shrimp and garlic in 1 tablespoon of the butter until shrimp are pink. Break bread into 1/2-inch pieces. Cut cheese into 1/2-inch cubes. Arrange shrimp, bread, and cheese in several layers in a greased casserole dish. Pour melted butter over the mixture. Add mustard, salt and pepper, rosemary, and nutmeg to beaten eggs. Add the milk to egg mixture. Pour over the shrimp. Let stand for 3 hours in refrigerator (you may let it sit overnight).

Heat oven to 350°F. Bake casserole for 1 hour. Yields 4 servings.

Jeanne Pettersen, Tidewater Unit

ARUGULA CAPPELLINI WITH LEMON CAPER SAUCE

1 1/2 pounds cappellini noodles

4 tbsp. olive oil

2 cloves garlic, crushed

4 tbsp. capers, rinsed

1 tbsp. seeded and diced chile
    pepper

2 tsp. grated lemon rind

3 tbsp. fresh lemon juice

1/4 cup dry white wine

4 cups chopped arugula

3/4 cup shaved fresh Parmesan

Freshly ground black pepper

Cook the noodles al dente.

In a large saucepan over medium-high heat, sauté the garlic in the olive oil. Add capers, chile, lemon rind, wine, and lemon juice and heat through.

Drain the pasta, add to garlic mixture. Toss in the arugula and Parmesan to combine. To serve, top with a generous sprinkling of black pepper. Yields 6–8 servings.

Anna Reich, Potomac Unit

CHEESE TORTELLINI WITH FENNEL CREAM SAUCE

1 pound fresh or frozen cheese
    tortellini

2 tbsp. olive oil

2 cloves garlic, minced

2 shallots, chopped

1 fennel bulb, thinly sliced

1 pint heavy cream

1/2 cup shredded fresh Parmesan
    cheese

1/2 tsp. salt

1/2 tsp. ground fennel

1 tbsp. chopped fennel tops

1 tbsp. chopped fresh Italian
    flat-leaf parsley

Freshly grated nutmeg for garnish

Bring a large pan of water to a boil. While waiting, prepare the sauce.

Heat olive oil in a saucepan, then add shallots, chopped fennel, and garlic. Cook over low heat until vegetables begin to soften, about 5–7 minutes. Keeping the heat low, add cream and heat through. Stir in Parmesan cheese and cook until mixture begins to thicken slightly. Stir in salt, ground fennel, fennel tops, and parsley. Blend thoroughly and heat through. Set aside.

Drop fresh or frozen tortellini into boiling water and cook according to package directions. Drain and place in a serving bowl. Pour cream sauce over top and toss to coat. Grate fresh nutmeg over top and garnish with an additional sprig of fennel.

Katherine K. Schlosser, North Carolina Unit

RIGATONI WITH FRESH TOMATO PASTA SAUCE

10 fresh plum tomatoes

4 garlic cloves

4 tbsp. balsamic vinegar

1 ball fresh mozzarella cheese

10 large basil leaves

5 tbsp. olive oil

1 pound rigatoni pasta

Dice tomatoes. Put garlic through a garlic press. Cube mozzarella cheese. Chop basil. Combine these ingredients with the balsamic vinegar and olive oil in a large bowl. Allow to sit at room temperature for 6 hours.

Cook pasta according to package directions and drain. Toss hot pasta with tomato mixture. Serve immediately or allow to cool and serve cold.

Judy Creighton, Ridge and Valley Unit

HARVEST VEGETABLE BAKE

2 medium zucchini, sliced

2 yellow summer squash, sliced

1 large onion, sliced

3 large tomatoes, sliced

2 tbsp. olive oil

4 oz. goat cheese

1 tsp. salt

1/2 tsp. black pepper

1/3 cup sliced black olives, drained

3 tbsp. chopped fresh thyme

1 tbsp. chopped fresh savory

2 tsp. minced fresh rosemary

3/4 cup freshly grated Parmesan
cheese

Optional:

3/4 pound mild Italian sausage

Preheat oven to 375°F. If using sausage, crumble and fry in a sauté pan.

Brush olive oil across the bottom of a 9-by-13-inch baking dish. Line the pan with the sliced squash, half the tomatoes, and half the onions. Add the crumbled cheese and sausage, if using. Sprinkle with salt and pepper, half the thyme and half the rosemary. Spread olives across the dish.

Add another layer of tomatoes, onions, salt and pepper, thyme, and rosemary. Sprinkle Parmesan cheese over all.

Bake, uncovered, for an hour or so, until vegetables are tender and bubbly. Watch closely the last 15 minutes—if onions begin to burn, reduce heat and cover lightly.

Carol H. Biester, North Carolina Unit

tester's note: *I served this as a main dish—tasted great! A good vegetarian dish without the sausage.*

MEXICAN POTATO CAKE

....

Vegetable Layers

3 tbsp. canola oil

1 medium onion, peeled and
    chopped

8 medium white mushrooms, cut
    lengthwise into 1/4-inch slices

2 medium zucchini, cut in 1/4-inch
    chunks

1 large poblano pepper (about
    3.5 oz.), cored, halved length-
    wise, then crosswise into
    1/4-inch slices

2 small hot peppers, prepared as
    above

2 medium potatoes, peeled and
    chopped

2 medium tomatoes, chopped

1 tsp. salt

Freshly ground black pepper

Potato Layers

2 pounds potatoes

2 tbsp. unsalted butter, cut
    into thick pats

1 cup milk

2 eggs, beaten

2 tsp. salt

Freshly ground black pepper

Dash of freshly grated nutmeg

Additional Ingredients

A little butter for greasing

3 tbsp. dry bread crumbs

VEGETABLE LAYERS

Pour oil in a large cast-iron or heavy skillet and set over high heat. When hot, put in the onion. Stir and fry for 1 minute. Now put in the mushrooms. Stir and fry for another minute. Put in the zucchini and chile peppers. Stir and fry for 4–5 minutes. Add the tomatoes. Stir and fry for 2–3 minutes. Now turn the heat to low and cook, stirring, another 5–6 minutes or until all the vegetables are cooked through. Add the salt and pepper. Turn off the heat.

POTATO LAYERS

Scrub the potatoes, put them in a pot with water to cover, and boil. When done, peel them while they are still hot and mash coarsely with butter. Using an electric mixer, slowly add milk to the potatoes, then add the eggs, salt and pepper to taste, and nutmeg. Beat until smooth.

ASSEMBLY

Preheat oven to 350°F. Butter a 4-cup ovenproof soufflé dish and grease it well with 2 tablespoons of the butter. Divide the mashed potatoes into 3 parts and the vegetables into 2 parts. Line the bottom of the soufflé dish evenly with a layer of the potatoes. Top that with a layer of vegetables, then another layer of potatoes, another layer of vegetables, and a final layer of potatoes. Dust the top with the remaining 1 tablespoon bread crumbs. Put the soufflé dish in the top third of the oven and bake for 40 minutes. Yields 6 servings.

Jim Adams, former curator, National Herb Garden

PASTA PROVENÇAL

1 pound pasta

7 oz. feta cheese

10 sun-dried tomatoes in oil, finely chopped

1 tbsp. black-olive paste

1 tbsp. herbes de Provence

Cook noodles according to package directions. Drain, reserving ½ cup of the liquid, and keep noodles warm. Combine remaining ingredients; toss with noodles. Add reserved water and toss again.

Barbara Blackburn, Member at large, Great Lakes District

PORTOBELLO PASTA CASSEROLE

1 pound Portobello mushroom caps, sliced

1/2 pound white mushrooms, sliced

2 large sweet onions, thinly sliced

16 oz. penne pasta

4 oz. feta or bleu cheese, crumbled

7 tbsp. butter

1/4 cup soy sauce

1/4 cup honey

1/4 cup flour

1 cup skim milk

1 tbsp. chopped fresh thyme

2 tbsp. snipped fresh chives

Preheat oven to 325°F.

Using a large frying pan, caramelize the onions in 4 tablespoons butter. Add sliced mushrooms and cook until soft. Meanwhile, cook pasta according to package directions and set aside.

Butter a large shallow baking dish. Put pasta in the bottom of the dish and pour onion mixture over the top.

Using the same pan in which you cooked the onions and mushrooms, add 3 tablespoons butter and melt over medium heat. In a small bowl, whisk together the flour and milk, add to pan, and heat. When mixture is hot, add honey and soy sauce and cook until thick. Stir in the thyme to blend. Pour mixture over the pasta and mushrooms, then sprinkle crumbled cheese and snipped chives over the top. Bake uncovered for 25 minutes, or until heated through and bubbly.

Jenefer Brouse-Schmidt, Member at large, Mid-Atlantic District

RABBIT RUN SPINACH PIE

10 oz. frozen chopped spinach,
thawed and drained

1/2 cup small-curd cottage cheese

1 medium onion, chopped

2 tbsp. snipped fresh chives

1/2 tsp. curry powder

1/2 cup Bisquick

2/3 cup milk

2 large eggs

1/2 pound cheddar cheese, grated

4 strips bacon, cook until crisp

Preheat oven to 400°F. Grease a 9-inch glass pie plate.

Mix spinach, cheeses, and onions and pour into the pie plate. Stir together the remaining ingredients and pour over the spinach.

Bake for 30–35 minutes, or until a knife inserted in the center comes out clean. Let stand for 5 minutes before cutting.

You can add all sorts of things to this recipe, such as crab or turkey instead of the bacon. You can also add chopped peppers and ½ cup hot cheese. There is no limit to the combinations you can use. Of course, you must add your favorite fresh herbs to enhance the flavor!

Rosalinda R. Madara, Philadelphia Unit

TOFU CHILI

3 tbsp. olive oil

3 medium onions, chopped

2 celery stalks, chopped

4 garlic cloves, minced

1 1/2 pounds firm tofu, crumbled

1 tbsp. chopped fresh oregano

1 tbsp. chopped fresh basil

3 tbsp. chili powder

1 tsp. ground cumin

1 quart tomatoes

15 oz. tomato sauce

4 cups cooked pinto, kidney,
or black beans

1/4 tsp. black pepper

1 tsp. salt

4 ears of corn, kernels cut off

Heat oil. Add onions, celery, garlic, and tofu. Sauté until onions are transparent. Add herbs and spices; mix in tomatoes, tomato sauce, and corn kernels. Cook 15 minutes uncovered. Add beans, cover, and simmer for 1 hour.

Amy Willard Schiavone, Pennsylvania Heartland Herb Society

TORTELLINI WITH PEPPERS, ONIONS, AND PESTO

2 green bell peppers, cut in strips

2 red bell peppers, cut in strips

1 orange bell pepper, cut in strips

1 1/2 Vidalia or Walla Walla onions,
    sliced

Juice of 2 small limes

2 oz. soy sauce

Sun-Dried Tomato Tortellini (fresh)

Pesto (for a selection, see Simple
    Ideas, below)

Sauté peppers and onions in olive oil. Add lime juice and soy sauce. Cook until the onions begin to brown.

Prepare favorite pesto recipe.

Cook tortellini until done; drain, reserving 1/4 cup hot liquid. Mix pesto with 1/4 cup hot liquid, then toss with the pasta.

Place tortellini on a serving platter and top with the peppers and onions.

Mary J. Johnson, Roanoke Valley Unit

WHITE CHILI

2 medium onions, chopped

2 large cloves garlic, chopped

1 tsp. ground cumin

1 tbsp. chopped fresh oregano

1/2 cup chopped cilantro

1 (15-ounce) can garbanzo beans

1 (15-ounce) can cannellini beans

1 (15-ounce) can white shoepeg corn

2 whole chicken breasts, cooked
    and cut in small pieces

2 cubes chicken bouillon

2 cans undrained green chiles

1 cup Monterey Jack cheese, shredded

Combine all ingredients in a greased casserole. Bake for 1 1/2 hours. Serve with Monterey Jack cheese.

Elaine Livingston, New England Unit

VEGETARIAN HARVEST BOWLS WITH GINGER TAHINI SAUCE

....

Ginger Tahini Sauce

3/4 cup sesame tahini

1/2 cup plain yogurt

2 tbsp. fresh lemon juice

3 cloves garlic, pressed

1 (1-inch) piece fresh ginger, peeled
　　and minced

1 tbsp. chopped fresh parsley

1 tsp. chopped fresh rosemary

1/2 tsp. salt

1/2–1 cup water

Vegetable Bowls

2 white or sweet potatoes

1 tbsp. olive oil

1/2 tsp. salt

1 cup brown rice

2 1/2 cups vegetable stock

1 (15-ounce) can red beans, black
　　beans, cannellini beans, or
　　pinto beans

1 tsp. ground cumin

1/2 pound fresh green beans, cut
　　into 1-inch pieces

Other Ingredients

4 oz. feta cheese, crumbled

2 fresh tomatoes, seeded and
　　chopped

1/4 cup black olives, sliced

1/4 cup chopped fresh basil

3 tbsp. pine nuts, toasted

This recipe is inspired by a dish served at Angelica's restaurant in Boone, North Carolina. You may substitute fresh vegetables that you have on hand according to season. Corn and green beans would make good replacements for the peas and potatoes.

GINGER TAHINI SAUCE

Place all sauce ingredients except water in a blender or food processor and blend until smooth and creamy. With the motor still running, slowly add water a little at a time until sauce reaches a thick "dressing" consistency. Pour into a covered container and refrigerate for at least 4 hours to allow flavors to blend.

VEGETABLE BOWLS

Peel and quarter potatoes. Place in a roasting pan, sprinkle lightly with olive oil and salt. Roast in a 400°F oven for about 20 minutes. Remove from oven and keep warm.

Prepare rice, using vegetable stock as the liquid, according to package directions.

Heat red beans and cumin in a small saucepan; drain, set aside, and keep warm.

Cook fresh green beans in a small amount of boiling, salted water until tender. Drain and keep warm.

ASSEMBLY

Gently warm the Ginger Tahini Sauce in a small saucepan. Place 1/2 cup brown rice in bottom of each of 4 serving bowls. Add a layer of red beans and crumbled feta cheese on top of rice. Place a large spoonful of green beans over 1/3 of the bowl; arrange roasted potatoes over 1/3 of the bowl; add chopped fresh tomatoes to the last 1/3 of the bowl. Top each bowl with 1/2 cup warmed Ginger Tahini Dressing. Sprinkle with fresh basil, sliced olives, and toasted pine nuts. Yields 4–6 servings.

Katherine K. Schlosser, North Carolina Unit

ZUCCHINI-PESTO PASTA

6 small zucchini, julienned

Salt

1 1/2 cups fresh basil, chopped

2 tbsp. olive oil

3 tbsp. pine nuts

2 cloves garlic

1 cup freshly grated
    Parmesan cheese

1/2 tsp. salt

3 tbsp. butter, divided

1 pound pasta of choice,
    cooked according to
    package directions

Lightly sprinkle zucchini with salt and set aside to drain in a colander. Process basil, olive oil, pine nuts, and garlic in a blender until smooth. Add cheese, 1/2 teaspoon salt, and 2 tablespoons butter.

Sauté zucchini in 1 tablespoon butter for about 3 minutes—until crisp tender. Stir zucchini into the basil mixture and toss with hot pasta noodles. Yields 4 servings.

Myra O'Neill, South Jersey Unit

EARLY SPRING OMELET WITH CHERVIL

4 eggs, room temperature

1 tbsp. milk

1 tbsp. mayonnaise

1/4 tsp. salt

1/8 tsp. pepper

1 tbsp. chopped fresh chervil

1 tsp. chopped fresh chives

1 tbsp. butter

1/4 cup grated or sliced
    Gruyère cheese

Separate eggs. Beat the whites until frothy but not stiff. Beat yolks until light.

Add milk, mayonnaise, salt, pepper, chervil, and chives to the yolks, blending well. Fold in the egg whites.

Heat the butter in a sauté pan over medium-low heat. Pour in the egg mixture and cook over low heat until eggs rise and begin to set. Turn omelet and allow to finish cooking.

Sprinkle cheese over the top of the omelet. Fold omelet in half and carefully slide onto a warmed platter. Garnish with additional chopped chervil.

Chef Shad R. McLennan, Friend of the North Carolina Unit

RICOTTA AND HERB FRITTATA

8 large eggs

1/2 cup fresh ricotta

Salt and pepper

2 tbsp. olive oil

3 tbsp. chopped fresh basil

1 tbsp. chopped fresh marjoram

2 tsp. fresh thyme

1 cup chopped cooked ham

1 tbsp. freshly grated
   Parmesan cheese

Preheat oven to 500°F.

Break eggs into a bowl and whisk lightly.

Place ricotta in a small bowl, add basil, marjoram, thyme, ham, cheese, salt, and pepper to taste. Whisk 2 tablespoons of mixture into the eggs.

Heat oil over medium heat in a 12-inch ovenproof, nonstick skillet. Add egg mixture, reduce heat to low, and cook until set and slightly runny (2–3 minutes). Spoon remaining ricotta mixture over the eggs and place pan in the oven.

Bake for about 1 minute. Remove pan from oven. Using a rubber spatula, loosen frittata and slide onto a serving platter. Cut into wedges to serve. Yields 6 servings.

Joan Musser, North Carolina Unit

VEGETABLES AND
SIDE DISHES

SAUTÉED ASPARAGUS WITH WHITE TRUFFLE OIL

24 stalks thin asparagus, washed,
ends snapped, and drained
2 tbsp. butter
1 tsp. white truffle oil
2 tsp. sesame seeds
Coarse sea salt and freshly ground
black pepper

Toast the sesame seeds in a dry sauté pan over medium heat until just beginning to brown. Set seeds aside and wipe out the pan.

Melt butter in the sauté pan. Pat the asparagus dry and sauté over medium heat for 4–5 minutes. When finished cooking, drizzle the white truffle oil over the spears and sprinkle on the sesame seeds, stirring to coat. Season with coarse sea salt and freshly ground black pepper. Serve immediately. Yields 4 servings.

Chef Shad R. McLennan, Friend of the North Carolina Unit

LEMON BROCCOLI MARIGOLD

1 head broccoli
1 tsp. finely chopped onion
1/3 cup mayonnaise
1 tsp. fresh thyme
1 tbsp. fresh lemon juice
1 tsp. lemon zest
Calendula petals

Trim off large leaves of broccoli and remove tough stems. Wash and cut into separate pieces. Arrange broccoli on a plate with stems toward outside. Cover with plastic wrap to seal and microwave on high about 5 minutes, or until it is the way you like it. Arrange on serving plate.

Combine mayonnaise, lemon juice, onion, and thyme in a 1-cup measure. Microwave on high for 30–40 seconds, or until thoroughly heated. Pour over broccoli and sprinkle with lemon zest and calendula petals.

note: *A common name for calendula is "pot marigold."*

Barbara Brouse, Colonial Triangle of Virginia Unit

CITRUS BRUSSELS SPROUTS

1 pound Brussels sprouts, washed
    and trimmed
1 tsp. olive oil
1 garlic clove, minced
2 tbsp. marmalade (lemon, orange,
    or grapefruit)
1 packed tsp. chopped fresh
    lemon balm
1 tsp. balsamic vinegar
Salt and freshly ground pepper
    to taste

Steam the Brussels sprouts for about 12 minutes, remove from heat, and set aside. Sauté garlic in olive oil for 2–3 minutes, remove from heat, and stir in marmalade, vinegar, lemon balm, salt, and pepper. Pour dressing over Brussels sprouts and toss to coat.

Serve warm. Yields 3–4 servings.

Ed Pierzynski, South Jersey Unit

HONEY MINT CARROTS

2 cups peeled and sliced carrots
2 1/2 cups water
5 tbsp. whole fresh mint leaves
2 tbsp. unsalted butter
1/2 tsp. dry mustard
2–3 tbsp. honey
Freshly grated nutmeg

Heat water to boiling, add mint leaves, and steep for 5 minutes. Strain out the mint leaves; add carrot slices and simmer for 8–10 minutes, or until carrots are just soft. Drain carrots, then add butter, mustard, and honey. Stir to coat and serve hot, with a sprinkle of freshly grated nutmeg.

You can substitute gingerroot for the mint, using a 2-inch piece of fresh gingerroot in place of the mint leaves.

Pat Sagert, Member at large, Great Lakes District

VINAIGRETTE CARROTS

1 pound baby carrots, peeled
1/2 cup chopped fresh chervil
1/2 cup white wine vinegar
1/3 cup olive oil
1 1/2 tbsp. fresh lemon juice
1 tbsp. snipped fresh chives
Chive blossoms for garnish

In a saucepan, steam the carrots in a cup of salted water for 4–5 minutes. Rinse carrots in cold water and pat dry.

Whisk together the remaining ingredients and season with salt and pepper. Toss the carrots in the mixed dressing. Chill for at least 2 hours. Serve with a chive blossom garnish.

Eleanor Davis, Western Pennsylvania Unit

SAUTÉED SPICY COLLARDS

1 onion, sliced thinly

4 cloves garlic, slice thinly

3 tbsp. olive oil

1 tsp. cumin seeds

2 pounds fresh collard greens (or kale)

1/4 cup chopped fresh parsley

2 tsp. minced chile pepper of your
choice (or 1 tsp. crushed red
pepper flakes)

Thoroughly wash collards and remove tough stalks. Stack leaves on a cutting board and slice into thin strips. Set aside to drain.

Heat olive oil in a large sauté pan, then add onions and garlic. Cook over medium-high heat until onions begin to wilt. Reduce heat to medium and add cumin seeds, cooking until onions are thoroughly wilted and just beginning to brown on the edges. Add collards and parsley and cook until the collards have wilted, but do not overcook. Stir in chile peppers and heat through. Serve warm.

Katherine K. Schlosser, North Carolina Unit

SOUTHWEST FRIED CORN

2 large red skinned potatoes,
scrubbed and diced

1/2 tsp. cumin seed

4 tbsp. olive oil

1 large sweet onion, coarsely
chopped

6 ears of corn, kernels removed

1 cup milk

1/2–1 chipotle pepper, chopped

3 tbsp. chopped fresh parsley

2 tbsp. chopped fresh cilantro

Heat oil in a heavy skillet. Sauté potatoes and cumin seeds for about 10 minutes, then add onion and continue to stir until slightly browned. Add corn kernels and milk, stirring frequently until most of liquid is evaporated. Remove from heat and stir in chipotle pepper and herbs. Season with salt and pepper and serve hot.

Good as an accompaniment to grilled chicken or fish.

Ed Pierzynski, South Jersey Unit

SOUTHWESTERN CORN

4 ears corn, kernels cut off

3 tomatoes, seeded and chopped

1/4 cup sliced green onions

1/4 cup chopped green pepper

2 cloves garlic, minced

1 (14-ounce) can black beans, rinsed
   and drained

1/4 cup chopped fresh cilantro

Salt to taste

Combine first 5 ingredients and sauté over medium high heat until tomatoes start to liquefy. Cover, turn heat to low, and cook about 10 minutes, stirring occasionally. Stir in black beans, cilantro, and salt. If the mixture looks dry, add 1/4 cup water. Heat just to boiling and serve.

Jane Thomson, Sangre de Cristo Unit

THYMELY MORELS

Fresh morels

1 egg, lightly beaten

1/4 cup milk

Crushed cracker crumbs

2 tsp. fresh thyme

2 tsp. snipped fresh chives

Vegetable oil for frying

Clean morels and cut in half. In a small bowl mix cracker crumbs with salt, pepper, thyme, and chives. In another small bowl stir together egg and milk.

Dip each morel in the egg mixture, then roll in cracker crumbs. Sauté over medium-high heat until lightly browned. Serve hot.

Gloria Brouse, Member at large, Central District

SAVORY ONIONS

6 large Vidalia onions

2 tbsp. butter

1 tbsp. chopped fresh savory leaves

Sea salt

Preheat oven to 350°F. Wash the onions without peeling them. Place in a shallow baking dish and bake for 1 1/2 hours or until tender. Remove from oven, remove the skins and season with butter, savory, and salt. Yields 6 servings.

To prepare dish in a microwave, remove skins from onions and place in a microwave-safe dish. Dot with butter and cook for 5 minutes on high. When done, remove from microwave and season with salt and fresh savory.

Eleanor Davis, Western Pennsylvania Unit

GREEN PEAS AND CUCUMBERS

1 cucumber, peeled and julienned

2 pounds green peas, shelled

4 tbsp. butter

1 tsp. chopped fresh mint

1 tsp. sugar

Salt and black pepper to taste

Place julienned cucumbers in a colander and sprinkle with salt. Allow them to drain while preparing peas.

Bring 1/2 inch of water to a boil and add cucumbers, peas, butter, and sugar. Cook for about 5 minutes. Stir in the fresh mint and serve hot.

Marion Foster, Tidewater Unit

FETA AND FENNEL POTATOES

6 large potatoes, peeled and sliced
into 1/4-inch rounds

2 tbsp. olive oil

1 onion, thinly sliced

1/2 fennel bulb, thinly sliced

1 1/2 cups heavy cream

3 oz. feta cheese

1 tbsp. finely chopped fennel tops

1/2 cup pecans, chopped

1/2 cup bread crumbs

1 tbsp. chopped Italian parsley

1/2 tsp. ground fennel

3 tbsp. butter, melted

Simmer sliced potatoes in water until just fork tender. Cool and set aside.

Heat olive oil in a sauté pan over medium heat. Add onions and fennel bulb, cooking until tender and browned. Slowly add the cream and bring to a simmer while stirring. Add feta cheese and ground fennel, stirring until cheese is melted. Season with salt and freshly ground black pepper to taste. Add cooked potatoes, stirring to coat. Put pecan pieces in a dry sauté pan and toast over medium heat until just beginning to brown. Pour pecans into a small bowl. Add bread crumbs, Italian parsley, ground fennel, and melted butter. Toss together to blend.

Pour potato mixture into a buttered baking dish and top with pecan mixture. Bake at 350°F for about 30 minutes, or until bubbly around the edges.

Katherine K. Schlosser, North Carolina Unit

HARVEST MASHED POTATOES

4 large red potatoes (about 2 pounds)

2 medium sweet potatoes
(about 1 1/2 pounds)

1/4 cup butter

1/2 cup milk

1/4 cup sour cream

1/4 cup freshly grated Parmesan
cheese

1 tbsp. horseradish

1/4 tsp. salt

1/4 tsp. pepper

1/4 tsp. cinnamon

1/8 tsp. freshly grated nutmeg

Peel potatoes and cut into 1-inch pieces. Cook until tender (about 15 minutes) in a large pan of boiling salted water. Drain and place in a large bowl.

Add all remaining ingredients. Mash with potato masher until smooth. These are not whipped potatoes—they will have a texture (lumpy) to them. If you prefer them whipped, add a little more milk and butter and whip with electric mixer. If you prefer a smoother texture, add a little more milk. Top with additional butter if desired.

Barbara Brouse, Colonial Triangle of Virginia Unit

ROSEMARY POTATO CASSEROLE

2 pounds potatoes, peeled
and sliced

4 tsp. chopped fresh rosemary
leaves

1/2 cup butter

Freshly ground black pepper

1 cup milk or half-and-half

1 tbsp. flour

1/4 tsp. salt

Preheat oven to 375°F. Place half the prepared potatoes into a large, buttered baking dish. Top with half the rosemary leaves, 1/4 cup butter, pepper, 1/2 cup milk or cream, 1 tablespoon flour, and a little salt. Put remaining potatoes on top, then add the rest of the rosemary, pepper, milk or half-and-half, and dot with the remaining butter.

Cover and bake for 45 minutes to 1 hour, until potatoes are soft. Remove cover and bake for an additional 15–20 minutes, or until the top begins to brown. Yields 4–6 servings.

Eleanor Davis, Western Pennsylvania Unit

SAVORY OVEN-ROASTED POTATOES

2 pounds each red new potatoes
  and sweet potatoes, peeled
  and cut in 1 1/2-inch chunks
1 large yellow onion, peeled and
  cut in 1 1/2-inch chunks
1 red bell pepper, cored and sliced
  into thin, 2–3-inch pieces
4 tbsp. extra virgin olive oil
2 tbsp. finely chopped fresh
  rosemary
2 tsp. mashed garlic
1/2 tsp. salt
1/4 tsp. freshly ground black pepper
Additional salt and pepper to finish
Chopped fresh parsley for garnish

Prepare vegetables as indicated. Place potatoes in cold water if preparing ahead of time. When ready to cook, preheat oven to 350°F. Drain potatoes and pat dry with terrycloth or paper towels. Place in a large bowl along with onion and red peppers. In a small bowl, blend olive oil, rosemary, and garlic. Drizzle the seasoned oil over the vegetables and toss lightly to coat evenly. Season with salt and pepper. Turn vegetables out onto a large heavy baking sheet and bake for about an hour, turning several times.

Raise oven temperature to 400°F during the last 10–15 minutes of baking if needed to brown; taste and adjust flavor with salt and pepper. Serve in a warm platter garnished with chopped fresh parsley. Yields 8 generous servings.

This recipe is easily varied with other vegetables: carrots, turnips, hard winter squashes or eggplant can be added with potatoes; soft vegetables such as broccoli, cauliflower, green beans, chiles, mushrooms, tomatoes, zucchini, or yellow squash should be added during last 20–25 minutes of cooking.

Madalene Hill and **Gwen Barclay**, The Flavour Connection, Pioneer Unit

SCALLOPED POTATOES

3 tbsp. butter
1 tbsp. flour
1 cup grated Parmesan cheese
1 1/2 cups milk
2 tbsp. chopped chives
2 tsp. fresh dill weed
6 large potatoes, peeled and
  thinly sliced
1 onion, thinly sliced
1/4 cup chopped fresh parsley
Dash of salt

Preheat oven to 375°F. Melt the butter over medium heat, then stir in the flour. Add milk slowly, stirring constantly to keep consistency smooth. Stir in Parmesan cheese. Cook over medium heat until thickened.

Place sliced potatoes, onions, and herbs in a buttered 9-by-13-inch baking dish. Add the white sauce. Salt to taste. Bake for about 1 hour, until potatoes are tender and beginning to brown.

Lorraine Kiefer, South Jersey Unit

RICE PILAF WITH HERBS

1/4 pound butter

4 oz. uncooked angel-hair pasta

26 oz. vegetable or chicken broth
   (in cans)

1 cup raw basmati rice

2 tbsp. fresh thyme, sage, parsley,
   tarragon, or herb of choice (may
   also use a combination of herbs,
   depending on what is in season)

Salt and pepper to taste

Optional:

1 cup shredded cooked chicken

Place butter in a large sauté pan, heating over medium heat. Break up pasta and add to butter, quickly heating until pasta just begins to brown.

Carefully stir in chicken or vegetable broth. Heat to boiling, then reduce to a simmer. Add 1 cup rice, herbs of choice, salt, and pepper.

Cover and cook until rice has absorbed liquid. This usually takes about 30 minutes, but follow the directions on rice.

If desired, 1 cup of shredded cooked chicken may be stirred in. Heat through and serve with a parsley garnish.

Margaret (Peggy) Ellmore, Virginia Commonwealth Unit

BASIL ZUCCHINI BAKE

6 strips bacon

3 tbsp. bacon drippings

1/2 stick butter

2 medium onions, chopped

5 medium zucchini, sliced

1 tbsp. chopped fresh basil

1 tbsp. sugar

1 tsp. salt

2 cups fresh tomatoes (canned
   tomatoes may be substituted
   out of season)

1 cup grated cheddar cheese

Preheat oven to 350°F. In a large skillet, fry the bacon strips. Drain the bacon, reserving fat, and crumble the bacon.

In 3 tablespoons bacon drippings and butter, sauté chopped onion until slightly browned. Add sliced zucchini. Cook 3–4 minutes over medium heat, stirring occasionally. Add sugar, salt, and tomatoes. Cover and simmer until squash is tender. Add fresh basil.

Pour mixture into a greased 2-quart casserole. Sprinkle with bacon and grated cheese. Bake for 20 minutes.

Mary J. Johnson, Roanoke Valley Unit

HARVEST BAKE

2 medium zucchini, sliced

2 yellow summer squash, sliced

1 large onion, sliced

3 large tomatoes, sliced

3/4 pound mild sausage, cut in
small pieces (optional)

4 oz. goat cheese

1/3 cup black olives, drained
and sliced

3 tbsp. fresh thyme

2 tsp. minced fresh rosemary

Olive oil to drizzle

Salt and pepper to taste

1 cup grated Parmesan cheese

Fry the sausage in the sauté pan until done. Set aside. Preheat oven to 375°F.

Drizzle olive oil in bottom of a 9-by-13-inch or paella pan. Brush to cover the bottom. Line the pan with squash slices, then add half the sliced tomatoes. Layer the onions next. Add goat cheese and prepared sausage. Sprinkle with salt and pepper, half the thyme, and half the rosemary. Top with half the olives.

Repeat above step, using the remaining ingredients. Drizzle the top lightly with olive oil and sprinkle generously with Parmesan cheese. Cover pan loosely with aluminum foil and bake for 30 minutes. After 30 minutes, remove aluminum foil and continue baking for another 30 minutes. Serve warm.

Carol H. Biester, North Carolina Unit

ONSLOW SLUMGULLION

2 small eggplants

2 tbsp. olive oil

1 large onion, chopped

5 cloves garlic, minced

2 red bell peppers, seeded and
chopped

2 yellow bell peppers, seeded
and chopped

2 zucchini, sliced

8 oz. fresh mushrooms, sliced

1 large can Italian tomatoes,
chopped (with liquid)

2 tsp. chopped fresh oregano

2 tsp. chopped fresh basil

2 tsp. fresh thyme

Red pepper flakes to taste

Salt and pepper to taste

Wash and slice eggplants. Lay slices on paper towels and sprinkle liberally with coarse salt. With additional paper towels, repeatedly pat the slices, soaking up excess water from the eggplant.

Heat olive oil in a large pan. Add onions and garlic and cook over low heat until translucent. Add peppers, zucchini, eggplant, and mushrooms and cook until tender—about 30 minutes. Add tomatoes, herbs, and seasonings and simmer over low heat until liquid is reduced and thick. Serve over rice.

Elaine H. McCall, North Carolina Unit

MEXICAN SUMMER VEGETABLES

1 cup finely chopped onion

2 tbsp. vegetable oil

1 garlic clove, minced

2 cups sliced summer squash or
zucchini, or a combination

1 roasted red bell pepper, peeled
and diced

2 chile peppers, roasted, peeled,
seeded, and diced

2 fresh tomatoes, chopped

3 cups corn kernels, stripped from
the cob or frozen

1/2 cup lightly packed fresh cilantro leaves, chopped

1/2 tsp. ground coriander seed

1/4 tsp. ground cumin seed

1 cup grated cheddar cheese

To roast the peppers, wash, dry, and place them under the broiler until skins begin to blister and blacken, usually just a few minutes. Remove with tongs and place in a paper bag. Wait about 5 minutes, then shake the bag vigorously to loosen the skins. Remove from bag and peel off the blackened outer skin. Handle the chile peppers with gloves, as they can burn your fingers, and don't touch your eyes until after you have finished and thoroughly washed your hands.

In a large saucepan, sauté the onion until soft. Add the squash and continue cooking for another 4 minutes. Add the minced garlic and cook for another 1–2 minutes. Add the peppers, corn, and tomatoes; cook, covered, over moderate heat for 5 minutes.

Add cilantro, cumin, and coriander, stirring thoroughly. Serve in warm bowls garnished with grated cheddar cheese. Yields 6 servings.

Eleanor Davis, Western Pennsylvania Unit

OVEN-FRIED SUMMER SQUASH

2 medium yellow summer squash

1/2 tsp. salt

1/2 tsp. freshly ground black pepper

2 slices soft whole-wheat bread

2 tbsp. freshly grated
Parmesan cheese

1 tbsp. finely chopped fresh parsley

2 tsp. chopped fresh basil

1 clove garlic, finely minced

1 egg, lightly beaten

Preheat oven to 450°F. Spray a cookie sheet with cooking oil to lightly coat. Wash and cut squash into thick slices; season with salt and pepper.

In a food processor, combine bread, cheese, basil, and parsley. Process until fine, put into a small bowl, and set aside.

Lightly beat the egg and garlic in a small bowl. Dip squash slices into egg mixture, then into crumbs, coating all sides. Place on a cookie sheet and bake for 10–12 minutes or until tender.

Elaine Kimmerly, Frankenmuth Mid-Michigan Unit

ZUCCHINI "CRAB" CAKES

1 medium zucchini, peeled and
grated
1 egg, lightly beaten
2 tbsp. mayonnaise
1 tsp. crab seasoning (Old Bay
or other)
1 cup bread crumbs, plus extra
for coating
1/4 cup freshly grated Parmesan
or pecorino cheese
1 tsp. fresh thyme
1 tsp. chopped fresh Greek oregano
1 tsp. chopped fresh basil
Vegetable oil for frying

Squeeze the excess moisture from the zucchini. Place in a large bowl and mix in all other ingredients except oil. Form into patties and coat with additional bread crumbs.

Fry in vegetable oil until golden brown on each side. Turn only once and take care that they do not fall apart. Serve with a fresh salsa or cocktail sauce.

Ed Pierzynski, South Jersey Unit

SPICY TOMATO GRITS

2 bacon slices, chopped
28 oz. chicken broth
1/2 tsp. salt
1 cup quick-cooking grits
2 large tomatoes, peeled, seeded,
and chopped
2 tbsp. chopped green chiles
1 cup shredded cheddar cheese

Cook bacon in a large, heavy saucepan until crisp, reserving drippings in pan. Gradually add chicken broth and salt; bring to a boil.

Stir in the grits, tomato, and chiles; return to a boil, stirring often. Reduce heat and simmer, stirring often, for 15 minutes.

Stir in shredded cheddar cheese. Cover and let stand for 5 minutes. Yields 6 servings.

Barbara Brouse, Colonial Triangle of Virginia Unit

DESSERTS

CHOCOLATE ENCHANTMENT BROWNIES

Brownies

1 cup sugar

1/2 cup margarine

4 eggs

1/2 tsp. salt

1 tsp. vanilla

16 oz. chocolate syrup

1/2 cup walnuts

1 cup flour

Second Layer

2 cups confectioners' sugar

2 tbsp. crème de menthe

1/2 cup margarine

Topping

6 tbsp. butter, no substitutes

6 oz. chocolate chips

45 fresh mint leaves for garnish

Preheat oven to 350°F. Grease and flour a 9-by-13-inch pan. In a large bowl, mix the brownie ingredients thoroughly. Spread the mixture in the prepared pan. Bake for 30–40 minutes, or until toothpick inserted in the center comes out clean. Set the pan aside to cool.

In a small bowl, mix the ingredients for the second layer and spread over the cooled brownies. In a small pan, melt the butter and chocolate chips together, stirring. Cool slightly and pour over the second layer. Refrigerate until the topping is set, then cut into squares. Garnish each with a mint leaf. Yields 45 brownies.

Barbara Brouse, Colonial Triangle of Virginia Unit

CRANBERRY NUT BARS WITH ROSEMARY

10 tbsp. unsalted butter, cut into
pieces

1 2/3 cups firmly packed light
brown sugar

1 1/2 cups unbleached flour

Pinch salt

3 extra-large eggs

1 1/2 tsp. pure vanilla extract

Zest of 1 orange

1/2 tsp. salt

1 1/2 tsp. baking powder

Generous cup of hazelnuts,
coarsely chopped, or pecan or
walnut halves

Scant cup dried cranberries or
dried cherries, rough chopped

3–4 tbsp. fresh minced
rosemary leaves

Preheat oven to 375°F and lightly butter a 9-by-13-inch pan.

In a food processor or a bowl, combine the butter, 2/3 cup brown sugar, 1 1/4 cups of the flour, and pinch of salt. Process, or mix in a bowl with a pastry blender, until crumbly. Pat the crust into the prepared pan and bake until just barely golden brown, 12–14 minutes. Remove from oven and let cool a bit. Reduce oven temperature to 350°F.

In the food processor or a bowl, beat the eggs with the remaining cup of brown sugar and blend well. Add the vanilla, orange zest, remaining 1/4 cup of flour, 1/2 teaspoon of salt, and baking powder and blend well. Stir the rosemary into the batter. Evenly spread the nuts and cranberries over the crust. Pour the egg mixture over the nuts and cranberries on the crust.

Bake for 22–25 minutes, or until the center is baked and the bars are a deep golden brown. Cool the pan on a baking rack and then cut into bars.

These buttery bars are full of flavor—tart with dried fruit, sweet with brown sugar, chock full of nuts—and fragrant with a pleasant surprise of rosemary. Use the larger amount of rosemary for a stronger herb flavor, or the smaller quantity for a milder taste. I like these best when made with hazelnuts that have been toasted and rubbed from their skins, but pecans and walnuts are equally good. For smaller bars, divide the pan into rows of 4 by 8 pieces, and for larger bars, cut them into 4 by 6 pieces. Store the bars in an airtight container. Yields 24–32 bars.

Susan Belsinger, Potomac Unit

GINGER COOKIES

2/3 cup oil

1 cup sugar

1 egg

1 tbsp. molasses

1 tbsp. grated fresh ginger

2 cups all-purpose flour

2 tsp. baking soda

1 tsp. ground ginger

1 tsp. cinnamon

Dash salt

Preheat oven to 350°F. Mix the oil, sugar, egg, molasses, and fresh ginger. Sift flour, baking soda, ground ginger, cinnamon, and salt. Add dry ingredients to egg mixture and blend well. Roll into quarter-sized balls, roll in additional granulated sugar, and place on an ungreased cookie sheet.

Bake for 10–12 minutes, or until lightly browned. Yields 4 dozen cookies.

Mattie McReynolds, Member at large, Southeast District

HERBAL SHORTBREAD COOKIES

1 cup (2 sticks) unsalted butter, room temperature, cut up

1/2 cup confectioners' sugar or 1/2 cup packed brown sugar

2 cups unsifted all-purpose flour

1/2 tsp. salt

1 tbsp. herb of choice:
lavender flowers, calendula flower petals, candied ginger, rosemary, lemon balm

Preheat oven to 325°F. In an electric mixer (or with a wooden spoon), beat together the softened butter and sugar until smooth. Sift flour and salt on top of mixture and sprinkle in herb of choice; blend all together just until ball begins to form.

On a floured surface, roll out to a circle or square shape, about 1/4–1/2-inch thick. When you have the shape you want, move the dough to an ungreased baking pan. Cut wedges or small squares in the dough, but do not pull apart.

Bake for 25 minutes or until top is dry and just turning golden. Take a sharp knife and cut through the marked areas.

Cookies will keep well in an airtight container.

Debby Accuardi, Member at large, West District

LAVENDER COOKIES

4 oz. (1 stick) unsalted butter, softened
1/3 cup light brown sugar
1 1/4 cups self-rising flour
1 tbsp. lavender flowers (dried)
Pinch salt
Confectioners' sugar for garnish

In a bowl, cream the butter, brown sugar, and salt until light. Add the flour and lavender. Mix well, set in refrigerator, and chill for about an hour.

Preheat oven to 400°F. Grease a heavy cookie sheet.

Turn dough out onto a lightly floured board and roll 1/3-inch thick. With a small biscuit cutter, cut the dough into rounds. Place on the cookie sheet and bake for 8–10 minutes, or until a delicate brown. Cool on a wire rack, sprinkling with confectioners' sugar while still warm.

Alma de la Guardia, Nashville Unit

LEMON MADELEINES

3 eggs, plus 1 egg yolk
2/3 cup superfine sugar
2 tbsp. lemon juice
1 tsp. pure vanilla extract
1/8 tsp. salt
1/2 cup unsalted butter, melted
24 lemon balm leaves, chopped
1 1/4 cups all-purpose flour, sifted

Preheat oven to 375°F. Lightly grease madeleine pans.

Beat eggs and yolk until light in color, about 5 minutes. Beat in lemon juice, vanilla, and salt. Fold in flour and sugar, mixing well. Drizzle butter over the batter and fold in. Refrigerate batter for 30 minutes.

Spoon 1 tablespoon batter into each madeleine mold and top with a lemon balm leaf; cover with more batter. Bake for 20–25 minutes.

Myra O'Neill, South Jersey Unit

LILLIAN'S LEMON DOODLES

1 cup butter, softened

1 1/2 cups sugar

2 eggs

2 tbsp. fresh lemon verbena, finely chopped

2 3/4 cups all-purpose flour

1 tsp. cream of tartar

1 tsp. baking soda

Grated peel from 1 lemon

1 tsp. vanilla

Lemon Glaze

1 stick butter, melted

1 box confectioners' sugar

1 tsp. pure vanilla extract

Juice of 1 lemon

1–2 drops of milk

Cream butter, sugar, lemon verbena, and eggs. Sift together dry ingredients; stir into creamed mixture. Chill about 1 hour.

Preheat oven to 375°F. Remove dough from refrigerator, roll into balls the size of a cherry, and bake for about 10 minutes. Cool and frost with Lemon Glaze.

LEMON GLAZE

Beat together butter, confectioners' sugar, lemon juice, and enough milk to make a spreading consistency.

Lorraine Kiefer, South Jersey Unit

ROSEMARY FOR REMEMBRANCE SHORTBREAD COOKIES

2 tbsp. fresh rosemary

1 cup butter, at room temperature

2/3 cup confectioners' sugar

1/8 tsp. salt

1 tsp. pure vanilla extract

2 cups sifted all-purpose flour

2/3 cup chopped pecans

Preheat oven to 350°F.

Turn food processor on and throw in the rosemary leaves to chop. Remove lid and add all remaining ingredients except pecans. Process until smooth. Remove batter from processor and stir in the chopped pecans.

Measure out dough by the tablespoonful. Roll each into a small ball, flatten to about 1/2-inch thick, and place 2 inches apart on an ungreased cookie sheet.

Bake for about 20 minutes, or until cookies are lightly browned. Allow to cool on cookie sheet for 10 minutes, then remove to cool completely.

Store in a tightly covered tin.

Mary Remmel Wohlleb, Arkansas Unit

THREE-SEED COOKIES WITH HERBS

3 sticks unsalted butter, softened

1 cup light brown sugar

1 cup sugar

4 large eggs

1/2 tsp. orange or lemon oil,
  optional

1 tsp. pure vanilla extract

2 tsp. orange or lemon zest

1/2 cup packed orange mint or
  lemon balm leaves, or 1/3 cup
  lemon verbena leaves, very
  finely chopped

2 cups unbleached flour

1 cup whole-wheat flour

3/4 tsp. salt

1 1/2 tsp. baking soda

1/2 cup rolled oats

1/4 cup poppy seed

1/4 cup sesame seed

1/4 cup flaxseed

Preheat oven to 350°F. Lightly butter baking sheets.

In a bowl, food processor, or mixer, beat the butter with the white and brown sugars until blended and fluffy. Beat in the eggs, one at a time. Add the citrus oil, vanilla, zest, and herbs and blend well.

In a mixing bowl, combine flours, salt, baking soda, oats, and seeds. Add the dry ingredients to the wet and blend well.

Drop the dough by rounded teaspoons onto baking sheets. Bake until golden brown on the edges—about 10–12 minutes. Remove from baking sheets and let cool on racks. Store in a tightly covered container.

I first created this recipe using orange mint and orange zest. It also works well with lemon balm or lemon verbena and lemon zest. These good-for-you cookies are full of flavor; the recipe can easily be halved. I make a big batch and freeze some to have on hand.

Susan Belsinger, Potomac Unit

CARDAMOM APPLES WITH BAY LEAF CREAM

4 apples, peeled, halved, and cored

1 orange

1 cup sugar

1 cup water

seeds from 8 cardamom pods

1/4 cup plus 2 tsp. brown sugar

4 tbsp. butter, cut in pieces

1/2 cup heavy cream

2 fresh bay leaves

2 tsp. brown sugar

Preheat oven to 350°F. Remove zest from orange and cut into thin strips. Juice the orange.

Place sugar, water, and cardamom seeds into a saucepan and bring to a boil. Add halved apples and simmer for 3 minutes. Remove from heat and allow apples to cool in the liquid. Remove apples from liquid and drain.

Heat cream and 2 teaspoons brown sugar in a small saucepan just to the boiling point. Remove from heat, add fresh bay leaves, cover, and allow to steep for 30 minutes. Remove bay leaves and chill the cream in the refrigerator.

Combine 1/4 cup brown sugar and butter in a small baking dish. Carefully lay the apples on top of brown sugar, flat side down. Pour orange juice and zest over apples. Bake for 10 minutes.

Turn apples in the orange syrup and return to oven for 10 minutes. Remove apples from the syrup and place in individual serving dishes. Drizzle a little of the orange syrup over the apples and add a spoonful of bay leaf cream in the apple hollow. Yields 8 servings.

Katherine K. Schlosser, North Carolina Unit

CRANBERRY LIQUEUR CAKE

1 3/4 cups sugar

3 sticks butter

6 eggs

3 1/2 cups cake flour

1/2 tsp. salt

1/2 tsp. baking soda

1/4 tsp. mace

1 cup sour cream

1/2 tsp. brandy extract

1/2 tsp. rum extract

1 tsp. vanilla

3 tbsp. cranberry liqueur

1 cup fresh cranberries, chopped
    lightly

1/2 cup pecans or walnuts,
    chopped

1 tsp. chopped fresh rosemary

Cranberry Liqueur Frosting

1 stick butter, room temperature

1 pound confectioners' sugar

3 tbsp. cranberry liqueur

Enough milk to achieve desired
    consistency

Preheat oven to 325°F. Grease and flour a 10-inch tube pan.

Cream sugar and butter until light and fluffy. Add eggs, one at a time, beating after each addition. Add brandy, rum, vanilla, and cranberry liqueur and beat well. Sift together the flour, salt, baking soda, and mace. Add to creamed mixture, alternating with sour cream, beating after each addition. Fold in cranberries, nuts, and rosemary.

Pour into prepared pan and bake for 1–1 1/2 hours or until cake tests done with a cake tester. Remove from oven and cool for 15 minutes, then remove from pan. Allow to cool for another 30 minutes, then frost with Cranberry Liqueur Frosting.

CRANBERRY LIQUEUR FROSTING

Mix all ingredients until thoroughly blended.

Lorraine Kiefer, South Jersey Unit

LEMON BALM CAKE

1 stick butter, room temperature

1/4 cup finely chopped lemon
  balm leaves

1 cup sugar

2 large eggs

1/8 tsp. salt

1 1/2 cups cake flour

1 tsp. baking powder

Grated rind of 1 lemon

1/4 cup pecans, finely chopped

Glaze

Juice of 1 lemon

1/2 cup granulated sugar

1/2 cup hot water

1/4 cup lemon balm leaves, minced

Preheat oven to 350°F. Grease and flour bottom and sides of a large loaf pan (or 2 small).

Cream butter with lemon balm. Add sugar and eggs and beat well. Sift together the salt, cake flour, and baking powder. Add sifted ingredients to creamed ingredients and beat together. Stir in the lemon zest and pecans, then pour into prepared pan. Bake for 30–45 minutes (depending on size of pan), or until a tester inserted into center of cake comes out clean.

While cake is baking, blend together glaze ingredients.

When cake is removed from the oven, pour the glaze over the top and allow it to sit in the pan for several hours. Remove from pan and wrap tightly with plastic wrap. Allow to sit overnight for flavors to blend.

Arlene Popko, Western Pennsylvania Unit

LEMON CARAWAY CAKE

1 1/2 cups butter

1 cup brown sugar

3 eggs, separated

2 cups all-purpose flour

2 tsp. baking soda

2 tsp. caraway seeds

Juice of 2 large lemons

Zest from 2 lemons

3 cups confectioners' sugar

Preheat oven to 350°F.

Line the bottom of an 8-inch round cake pan with waxed or parchment paper. Grease the paper and the sides of the pan. In a bowl, cream together 3/4 cup butter, brown sugar, and zest from 1 lemon. Beat in the egg yolks, then stir in flour, soda, caraway seeds, and 3 tablespoons lemon juice. Beat egg whites until stiff; fold into the batter.

Bake for 1 hour. Turn out of pan and onto wire rack. Cool for 1 hour.

Cream remaining butter, zest from 1 lemon, and remaining lemon juice. Gradually add the confectioners' sugar. Spread on the cooled cake.

Best eaten the next day.

Eleanor Davis, Western Pennsylvania Unit

MABEL GREY POUND CAKE WITH LIMONCELLO

1 package lemon cake mix

1 package lemon instant
   pudding mix

1/2 cup water

1/2 cup oil (not olive)

4 large eggs

1 tbsp. finely chopped Mabel Grey
   pelargonium leaves

1 cup chopped pecans

Finely grated rind of a large lemon

1/2 cup limoncello

Sauce

1 cup sugar

1 stick butter

1/4 cup water

1/4 cup limoncello

Preheat oven to 350°F.

Mix all cake ingredients together and beat for 3 minutes. Pour into a lightly greased and floured Bundt or tube pan and bake for 50–60 minutes. Check the cake at 50 minutes and continue baking until done. Remove from oven and make the following sauce.

In a saucepan, heat sugar, butter, and water for 2–3 minutes or until the sugar is completely dissolved. Remove from the stove and add the limoncello. Use a cake tester to make small holes in the cake. Slowly spoon or pour the sauce all over the hot cake. Leave in the pan until cool and then turn out on a serving dish.

Caroline Amidon, Philadelphia Unit, and
Joyce Brobst, Pennsylvania Heartland Unit

note: **Limoncello** is a traditional lemon liqueur made in Italy—see recipe for Lemon Liqueur in the Beverages section.

MINT CHOCOLATE POUND CAKE

1 cup butter

1/2 cup solid shortening

3 cups sugar

5 eggs

3 cups flour

1/4 tsp. salt

1/2 tsp. baking powder

1/2 cup cocoa

2 tsp. Ceylon cinnamon

1 1/2 cups milk

1 tsp. pure vanilla extract

1 tbsp. chopped fresh mint

Preheat oven to 350°F. Grease and flour a tube pan.

Cream butter, shortening, and sugar. Add eggs and beat at high speed for 3 minutes.

Sift dry ingredients, then toss in chopped mint. Add, alternating with milk, to the creamed mixture. Beat until smooth. Blend in the vanilla.

Pour into prepared pan and bake for 30 minutes. Reduce heat to 325°F and bake for an additional 45 minutes, or until a toothpick inserted in center comes out clean.

Cool for 10 minutes in pan, then turn out onto a wire rack to cool. Allow to sit for at least a day for flavors to blend and texture to develop.

Mary and **Jerry Johnson**, Roanoke Valley Unit

SAFFRON CAKE

1/2 cup butter

1 cup brown sugar

1 cup currants (dried)

3 tbsp. golden raisins

1 cup water

1 egg, lightly beaten

1/2 tsp. cinnamon

1/2 tsp. mace

1/4 tsp. ground cloves

1 tsp. powdered saffron

2 cups cake flour

2 tsp. baking powder

1 tsp. grated lemon peel

1 1/2 cups milk

Add saffron to 1 tablespoon hot water and set aside. Bring 1 cup of water to a boil, remove from heat, and add raisins and currants, setting aside to plump.

Grease and flour the bottom and sides of 8-inch cake pan or Bundt pan. Preheat oven to 350°F.

Sift together the flour, cinnamon, mace, cloves, and baking powder. Stir in the lemon peel.

Put raisins and currants into a colander to drain.

Cream butter and sugar until light and fluffy. Add the dissolved saffron and beat well. Combine milk and beaten egg, then add sifted dry ingredients and beaten egg mixture alternately to the creamed butter and sugar.

Stir the drained raisins and currants into the batter. Pour batter into prepared pan and bake for 1 1/2 hours.

Eleanor Davis, Western Pennsylvania Unit

FRESH FRUIT WITH MINT

1 whole fresh pineapple

1/2 cup sugar

3/4 cup fresh mint leaves,
coarsely chopped

1 pint fresh strawberries

Fresh sprigs of mint for garnish

Cut off the top and bottom of the pineapple. Peel and slice into rings. Sprinkle sugar and mint over the pineapple. Store in a plastic bag in the refrigerator for at least 6 hours. Wash and hull the strawberries. Add to the pineapple and serve garnished with sprigs of fresh mint.

Jennifer F. Jordan, Tidewater Unit

CARRIE'S PLUM PUDDING AND SAUCE DELICIOUS

Plum Pudding

1 cup brown sugar

1 cup chopped suet

2 large apples, chopped with
the skins on

1 cup raisins

1 cup nut meats

2 cups flour

1 tsp. baking soda

2 tsp. cinnamon

1/4 tsp. ground cloves

1/4 tsp. freshly grated nutmeg

1 cup milk

Sauce

1 cup sugar

1/2 cup butter

4 egg yolks, well-beaten

4 oz. lemon juice or brandy

Pinch of salt

1 cup warm cream

PLUM PUDDING

Mix all pudding ingredients together. Pour into a lightly greased 2-quart heat-resistant container and cover tightly. Place on a rack in a deep pot. Add boiling water to the pot to a depth of 1 inch. Cover and keep just under the boiling point, adding more water as needed. Steam 2 hours. Remove pudding container from outer pot and cool for 15 minutes. Turn upside down on serving dish.

SAUCE

Cream butter and sugar until light. Add beaten egg yolks. Stir in lemon juice or brandy. Add a pinch of salt and 1 cup warm cream. Beat mixture well. Place in a saucepan and cook, stirring constantly, until thickened. Do not allow to boil.

Virginia Chaney, Central Ohio Unit

GERI'S CHOCOLATE POTS DE CRÈME

1 1/2 cups cream (may substitute
    evaporated skim milk)
12 oz. semisweet chocolate chips
3 eggs
1/4 cup Tia Maria or Kahlua coffee
    liqueur

*This is the easiest and most elegant dessert—my old standby.
Plus, it must be made the night before!*

Heat cream just to the boiling point. Pour chocolate
chips and hot cream in blender simultaneously while blending. Add eggs and liqueur while you continue to blend.

Pour into demitasse cups or tiny cups and refrigerate
for 8 hours. Serve with a dollop of whipped cream and a
chocolate-covered espresso bean.

Geri Laufer, Chattahoochee Unit

LAVENDER ICE CREAM

2 eggs
1 cup lavender syrup (see below)
1/4 cup milk
2 cups whipping cream
1 tsp. pure vanilla extract

Lavender Syrup
2 cups water
2 cups sugar
2 tbsp. dried lavender flowers

Blend eggs, 1 cup lavender syrup, and milk in a blender.
Stir in the cream and vanilla. Freeze in an ice-cream maker.

LAVENDER SYRUP

Boil sugar and water for 5 minutes. Add lavender flowers
and allow to steep for 30 minutes. Strain and refrigerate.

Anne Abbott, New Orleans Unit,
North Carolina Unit, Potomac Unit

LAVENDER RASPBERRY CHEESECAKE

Crust

1/4 cup pecans

1 1/4 cups graham-cracker crumbs

1/3 cup butter, melted

First Layer

1 cup low-fat cottage cheese

1 cup cream cheese

2 eggs

2/3 cup sugar

1 tsp. dried lavender flowers

Second Layer

1 pint plain yogurt

1/3 cup confectioners' sugar

1 tsp. lemon juice

Garnish

1 pint raspberries

1/2 cup lavender jelly (see recipe
   under Simple Ideas)

Preheat oven to 350°F.

Combine crust ingredients and press into an 8-inch springform pan. Bake for 10 minutes.

Combine ingredients for first layer and pour into the pie crust. Bake for 40 minutes or until knife inserted in center comes out clean. Cool.

Combine ingredients for second layer and spread over cooled first layer. Bake for 20 minutes or until knife inserted in center comes out clean.

Arrange raspberries on top of cooled cheesecake. Heat jelly in microwave just to melting point, then pour over the raspberries. Allow to cool so the jelly will reset.

Barbara Brouse, Colonial Triangle of Virginia Unit

LEMON BASIL TEA BREAD

1 cup sugar

6 tbsp. unsalted butter, softened

2 eggs

6 tbsp. milk

2 tbsp. fresh lemon juice

1 1/2 cups all-purpose flour

1 tsp. baking powder

1/8 tsp. salt

2 tbsp. chopped fresh basil

Zest of 1 lemon

Glaze

1/2 cup sugar

3 tbsp. fresh lemon juice

Preheat oven to 350°F. Grease a loaf pan.

In a large bowl, cream butter and sugar. Add eggs, one at a time, beating well after each. Blend in milk, then lemon juice.

In a small bowl, sift together flour, baking powder, and salt. Stir in fresh basil and lemon zest.

Slowly add flour to creamed mixture, blending thoroughly. Pour into prepared pan and bake for 30–40 minutes, or until bread tests done when a toothpick is inserted in the center.

While bread is baking, prepare glaze by stirring lemon juice into the sugar in a small bowl. Stir periodically to make sure the sugar dissolves.

Remove bread from oven and cool in pan for 10 minutes, then turn out onto a wire rack with waxed paper beneath the rack. Brush glaze over all sides of the bread. Allow to cool completely.

Edna Wilson, North Carolina Unit

ALMOND PIE CRUST

1 cup ground toasted almonds (or
    pecans, walnuts, or hazlenuts)
1 1/4 cups flour
2/3 cup butter
1/2 tsp. salt
1/2 tsp. freshly grated nutmeg
1 tbsp. sugar
1/3 cup cold water

Combine flour, almonds, nutmeg, and salt in a bowl. Cut in butter with a pastry blender until mixture resembles small peas. Add water 1 tablespoon at a time, tossing with fork until all flour is moistened, not wet. Dough should just hold together when pressed together with fingers.

Lightly press into a flat round shape. Roll out into a circle, 1 inch larger than top of pie plate. Fit into the pie plate. Use remainder for top of pie. Roll to 1/2 inch beyond top rim of pie. Moisten edges of pie and cover. Decorate with any remaining dough, leaving holes for steam to escape.

Crimp edges together tightly with fork or fingers. Bake as directed.

note: *To toast almonds, heat them in a dry frying pan, then grind in a processor and measure to 1 cup (or you can buy them already ground).*

Mary Young, South Jersey Unit

GINGER PUDDING PIE

22 ginger snaps, finely crushed
    (about 1 1/2 cups crumbs)
1/3 cup melted butter or margarine
2 tbsp. sugar
1 (4.6-ounce) package vanilla
    pudding mix (not instant)
3 cups milk
1 (3-inch) piece fresh gingerroot,
    peeled and sliced into
    9 (1/4-inch) slices

Preheat oven to 350°F. Mix the ginger snap crumbs, melted butter, and sugar together and press on the bottom and up the sides of a 9-inch pie plate. Bake for 8 minutes. Remove from oven and cool.

In a saucepan, bring milk just to a boil. Remove from heat and add the ginger slices. Cover and allow to steep for 30 minutes. Strain out the ginger. Return to heat and add the pudding mix. Stirring constantly over medium heat, bring the mixture to a full boil.

Remove from heat and pour into the prepared pie shell. Allow to sit for at least 3 hours before serving.

Billi Parus, Tidewater Unit

REXFORD'S SWEET POTATO PIE

1/4 cup butter, softened

1/2 cup sugar

2 cups cooked, mashed sweet
potatoes (microwave in skins,
if desired)

3 eggs

1/4 cup peach brandy

1 tsp. lemon zest

1 tbsp. lemon juice

1 tsp. pure vanilla extract

1/2 tsp. freshly ground nutmeg

1 vanilla wafer pie shell, or
crust of choice

Preheat oven to 375°F. Cream butter and sugar in a mixing bowl, beating well. Add potatoes; beat at medium speed with an electric mixer until well blended. Add eggs, one at a time, beating well after each addition.

Place brandy in a small pan; heat just until warm (do not boil). Add brandy, lemon zest, lemon juice, vanilla, and nutmeg to sweet potato mixture; stir until well blended.

Pour mixture into pastry shell. Bake for 30–40 minutes, or until a cold knife inserted in center of pie comes out clean.

Rexford H. Talbert, North Carolina Unit

RHUBARB CUSTARD PIE

3 eggs

3 tbsp. milk

2 cups sugar

3 tbsp. quick-cooking tapioca

Pie crust for 9-inch pie

4 cups diced rhubarb

2 tsp. butter

Cinnamon to sprinkle

Preheat oven to 425°F. Prepare favorite single-crust pie crust.

In a mixing bowl, beat eggs lightly; blend in milk. Combine sugar and tapioca; stir into egg mixture. Place crust in a pie plate; add the rhubarb. Pour egg mixture over the rhubarb. Dot with butter. Sprinkle with cinnamon.

Bake for 15 minutes, reduce heat to 350°F. Bake 35–40 minutes longer, or until lightly browned. Cool and serve.

Betty Klingaman, Member at large, Mid-Atlantic District

tester's note: *Try this with Deni Bown's Rose Geranium–Scented Celtic Cream (page 223).*

SUGAR-FREE GINGER PUDDING PIE

2 (1-ounce) packages instant
    vanilla pudding (fat-free,
    sugar-free)
3 cups milk
1 (4-inch) piece fresh gingerroot,
    peeled and sliced into
    1/4-inch slices
1 (5.5-ounce) package sugar-free
    gingersnap cookies, finely
    crushed
1/2 cup melted "I Can't Believe It's
    Not Butter" (stick type)

Preheat oven to 350°F. Mix the ginger snap crumbs and melted margarine and press on the bottom and up the sides of a 9-inch pie plate. Bake for 8 minutes. Remove from oven and cool.

Bring 3 cups of milk just to a boil. Remove from heat and add the ginger slices. Cover and allow to steep for 30 minutes. Strain out the ginger and refrigerate until cold. Pour milk and 2 packages of pudding mix into a bowl and mix vigorously. This will begin to thicken immediately. Pour into previously prepared pie shell. Refrigerate for 1 1/2 hours, or until set.

Billi Parus, Tidewater Unit

ROSE PETAL TRIFLE

2 cups sweetened whipped cream
2 drops rose extract
1 pound cake
1 box vanilla instant pudding
    (make according to directions
    on package)
1 cup Rose Petal Jam (see recipe
    in Simple Ideas)
Crystallized rose petals

Scent the whipped cream by adding 2 drops of rose extract. (Do not add more and be sure you are using rose extract, not rose water.)

Using a large attractive glass bowl, layer slices of the pound cake, rose petal jam, vanilla pudding, and rose-scented whipped cream. End with a layer of whipped cream and garnish with crystallized rose petals.

Rose petals may be crystallized by first rinsing rose petals (use only those that have never been sprayed with pesticides), then allowing them to drain until dry. Mix a little powdered egg with water to a viscous consistency. Dip rose petals into egg white blend, then into a fine white sugar, coating both sides. Place petals on a wire rack and allow to dry completely. Store in a tightly covered container, separating layers with waxed paper.

Marie G. Fowler, Arkansas Unit

ROSE GERANIUM–SCENTED CELTIC CREAM

12 fresh bay leaves (do not use dried leaves)

8 rose-scented geranium leaves

10 oz. cream

1/4 cup sugar

2 large egg yolks

12 oz. mascarpone cheese

Cut fresh bay leaves and rose geranium leaves into small pieces with scissors. Add cream and put into a heatproof bowl. Place the bowl over a pan of hot water and heat very gently until the cream is warm. Remove from heat, cover, and leave to infuse for 10 minutes. Strain, discarding leaves.

Return cream to heatproof bowl; add sugar and egg yolks. Whisk briefly to blend, then warm gently over hot water again until thickened, stirring occasionally. Stir the custard into the mascarpone to make a smooth sauce.

This recipe is an adaptation of one by Clare Ferguson in *Gourmet Vegetarian Microwave Cookery*, published by Grub Street, London, in 1986. It works very well with a rhubarb compote, balancing the tartness of the rhubarb.

Deni Bown, Member at large, England

THE PERFECT MARRIAGE

Strawberries

Confectioners' sugar

Cointreau

Violas for garnish

Place 5 ripe strawberries on a plate for each diner. Pile a tablespoon of confectioners' sugar on the plate. Add a wide-mouthed liqueur glass of Cointreau to each plate. Decorate plate with a viola.

Guests may dip their strawberries into the Cointreau, then the confectioners' sugar.

Lory Doolittle, Connecticut Unit

SIMPLE IDEAS
Sauces, Blends, and Extras

Chutneys—Salsas—Relishes

CRANBERRY SALSA

2 cloves garlic

1 small red onion, peeled and
quartered

1 green bell pepper, rinsed,
quartered, and seeded

1/2–1 cup sliced pickled jalapeños
(according to taste)

2 tbsp. fresh cilantro leaves, rinsed
and patted dry

1 (6- to 8-ounce) jar cherry jelly or jam

2 tbsp. apple cider vinegar

3 bags Craisins (sweetened dried
cranberries)

Freshly ground black pepper to taste

Mince garlic in food processor. Add onion, green pepper, jalapeños, and cherry jam. Pulse until ingredients have a coarse-relish consistency. Pour into a large bowl and add remaining ingredients, stirring thoroughly. Refrigerate overnight.

May be served as a dip or condiment. It is especially nice with Thanksgiving dishes and smoked salmon. Keep refrigerated.

Mary Remmel Wohlleb, Arkansas Unit

RAINBOW SALSA

1/2 cup diced fresh pineapple

1/2 cup diced mango or peach

1/2 cup diced green onion

1/2 cup diced green bell pepper

1/2 cup diced, seeded tomato

Juice of 1 lime

1 diced jalapeño pepper

1 tbsp. chopped fresh cilantro

Place all ingredients in a processor and pulse until finely chopped but not pureed.

Jennifer F. Jordan, Tidewater Unit

GERI'S GOOD-ON-ANYTHING CRANBERRY CHUTNEY

2 cups water

2 cups sugar

2 tbsp. molasses

2 large Granny Smith applies, sliced and diced

12 oz. fresh cranberries

1 cup raisins

1/3 cup red wine vinegar

2 tbsp. finely minced fresh gingerroot

2 tsp. hot curry powder

1 tsp. salt

1/3 tsp. Tabasco sauce

In a heavy saucepan, bring water and sugar to a boil; simmer until sugar is dissolved. Add molasses and apples. Bring back to a boil, then reduce heat and simmer 10 minutes, until apples are tender. Add cranberries and remaining ingredients.

Stir and bring back to a boil, then simmer for another 20 minutes. Store in covered jars in the refrigerator.

Keeps a whole year under refrigeration, but I'll bet it won't last that long!

Geri Laufer, Chattahoochee Unit

MANGO APPLE CHUTNEY

10 pounds peeled, sliced mangoes

1/4 cup salt

5 pounds dark brown sugar

6 cups cider vinegar

6 Granny Smith apples, peeled and diced

1 1/2 cups blanched slivered almonds

4 lemons, thinly sliced and quartered

2 large onions, chopped

1 1/2 cups candied citron

2 pounds seedless golden raisins

2/3 cup grated fresh gingerroot

1 cup chopped candied ginger

3 cloves garlic, finely chopped

1 tbsp. red pepper

Sprinkle mangoes with salt and let stand overnight or while preparing the rest.

Boil sugar and vinegar together for 5 minutes. Add drained mangoes and other ingredients. Simmer for 1–2 hours, until mangoes are tender and the juices have thickened. Pour boiling chutney into hot sterilized jars and cap with hot lids, making sure to clean the lips of the jars before placing two-part lid on. Process in boiling water bath for 10 minutes. Yields about 30 half-pint jars.

Caroline Amidon, Philadelphia Unit

tester's note: *I was the happy recipient of a prepared jar of this wonderful chutney. This is a great recipe to make with holiday giving in mind!*

RED PEPPER RELISH

4 cups finely chopped sweet red
    peppers ("lipstick" pimientos
    are best)
2 tbsp. sea salt
1 1/2 cups cider vinegar
3/4 cup sugar
1 tsp. fresh fennel seeds

Mix peppers and salt in a glass bowl, let stand overnight in the refrigerator. Drain peppers. Combine peppers with remaining ingredients in a stainless steel pot. Bring to a boil, lower heat, and cook, stirring occasionally, until mixture thickens slightly. If liquid boils down too much, cover the pan. Spoon relish into sterilized 8-ounce jars. Screw on tops and process in a boiling-water bath for 10 minutes. Yields 3 jars.

Nancy B. Hanst, Western Pennsylvania Unit

SAGE RELISH

4 tbsp. fresh sage leaves
2 tbsp. salt
2 tbsp. grated lemon peel
1 tbsp. lemon juice
1/8 tsp. cayenne pepper
2 cups dry red wine
1/8 tsp. freshly grated nutmeg

Mix all ingredients and refrigerate, covered, for 2 weeks. Shake well each day. On last day, do not shake; filter using a dampened coffee filter. Store tightly covered in the refrigerator. To use, mix a tablespoonful in gravy for pork or chicken.

Eleanor Davis, Western Pennsylvania Unit

Marinades and Sauces

ANNIE'S ROSEMARY MARINADE

1 cup Italian salad dressing

2 tbsp. Worcestershire sauce

1/4 cup soy sauce

2 tbsp. honey

2–3 tbsp. fresh rosemary

Mix all ingredients. Marinate chicken or pork several hours or overnight. Cook according to recipe being used.

Marilyn Rhinehalt, Western Reserve Unit

BORDELAISE SAUCE

1/2 cup sliced fresh mushrooms

1 tbsp. butter

2 tbsp. flour

1 1/2 cups beef stock

1 tbsp. lemon juice

1/4 cup red wine

1/4 tsp. pepper

1/4 tsp. garlic powder

1/2 tsp. chopped parsley

1 tsp. tarragon

1 tbsp. minced onion

1 bay leaf

1/4 tsp. thyme

Freshly ground black pepper

Sauté mushrooms in butter; add flour, then beef stock, lemon juice, and red wine. Stir constantly over low heat until thickened. Add remaining herbs and seasonings.

Lori Schaeffer, Pennsylvania Heartland Unit

LEBANESE ONION SAUCE

4 large onions, sliced
6 tbsp. butter
2 tsp. spice mixture (see below)

Spice Mixture
1 tbsp. cinnamon
1 tbsp. paprika
1 tbsp. salt
3/4 tsp. cayenne pepper

Warm a heavy pan over low heat and add butter. As butter begins to melt, toss in onions and cook, stirring frequently, for 30–40 minutes. Keep heat low to avoid burning the butter. When onions are done, sprinkle the spice mixture over the onions and toss thoroughly.

Serve the Lebanese Onion Sauce with meatloaf, with chopped tomatoes as a garnish. You might also try adding a bit of the spice mixture to your favorite meatloaf recipe.

SPICE MIXTURE

Stir spices together and keep in a tightly covered jar.

Ruth Mary Papenthien, Virginia Commonwealth Unit, Colonial Triangle of Virginia Unit

tester's note: *I served this with meatloaf, as recommended. The entire family thought it was delicious—it made an ordinary meal different and special.*

LIME VINAIGRETTE

1/4 cup extra virgin olive oil
1/4 cup fresh lime juice
1/4 cup water
2 large cloves garlic
1 tsp. seeded and chopped jalapeño
    or Serrano pepper
1/2 tsp. salt
1/8 tsp. ground black pepper
1 tbsp. Dijon mustard
2 tbsp. chopped fresh basil
2 tbsp. chopped fresh spearmint

Combine all ingredients except herbs in a blender or processor and blend until smooth. Add basil and spearmint, just blending to mix. Use as a marinade or basting sauce, or as a topping for grilled or roasted meats, poultry, seafood, or vegetables.

Add additional oil, lime juice, and water to thin and use as a salad dressing for greens or vegetables. Adjust salt as needed. Yields about 1 cup.

Madalene Hill and **Gwen Barclay,** The Flavour Connection, Pioneer Unit

tester's note: *I used this as a marinade and basting sauce for pork spareribs. It was outstanding—rave reviews from tasters!*

MOTHER'S PLUM CATSUP

5 pounds red or purple plums,
    washed and pitted
3 pounds sugar
1 cup cider vinegar
1 tbsp. ground cloves
1 tbsp. ground cinnamon

Combine all ingredients in a large, heavy kettle, mixing well. Boil slowly for 1 hour or until thickened. As catsup thickens, stir frequently as it will scorch easily.

If desired, strain out the plum skins, using a food mill.

Fill sterilized 8-ounce jelly jars, affix seals and lids; process in a boiling-water bath for 10 minutes. Yields ten 8-ounce jars.

Excellent served with ham, pork, or poultry.

Shirley A. Ricketts, Western Reserve Unit

MUSTARD DILL SAUCE

1/2 cup fresh dill, chopped
1/2 cup Dijon mustard
1 tbsp. honey
3 tbsp. dill white wine vinegar
3 tbsp. plain yogurt
1/2 cup olive oil

In a blender, combine all ingredients except the oil. With the motor running, slowly add the oil. Blend until thick and smooth. Place in a covered container and refrigerate.

Serve with steamed vegetables, grilled chicken, or fish.

Eleanor Davis, Western Pennsylvania Unit

MY SECRET HERB BUTTER

3/4 cup butter, softened
1/3 cup cut celery leaves, packed
1 tbsp. fresh sage
1 tbsp. fresh thyme
1/3 cup chopped fresh parsley
1/3 cup green onions, including tops
1 tbsp. fresh marjoram
1/4 tsp. freshly ground black pepper

Blend or process all ingredients until well blended. May be stored in the refrigerator for 1 week.

Mary Nell Jackson, North and Central Texas Unit

tester's note: *Can be used to baste turkey or chicken when grilling or roasting. Very good spread on hot French bread or on a baked potato.*

TARRAGON BUTTER

1 cup softened butter

2 tsp. fresh tarragon, minced

1 tsp. fresh parsley, minced

1 tsp. fresh lemon juice

Work herbs and lemon juice into the softened butter. Cover tightly and refrigerate until ready to use.

Marie G. Fowler, Arkansas Unit

PIQUANT GREEN SAUCE FOR MEATS

1/2 cup extra virgin olive oil

2 tbsp. white wine vinegar

2 tbsp. water

1/4 tsp. sugar

1/2 tsp. salt

1/4 tsp. freshly ground black pepper

1 tbsp. each chopped fresh chives,
   sorrel, parsley, watercress or
   nasturtium leaves, savory, dill,
   tarragon, and chervil (if some
   seasonal herbs are not available, use more of others)

1 tbsp. finely chopped yellow onion

1 tbsp. finely chopped leeks, white
   portion only

2 hard-boiled eggs, finely chopped

Using a wire whisk, combine olive oil and vinegar in a medium bowl to emulsify. Add sugar, salt, and pepper, mixing well. Fold in chopped herbs, onion, leeks, and eggs; taste for seasoning. Serve at once or within several hours to maintain texture of eggs. Serve with cold or hot meats and poultry. Also good with duck.

In the style of Frankfurt, Germany, this condiment is the perfect foil for rich meats and poultry.

Madalene Hill and **Gwen Barclay**, The Flavour Connection, Pioneer Unit

ROASTED TOMATO PASTA SAUCE WITH FRESH HERBS

2 tbsp. olive oil

4 large tomatoes, halved

1 large red onion, sliced

3 cloves garlic, sliced

2 tbsp. fresh basil

2 tbsp. fresh oregano

1 tbsp. fresh lemon thyme

1/2 cup sliced Kalamata olives

Preheat oven to 400°F.

Coat the bottom of a roasting pan with olive oil. Separate the onion into rings and layer them on the bottom of the pan. Scatter the fresh herbs over the onions, then spread olives over the pan. Lay tomatoes cut side down on top, packing closely. Roast for 30–40 minutes. The skins should just be browning. Remove from the oven. When cooled a bit, lift off the tomato skins. Pulse the vegetables briefly in a blender; the sauce should be chunky.

Serve over hot pasta.

Marilyn Kushner, Northern California Unit

SAGE BUTTER FOR FISH

1/2 cup butter (1 stick)

2 tbsp. chopped fresh sage

1 tbsp. lemon zest

1 tbsp. lemon juice

Sea salt to taste

White pepper to taste

Slowly melt butter in a small saucepan. Stir in sage, lemon zest, lemon juice, salt, and pepper. Brush generously over fish of choice (tuna or salmon are good choices) prior to grilling, broiling, or baking.

Katherine K. Schlosser, North Carolina Unit

SESAME GINGER SAUCE

1/2 cup rice wine vinegar

1/3 cup tamari sauce

1/3 cup canola oil

2 tbsp. honey

2 tbsp. grated fresh ginger

1 clove garlic, crushed

1 tbsp. tahini

Blend ingredients and store in a covered container in the refrigerator. Good as a seasoning for pan-seared or grilled salmon or tuna filets.

Katherine K. Schlosser, North Carolina Unit

SOFRITO

1 head garlic

2 seeded green peppers

2 medium onions

6 tbsp. fresh basil

6 tbsp. fresh oregano

6 tbsp. fresh rosemary

6 tbsp. cilantro, or more to taste

White wine vinegar

Blend all ingredients with enough vinegar to make a thick paste. Adjust seasoning with freshly ground black pepper as you wish. Keep refrigerated.

Dorothy Bonitz, North Carolina Unit

tester's note: *I received a gift of a prepared jar of Sofrito. It is a fabulous, fresh-tasting condiment for use with bean dishes, meats, eggs, or just on a cracker!*

STEVE'S PORK TENDERLOIN MARINADE

1/2 cup balsamic vinegar

1/2 cup olive oil

1/2 cup chopped shallots

2 tbsp. fresh rosemary

1 tbsp. sugar

2 cloves garlic

Puree all ingredients. Place meat in a recloseable plastic bag with the marinade and refrigerate for 2–3 hours or overnight.

Marilyn Rhinehalt, Western Reserve Unit

Pesto

AVOCADO CILANTRO PESTO

1/4 cup pine nuts

2 cups cilantro, chopped

1 cup parsley, chopped

1/2 cup avocado, peeled

1/2 cup olive oil

1/4 cup fresh lemon juice

Salt and pepper to taste

1/2 cup freshly grated Parmesan
cheese

Combine all ingredients in a food processor until smooth. Stir into soups and stews or mix with sour cream as a spread. Mix into sour cream and use in place of butter on baked potatoes.

Debra Seibert, Rocky Mountain Unit

PESTO GENOVESE

2 cups solidly packed basil (lettuce
leaf or sweet basil)

1/3 cup pine nuts, lightly toasted

1/2 tsp. salt

1/8 tsp. freshly ground black pepper

1/2 cup freshly grated
Parmesan cheese

1/4 cup freshly grated
Romano cheese

3 garlic cloves, chopped

1/2 tsp. finely chopped fresh
marjoram

1/2 cup extra virgin olive oil

Put all ingredients in a food processor in the order listed, processing lightly after each addition. Slowly add oil, blending all ingredients well.

Store in tightly covered container in refrigerator; use within a week. You may also freeze the pesto for up to 3 months.

Use in most recipes calling for pesto; stir a spoonful into fresh tomato soup; add a little to spaghetti sauce; serve over hot pasta with a little extra oil or butter.

Eleanor Davis, Western Pennsylvania Unit

BASIL PESTO

5 cloves garlic, peeled and sliced

1/4 cup pine nuts

4 cups basil leaves

Salt

1/2 cup freshly grated Parmesan
cheese

3/4 cup olive oil

Combine the garlic and pine nuts in a large mortar and crush into a smooth paste. Add the basil to the mortar, a handful at a time, crushing the leaves against the sides with the pestle. The mixture will be like a coarse, thick paste until the oil is added. Add a few pinches of salt to the basil.

Stir in the cheese. Drizzle the olive oil in slowly, a bit at a time, as you work it in. The pesto should become very smooth. (If using a food processor, follow the same order, processing to desired consistency.)

If serving over pasta, cook pasta until it is al dente. Toss the pasta with the pesto using a few tablespoons of the hot pasta water to thin the pesto so that it coats the pasta evenly. Serve immediately.

A little pesto makes a good sauce for grilled or roasted fish and vegetables, especially salmon, potatoes, eggplant, tomatoes, and squash, as well as a tasty garnish for vegetable soups. A delicious dip can be made by mixing pesto with an equal amount of sour cream; serve with fresh vegetable crudités. Pesto is best when used immediately, though it will keep in the refrigerator for 3 or 4 days. The top layer will darken some, just stir to remix.

Susan Belsinger, Potomac Unit

BASIL AND OREGANO PESTO

2 cups fresh basil leaves

3 tbsp. fresh oregano leaves

2 cloves garlic

1/4 cup freshly grated Parmesan
cheese

1/4 cup walnuts

1/2 cup olive oil

Salt and pepper

Combine the basil, oregano, garlic, cheese, and walnuts in a food processor. With the machine running, slowly add the olive oil through the filler tube. Season with salt and pepper and process to desired consistency. Store tightly covered in the refrigerator for up to a week, or freeze.

Joe Money, South Jersey Unit

SUN-DRIED TOMATO PESTO SAUCE

2 cloves garlic

2 cups fresh basil leaves

5 sun-dried tomatoes, reconstituted

1/2 cup olive oil

1/4 cup pine nuts

1/4 tsp. coarse salt

1/4 cup freshly grated Parmesan
   cheese

Place garlic, basil, sun-dried tomatoes, and oil into a food processor. Process until tomatoes are coarsely chopped. Add pine nuts, salt, and cheese; process just to mix. Check seasoning and adjust salt if necessary. Yields 3/4 cup.

Laurel Keser, South Jersey Unit

SPRING PESTO WITH CHERVIL AND PINE NUTS

2 cups fresh chervil

1/4 cup freshly grated Parmesan
   cheese

1/4 cup toasted pine nuts

1/3 cup olive oil

1 clove garlic, sliced

Salt and pepper to taste

Toast pine nuts in a dry sauté pan for 2–3 minutes, or just until the nuts take on a golden color. Remove from heat and place the nuts in a dish until ready to use. Wash and dry the chervil and mince the garlic.

Combine chervil, Parmesan, pine nuts, garlic, and 2 tablespoons of olive oil in a food processor. Pulse lightly to ensure that ingredients are well combined. Add additional olive oil as necessary to make a thin paste, leaving bits of chervil still visible. Season with salt and pepper, then store in the refrigerator for up to 3 days. If you will be keeping the pesto longer, freeze in an ice cube tray, then pop the cubes into a plastic bag and seal.

Katherine K. Schlosser, North Carolina Unit

CANDIED ORANGE PEEL

2–3 large oranges with thick skins

2 cups sugar

1 cup water

1 cup sugar or more

Score the orange in quarters and peel from orange. Don't worry about removing white part of peel. Slice the orange peel into 1/2-inch strips. Soak these slices in a bowl covered with cold water overnight, making sure the orange peel is underwater.

In the morning, drain and rinse the peel. Using a large pan, cover orange peel with water again and simmer until tender, up to an hour. When peel is easily pierced with a fork, drain well in a colander.

While draining, prepare a sugar syrup with 2 cups sugar to 1 cup water; bring to a boil and simmer for 5–10 minutes. You should have enough sugar syrup to cover the orange peel.

Simmer the orange peel in the sugar syrup (do not allow to boil) until it is transparent. This will take up to an hour and the syrup will thicken.

Drain orange peel well in a colander, taking care not to burn yourself with the hot syrup. When cool and not wet with the syrup, mix peel with white sugar to coat. Arrange on waxed paper-lined baking sheets so the pieces do not touch one another. Allow to dry overnight. Store in a covered tin.

This sounds like a lot of work, but you don't need to stand over it while it is cooking. However, you should plan to be home the day you make the recipe so you can check it while it is cooking. The important thing is to not remove the peel from the syrup until it has absorbed the syrup or it will not absorb the sugar and will remain too soft.

Betty Rea, Virginia Commonwealth Unit

tester's note: *This is the best candied orange peel I have ever had!*

CRANBERRY SAGE JELLY

3 tbsp. fresh sage, washed and
    patted dry
1 3/4 cups cranberry juice
2 cups sugar
1/4 cup lemon juice
1/2 cup bottled Certo

Wash and sterilize jars and tops. The recipe makes 3 cups, so select size and number of jars accordingly. Keep jars in hot water while preparing the jelly.

Pour cranberry juice and sage leaves into a stainless steel saucepan. Bring to boil, remove from heat, and let stand for 5 minutes. Strain out the sage leaves.

Add sugar and lemon juice to the cranberry juice. Bring to a boil. Stir in Certo and boil for 1 full minute. Remove from heat, skim off foam, and pack in sterilized jars.

Process according to the instructions with your canning equipment.

Adrienne Lind, Pennsylvania Heartland Unit

tester's note: *Has a great ruby color and good sage taste. Good accompaniment to chicken and turkey. Liquid Certo was not available, so I substituted a box of powdered pectin.*

HERB HONEY

1 cup honey
2 sprigs herb (rosemary, basil,
    lavender, or other)

Combine honey and herbs. Bring to a simmer in a small saucepan. Remove from heat and allow to cool. Store in a glass jar in the refrigerator.

Debra Seibert, Rocky Mountain Unit

LAVENDER JELLY

2 cups lavender infusion (see below)

1/4 cup fresh lemon juice

4 cups sugar

1 (3-ounce) envelope liquid pectin

Lavender Infusion

1/2 cup fresh lavender flowers
(unsprayed)

3 cups distilled water

Bring lavender infusion, lemon juice, and sugar to a boil, stirring constantly. Stir in liquid pectin and boil for 1 additional minute, stirring constantly.

Remove from heat and pour into sterilized glass jars. (Add a few flowers if desired.) Affix seals and lids; process in a boiling-water bath for 10 minutes. Yields 2 pints.

LAVENDER INFUSION

In a nonreactive pan, bring water to a boil and pour over the flowers; steep for 20 minutes. Strain and set aside.

Barbara Brouse, Colonial Triangle of Virginia Unit

LEMONGRASS SYRUP

2 cups water

1 cup sugar

2 cups lemongrass, cut into
1-inch pieces (may substitute
2 cups lemon verbena or
orange mint, chopped)

Using the bottom portions of lemongrass stalks, cut into 1-inch pieces. (Use the part that just gets up into the green; depending on your plant, that may be 6–8 inches up the stalk. Use a sharp knife and take care not to cut your hands on the sharp edges of the leaves.)

Combine water and sugar in a small saucepan. Bring to a boil, reduce heat, add lemongrass, and simmer for 10 minutes. Remove from heat and allow to steep for 30 minutes–1 hour. The syrup should be thickened and a pale golden yellow color. Strain out the lemongrass. Pour syrup into a sterilized glass bottle and store in the refrigerator.

This is very nice served over fruit, drizzled over ice cream or cake, or stirred into tea, lemonade, or a glass of dry white wine.

Katherine K. Schlosser, North Carolina Unit

NANCY HOWARD'S OPAL BASIL JELLY

1 cup cider vinegar

1 1/2 cups water

2 quarts loosely packed opal
basil leaves and flowers

Juice of 1 lemon

6 cups sugar

1 bottle pectin

Make an infusion of the opal basil: Bring to a boil cider vinegar, water, and opal basil leaves. Remove from heat and steep, covered, for 15 minutes. Add the juice of 1 lemon. Pour through a filter (try using a dampened coffee filter).

Bring 2 1/2 cups opal basil infusion and 6 cups sugar to a rolling boil. Add 1 bottle of pectin. Boil 1 minute. Pour into sterilized jars and top with hot lids. Invert jars for 5 minutes, then stand upright. Allow to cool undisturbed.

When cool, check seals. Any jars that are not sealed should be stored in the refrigerator.

Caroline Amidon, Philadelphia Unit

PYRACANTHA BERRY JELLY

6 cups ripe pyracantha berries

3 1/2 cups water

Juice of 1 grapefruit

Juice of 1 lemon

1 package pectin

5 1/2 cups sugar

Cook berries in water for about 20 minutes. Strain carefully, being sure not to get any seeds in the juice. Add grapefruit and lemon juice to make 4 1/2 cups liquid. Put juice into a stainless steel pan and add sugar. Bring to a boil and boil 5 minutes, stirring constantly and skimming foam as necessary. Add pectin and boil 1 additional minute.

Pour jelly into sterilized jars, affix lids, and process in boiling-water bath for 10 minutes.

Be absolutely certain that the berries you use have not been sprayed and have not been exposed to roadside fumes. Wash them carefully, and take care not to get seeds or leaves into your jelly (they contain prunasin, a cyanogenic glycoside, and are thus poisonous, but so are the pits and leaves of peaches because of the content of another cyanogenic glycoside, amygdalin!).

Barbara Brouse, Colonial Triangle of Virginia Unit

ROSE HIP SYRUP

1 cup rose hips

3/4 cup water

Juice of 1 lemon

1 1/2 cups sugar

1 package powdered pectin

3/4 cup water

Cut stems and ends of washed rose hips. Slit down the side and remove seeds. Place rose hips, 3/4 cup water, and lemon juice in a blender. Process until perfectly smooth. Gradually add 1 1/2 cups sugar, running the blender the entire time. Blend for another 5 minutes to make sure the sugar is completely dissolved.

In a saucepan, stir 1 package pectin into 3/4 cup water. Bring to a boil and boil hard for 1 minute. Pour this into the blender and blend for 1 minute more. Pour immediately into a sterilized jar with a nonmetal lid. Store in the refrigerator. Also freezes well in a freezer container.

Pour a little over ice cream, pancakes, or pound cake. Pour over fresh fruit and allow to marinate for an hour or so.

Be sure to use rose hips that have not been contaminated by pesticides or roadside fumes. *Rosa rugosa* produces large hips that make an easy job of extracting the pulp. Very high in vitamin C and has a lovely flavor.

Marilyn Sly, Connecticut Unit

ROSE PETAL JAM

1 cup strongly scented rose petals, tightly packed (use only unsprayed, organic roses)

1 cup water

1 cup sugar

1 cup honey

2 tbsp. lemon juice

1 package pectin, plus 3/4 cup water

Snip off the white base of each rose petal and put the petals in a blender with the water, honey, and sugar.

Mix the pectin and 3/4 cup water in a saucepan and bring to a boil, boiling hard for 1 minute, stirring constantly. Add the pectin mixture to the rose mixture in the blender and process until well blended. Pour into 4 sterilized pint jars and seal. Must be either refrigerated or frozen.

Marie G. Fowler, Arkansas Unit

RED HIBISCUS PEPPER JELLY

4 cups sugar

1 pouch liquid pectin

2/3 cup pickled jalapeños, drained and chopped

1/3 cup apple juice

1 tbsp. hibiscus tea leaves

2 tbsp. cider vinegar

Steep apple cider with tea to a brilliant red. In a 2-quart pot, mix sugar and pectin; let sit for 10 minutes.

Bring sugar mix to a boil; add remaining ingredients. Boil 1 minute more. Pour into sterilized canning jars, cover with lids and seals. Process in boiling water bath for 10 minutes, or freeze until ready to use.

Serving suggestions: Pour jelly over cream cheese or crème fraiche and serve crackers alongside. Mix pepper jelly with other jams, marmalades, or mustards to glaze roast pork, ham, duck, chicken, or turkey. Add 2–3 tablespoons to a basic vinaigrette for pizzazz!

Linda Franzo, New Orleans Unit

WILD STRAWBERRY GINGER JAM

2 cups crushed wild strawberries (use small, sweet domestic strawberries if wild are not available)

2 tbsp. crystallized ginger, cut into small pieces

2 tsp. fresh lemon thyme

3 1/2 cups sugar

1/2 of 1 pouch liquid pectin

Prepare home canning jars and lids according to manufacturer's instructions. Combine strawberries and ginger in a large saucepan. Add sugar, stirring to dissolve. Bring to a rolling boil over medium-high heat, stirring constantly. Stir in thyme, then stir in liquid pectin. Boil hard 1 minute. Remove from heat. Skim foam if necessary. Ladle hot jam into hot jars, leaving 1/4 inch headspace. Wipe jar rims clean, adjust caps, and process 10 minutes in a boiling-water canner.

Remove jars from canner and allow to sit for 24 hours. Check seals and store in a dark place. Any unsealed jars should be refrigerated. Yields about 4 8-ounce jars.

Katherine K. Schlosser, North Carolina Unit

Miscellaneous

ASPARAGUS IN GARLIC VINEGAR

3 pounds of pencil-thin asparagus

3 cups of rice wine vinegar

2 tsp. of pickling salt

4 tbsp. of sugar

1/4 tsp. black pepper

4 cloves garlic, thinly sliced

Wash asparagus and allow to dry. Lay the asparagus on a cutting board with the florets at one end. Cut the stalks 1 inch shorter than the height of the jars you will use. Insert asparagus tightly into hot, sterilized jars. Combine all remaining ingredients in a nonreactive pan and heat to a slow boil. Pour over the asparagus leaving a half inch of head space. Make sure you distribute the garlic as evenly as possible in the jars. Adjust the lids/seals and process in a boiling-water bath for 20 minutes. Allow to age for 30 days before using.

Joe Money, South Jersey Unit

NIGELLA STUFFED EGGS

12 hard-boiled eggs

2 tbsp. finely grated carrot

1/4 cup plain yogurt

1/4 cup sour cream

1 clove garlic, minced

1/4 tsp. salt

2 tsp. Nigella seeds

Peel eggs and slice lengthwise. Remove yolks. Combine yolks with the remaining ingredients and mix well. Fill whites with yolk mixture, mounding slightly.

Ann Wilson, Member at large, South Central District

CRANBERRY-ROSEMARY VINEGAR

Pack fresh or frozen whole cranberries into a glass bottle. Add leaves from 2 (6-inch) sprigs of rosemary. Pour white wine vinegar into the bottle to cover cranberries and rosemary. Cover and allow to sit for 2–3 weeks. Strain out the berries and rosemary.

Store in a glass bottle with a nonmetallic top.

Debra Seibert, Rocky Mountain Unit

SALT METHOD FOR PRESERVING BASIL, DILL, OR FENNEL

I have been using this method for many years. I watched my mother-in-law preserve her harvest when I was a young bride, and I have been doing it her way ever since (49 years).

In a wide-mouthed glass jar, alternate layers of kosher salt and fresh herbs. Cover with plastic lid and store in a dark, dry place. Allow to sit for at least two weeks.

When ready to use, break up any lumps that may have formed in salt. Carefully remove herbs for use in cooking, lightly brushing off salt. Reserve the flavored salt for cooking as well.

Alternatively, after 2–3 weeks, you may empty contents of jar into a food processor and chop lightly. Use as a seasoned salt.

Ellen Adams, Member at large, Great Lakes District

tester's note: *You can use this method with other herbs as well.*

GARAM MASALA

3 tbsp. black peppercorns

3 tbsp. whole coriander

2 1/2 tbsp. dark caraway seeds

1 (1-inch) stick cinnamon, broken

1 tbsp. cardamom seeds

1 tbsp. whole cloves

Grind all ingredients in a coffee grinder to a powder. Store in a tightly covered container.

This blend is good for seasoning vegetables, stews, and potatoes. It is also wonderful in tomato soup. Yields 3/4 cup.

Mary Remmel Wohlleb, Arkansas Unit

JAMIE'S DILL DIP MIX

1 cup dried minced onion

1 cup dried parsley

1 cup dried dill weed

1/3 cup sugar

1 tbsp. salt

1/2 tsp. garlic powder

1 1/4 tsp. celery salt

Blend ingredients thoroughly and store in the freezer.

To make dip, blend 3 tablespoons Jamie's Dill Dip Mix with 1 cup mayonnaise and 1 cup sour cream. Refrigerate and allow flavors to blend for several hours. Use as a dip for crackers, vegetables, or mix with hot potatoes, cauliflower, or beans.

Jamie H. Barrow, HSA President, 1992–94

LEMON-PEPPER SEASONING MIX

1 cup ground black pepper

1/3 cup dried lemon peel

3 tbsp. coriander seeds

1/4 cup dried minced onion

1/4 cup dried thyme leaves

Stir all ingredients and store in airtight jars. This seasoning adds a piquant flavor when used on grilled meats.

Jennifer F. Jordan, Tidewater Unit

LEG OF LAMB COATING

1/4 cup lemon juice

2 tsp. salt

2 cloves garlic, minced

1/4 tsp. pepper

1 tsp. paprika

1/2 cup minced fresh parsley

1 bay leaf

1/4 cup minced carrots

1/4 cup minced onion

1 tsp. fresh thyme

1/4 cup soft butter

2 tbsp. flour

2 tsp. prepared mustard

Thoroughly combine all ingredients. Spread over lamb and roast according to weight of the meat.

Henrietta McWillie, Member at large, Southeast District

SIMPLE IDEAS FOR USING HERBS

Rule of thumb for fruit and herb dressings—use 3 parts oil to 1 part vinegar.

Use fruit juices as a substitute for the vinegar. Possible combinations: orange juice with chocolate mint and lemon verbena; orange juice with orange mint; pineapple and mango juice with lemon balm, thyme, and cinnamon basil.

Kelly Wisner, Pennsylvania Heartland Unit

To your favorite pound cake recipe, add 1 heaping teaspoon chopped rosemary and 1/2 cup rosemary flowers.

Dorothy Bonitz, North Carolina Unit

Use herb vinegars when marinating meats for a special herb flavor.

Betty Rea, Virginia Commonwealth Unit

To your favorite egg salad recipe, add 1 tablespoon chopped fresh dill and 1 tablespoon capers.

Katherine K. Schlosser, North Carolina Unit

Cook green beans with a few sprigs of summer savory.

Betty Rea, Virginia Commonwealth Unit

Add chopped fresh basil to cream cheese and drained crushed pineapple.

Betty Rea, Virginia Commonwealth Unit

Arrange thick slices of tomatoes on a platter. Cover each slice with minced fresh basil and chopped chives. Cover with foil and place in refrigerator for several hours. To serve, sprinkle with oil and vinegar dressing.

Betty Rea, Virginia Commonwealth Unit

Add 1/4 cup rosemary blossoms to a vanilla, lemon, or carrot cake recipe.

Dorothy Bonitz, North Carolina Unit

Add 2 teaspoons garam masala or 1/2 teaspoon nutmeg to your favorite tomato soup. I have served this to guests and some guessed they were eating pumpkin soup!

Mary Remmel Wohlleb, Arkansas Unit

Work 4 teaspoons fresh herbs (parsley, thyme, savory, rosemary, oregano, or a combination) in your favorite pastry crust recipe for savory pies.

Ed Pierzynski, South Jersey Unit, and Eleanor Davis, Western Pennsylvania Unit

Stir 2 tablespoons finely chopped fresh rosemary into your favorite biscuit recipe.

Eleanor Davis, Western Pennsylvania Unit

Add orange mint or apple mint to cranberry juice. Let it stand at least 2 hours, then strain and serve.

Betty Rea, Virginia Commonwealth Unit

III The National Herb Garden: America's Garden

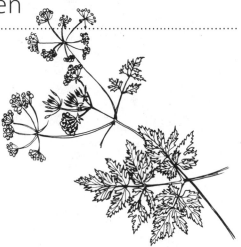

The National Herb Garden: America's Garden

Visitors to the National Herb Garden are often unaware that the paths they follow through the Garden trace the outline of an old-fashioned skeleton key, for the design is visible only from the air. Themed gardens create distinct spaces within the design, and they are connected so that visitors focus on one collection of plants at a time. Although a large garden, the National Herb Garden thus engenders an intimate atmosphere.

The shank of the key contains the Entrance Garden, which overlooks the Knot Garden. The Entrance Garden leads naturally into the Antique and Heritage Rose Garden, a garden especially beautiful in May but filled year-round with colorful herbs. The oval head of the key holds ten specialty gardens: the Dioscorides, Dye, Colonial, Native American, Medicinal, Industrial, Fragrance, Asian, Beverage, and Culinary Gardens, each of which is described in detail in the following pages.

The National Herb Garden is a zone 7 garden, featuring primarily plants that do well in the Washington, D.C., climate, though some of its plants are ordinarily found in warmer zones. The plants that are not winter hardy are kept in containers and wintered in the Garden's greenhouse. Other plants in the Garden are said to be hardy only to zone 8, but make it through the winter year after year.

The National Herb Garden is a garden for all, and it tries to have something of interest for each visitor. Herb Society of America members from across the United States are joining with the HSA's National Herb Garden committee to develop a trove of gardening experiences from various regions of the country, which will be shared with visitors to the Garden. From the casual one-time visitor to frequent visitors and re-

Design of the National Herb Garden showing the skeleton key shape

searchers, all are welcome to participate in this process. The Garden's staff and volunteers readily answer questions about the Garden and its plants, and they are eager to hear about plants from other areas of the country. Educational programs are open to the public, and changing educational displays in the Garden draw visitors' attention to a variety of horticultural issues.

Now, a short tour.

THE ENTRANCE GARDEN

Amid a cottage-garden bed filled with flashy flowers and delightful herbal fragrances, the National Herb Garden sign points the way to the Entrance Garden, which is a natural gathering area for many of the Garden's five hundred thousand annual visitors. The large circular garden, paved with red brick, features a small quiet fountain at its center and looks out over the U.S. National Arboretum meadow, with the Flowering Tree Walk and the Capitol Columns in the distance.

The entrance is flanked with large clay containers of *Rosmarinus officinalis* 'Tuscan Blue' topiaries, which spend winters in the greenhouse. On the edges of this garden are semicircular beds that hold changing displays of annual herbs. These beds give Garden interns an opportunity to show their creative horticultural skills. At various times, the beds have held displays of lime green and deep maroon potato vines, twining in and around 'Purple Ruffles' basil and purple pansies. A collection of basils of every imaginable type, underplanted with violas, made another pleasing and fragrant display. One year an enterprising intern created bamboo frames and painted them a brilliant red to set off the plants they held. The year of the Garden's twenty-fifth anniversary, the beds held a selection of silver-leaved herbs interspersed with white tulips. The beds change with the seasons and with the tastes of the intern, always demonstrating the attractiveness of herbs in landscape design.

Fruit-producing pomegranates, wintered in the greenhouse, are brought out in their concrete containers every spring in time to adorn the area with their blossoms and,

Entrance area with Capitol
columns in the distance

later, with their muted-red fruit. The pomegranates sit at the entrance to two magnificent grape arbors, each thirty feet long and twelve feet wide and sited along the length of the Knot Garden. They offer "a place for sitting, decoratively shaded with plants," which has been a traditional definition of *arbor* since the early eighteenth century.[1] The arbors, with benches placed along their sides, form a dense and verdant passageway to the other gardens.

In the distance are twenty-two tall neoclassical columns, erected by landscape designer Russell Page. The columns, quarried from sandstone in Virginia, were built in 1828 as a part of the East Portico of the Capitol. They were put in place before the dome of the Capitol was built, and it was soon realized they would have to be removed, for the dome was of such proportions that the columns appeared to offer inadequate support. As the story continues:

> An addition to the east side of the Capitol was proposed to eliminate this unsettling illusion, but it was not constructed until 1958. More time would pass before the columns would come to their final resting place. It was not until the 1980s that Arboretum benefactor Ethel Garrett took up the cause of establishing a permanent home for them.
>
> Russell Page, a close friend of Garrett's, and landscape designer visited the Arboretum in September 1984, only months before his death. He found the perfect site for them on the east side of the Ellipse where the grandeur of the columns would be in scale with the more than 20 acres of open meadow, a rarity in a built up city like Washington. The columns are set on a foundation of stones from the steps that were on the east side of the Capitol. Old identification marks from the quarry are still visible on some of the stones.
>
> A reflecting pool fed by a small rivulet of water than runs down a channel in the steps reflects the columns and provides sound and movement. Gently curved paths mowed in the Ellipse Meadow invite further exploration; you can easily walk across the Ellipse where you will find a capital, or top portion, of one of the columns. Here you can see the incredible detail that the stone carver incorporated into the design. Acanthus leaves are clearly visible, and the many layers of paint applied while the column was in place at the Capitol are evident on portions of the stone as well.[2]

To the left of the grape arbor is the Knot Garden, which is sunken several feet to provide visitors a full view of its design.

THE KNOT GARDEN

From the grape arbors, seven steps lead visitors into the Knot Garden, a formal design of three interwoven ribbons of dwarf evergreens (*Thuja occidentalis* 'Hetz's Midget', *Ilex crenata* 'Piccolo', and *Juniperus squamata* 'Blue Star', punctuated with

Knot Garden

Ilex cornuta 'Rotunda' and *Stachys byzantina* 'Big Ears').[3] Contrasting colors and a variety of textures emphasize the design of the knot. The whole is framed with English ivy (*Hedera helix* 'Thorndale') and surrounded by wide bluestone paths. To further highlight the design, the spaces between the living ribbons are filled with crushed stone. The intricate pattern is typical of traditional knot gardens, in which interwoven lines of plants create complex geometric designs. Evergreens were chosen for this garden instead of more traditional herbs in order to keep it attractive year-round.[4] Clay containers of scented geraniums (*Pelargonium* spp.) line the edges of the Knot Garden. These containers—a collection created when *Pelargoniums* were named Herb of the Year for 2006—are taken into the greenhouse during the winter. Along two sides, the Knot Garden is bordered by towering arbors, also typical of formal gardens of Italian, French, and Renaissance styles.

Knot gardens evolved from walled gardens of the Middle Ages, which were created to keep out animals and intruders.

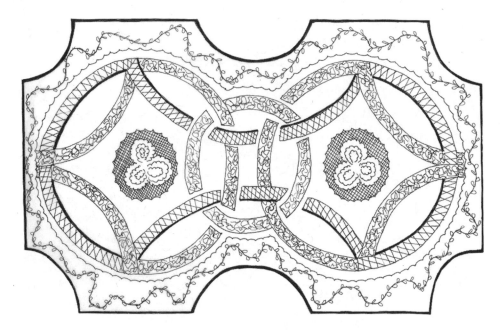

Knot Garden sketch

In addition to providing food and medicinal needs for their owners, knot gardens also served as pleasure gardens.[5] They have their origin in Francesco Colonna's *Hypnerotomachia Poliphili* (*The Strife of Love in a Dream*), published in 1499.[6] The book was acclaimed as much for its woodcuts (by an unidentified artist) as for its complicated plot. Many of the woodcuts are ornate flower-bed plans featuring geometric curves and loops, in which plants sometimes outline initials or eagles that appear in the story. These designs were adopted by gardeners, who followed them to create knot gardens using plants such as lavender, rue, cotton lavender, pennyroyal, thyme, basil, costmary, marjoram, and southernwood, as suggested by Colonna.[7]

By the mid-1500s, the book had been translated into French, and the woodcuts were as enthusiastically followed by French gardeners as they had been in Italy. Over time, however, the French devoted more energy to parterres, in which flowers and herbs were planted within cutwork patterns.[8] Parterres eliminated the interwoven effect of the knot garden and replaced it with symmetrically arranged shapes, each element of which was filled with flowers or attractive ground coverings.[9]

Tudor England eagerly adopted the knot garden. In 1502 "there is an entry in the household account of the unfortunate Edward Stafford, Duke of Buckingham, of the payment of 3s. 4d. to John Wynde, gardener, for diligence in making knottes in the Duke's garden."[10] From simple patterns of squares with dwarf shrubs and herbs and a central feature (usually a statue or a fountain), knot gardens matured into complicated geometric designs. John Parkinson's *Paradisi in Sole, Paradisus Terrestris* (1629) includes six drawings of "open knots proper for outlandish flowers."[11] Open knots incorporated flowering plants in the spaces created by the geometric designs.

Knot gardens remained popular in England and France throughout the sixteenth and seventeenth centuries. The English continued designing ever more intricate knot gardens, some of which evolved into elaborate designs known as mazes. Mazes provided for the delight and recreation of owners and their guests, who could spend hours walking through the designs. Some mazes had only one way in and out, while others had many dead ends, requiring repeated attempts to navigate them successfully. Retaining the shape of the original design required careful and frequent clipping (clippings were often used for strewing on the floors of homes), trimming roots, and replacing plants as they died out, making maintenance of mazes a costly pursuit.[12]

As Europeans arrived on North American shores, they brought familiar garden styles with them. Most of the early settlers, for reasons of expediency, interpreted these designs as basic parterres for kitchen and medicinal herbs. These early kitchen gardens were usually enclosed with fencing or thorny shrubbery to keep out animals, and the beds contained a mix of vegetables, fruits, and medicinals to meet the needs of the family. Gardens also sometimes contained favorite flowers. Many brought flowers with them on their voyages to America; others ordered them or traded them with friends. Gardens were planted to allow for easy access, and there was usually little thought given to design, with plants mixed within beds rather than separated by type. More elaborate knot gardens were reserved for estates developed by the wealthy.[13]

As fashion moved to a more natural style of gardening, knots were eventually abandoned. In 1625 Francis Bacon declared, "As for the making of knots, or figures, with divers coloured earths, that they may lie under the windows of the house on that side which the garden stands, they be but toys; you may see as good sights many times in tarts."[14] In the late 1700s Horace Walpole echoed Bacon's sentiments, ridiculing the "impotent displays of false taste" and bemoaning the fact that "the shears were applied to the lovely wildness of form with which nature has distinguished each various species of tree and shrub."[15]

Andrew Jackson Downing, a renowned landscape architect of the nineteenth century, moved the natural style forward in his widely distributed work, *A Treatise on the Theory and Practice of Landscape Gardening, Adapted to North America* (1849). Downing influenced the landscape not only of American cottages and modest homes, but also of great estates and public spaces. The natural style was well suited to America, and knot gardens fell by the wayside in the United States. "Whatever may have been the absurdities of the ancient style," Downing wrote, "it is not to be denied that in connexion with highly decorated architecture, its effect, when in the best taste—as the Italian—is not only splendid and striking, but highly suitable and appropriate." Still, he declared, "A stone hewn into a gracefully ornamented vase or urn, has a value which it did not before possess: a yew hedge clipped into a fortification, is only defaced. The one is a production of art, the other a distortion of nature."[16] As harsh as Downing was on the subject of frivolity in gardens, he did not dismiss the concept entirely: "Where a taste for imitating an old and quaint style of residence exists, the symmetrical and knotted garden would be a proper accompaniment; and pleached alleys, and sheared trees, would be admired, like old armor or furniture, as curious specimens of antique taste and custom."[17]

The Knot Garden at the National Herb Garden interprets traditional design with contemporary materials, recognizing the beauty and popularity of a garden style that has lasted more than four centuries.

ANTIQUE AND HERITAGE ROSE GARDEN

The path from the Knot Garden leads back up and through the second grape arbor into a series of beds defined by a cedar rail fence and another, smaller arbor. The beds hold a collection of species of "old" roses, which are defined as plants in existence prior to 1867.[18] Known for their beautiful flowers and exquisite fragrance, some old roses have large hips (the fruit of the rose), and most require less care and attention than modern roses demand.

Rose arbor and armillary

Roses are included in the National Herb Garden for their long history of use for healing, for their fragrance, and for their ornament. Early Chinese herbals record uses for *Rosa laevigata*, and in the first century CE, Pliny recorded thirty-two medicinal uses for roses. Roses were used internally for colds and asthma, gastritis, and the control of diarrhea. They were also used externally for skin problems and eye irritation. Rose hips are full of vitamin C. Deni Bown writes that "toward the end of World War II, when citrus fruits were unavailable, 120–450 tons of rose hips were gathered from the wild in Britain each year to make rosehip syrup as a vitamin C supplement for children."[19]

Roses are best known for their fragrance, which is extracted and distilled to create rose oil and rose water for soaps, cosmetics, and perfume. You can make a simple rose water by steeping a cup of fragrant rose petals (those grown without pesticides, of course) in a cup of boiling distilled water, much as you would for tea. Steep for five minutes, then strain out the petals. Reheat the rose water just to a boil, remove from heat, and add a fresh cup of rose petals. Allow to steep for an additional five minutes, strain, and cool. Keep in the refrigerator. Use your rose water to scent homemade soaps, or add it to your bath water. Rose petals are also a primary ingredient in potpourri and sachet recipes, and they make a tasty confection when candied or added to jams and jellies.

The following roses are represented in the Antique and Heritage Rose Garden:

Species roses are those which are found in nature and from which other roses have been bred. The five-petalled flowers, or multiples thereof, open in the spring. Though usually single, some are double or semidouble flowers, and others have been hybridized to create the double form.

Gallicas are among the oldest of cultivated roses and were used by thirteenth-century apothecaries to make confections and herbal remedies. The compact bushes often bear deep red flowers, sometimes with stripes. These roses bloom only once per season, and the dark green foliage turns reddish in the fall.[20]

Under the grape arbor

Damask roses, which date to 1573, come in shades of pink and white and are usually semidouble.[21] Most only flower in June and July, but the Portland Damask will bloom again in the autumn. Damasks are known for their perfume, and their flowers are collected for potpourri and fragrance oils. They are often upright and airy in structure, with heavy blossoms that pull their long canes toward the ground. York and Lancaster is a well-known Damask; it is a white-petalled flower interspersed with red.

Alba roses are known as the 'White Roses' of Shakespeare, though they actually range from white to a delicate blush. These fragrant roses, which bloom in the spring, date to 1597 and are thought to be a cross between *R. canina* and *R. gallica.*[22] The foliage has a bluish tinge, which, along with its upright growth habit, makes the plant a good choice for the back of a border.[23] Many of the Albas show resistance to pests and diseases.

Centifolias, which date from about 1580, are also known as cabbage roses for the many petals in each bloom.[24] The flowers are very full and very fragrant atop tall shrubs. These are the roses made famous in seventeenth-century Dutch and Flemish still-life paintings.[25]

Moss roses are descendants of Centifolias. Recognized in France as early as the late 1600s, they were bred heavily in the mid-nineteenth century. The name is descriptive of the mossy appearance of the stems, buds, and sepals. The Mosses have an upright habit with fragrant flowers, which are often soft to deep pinks and whites. Moss roses are prized especially for the beauty of their buds.[26]

China roses, known since the 1700s, are repeat bloomers from the spring through the fall. Their flowers come in a wide variety of colors, which makes up for what they lack in fragrance. China roses are parents of other classes of roses, such as the Teas, Noisettes, and Bourbons.[27]

Bourbon roses are named for the Isle of Bourbon (now Réunion) in the Indian Ocean, on which they were found in 1817. A natural hybridization of the Portland Damask and a pink China rose, they come in many colors. Their large, full, fragrant blooms generally repeat throughout the spring and summer.[28]

Noisettes are climbers with fragrant pink, white, red, or yellow flowers. They were developed as a cross between Chinese and Western roses by John Champney of South Carolina. Philippe Noisette of Charleston raised a French cross from a second-generation Noisette and sent it to Paris in 1819.[29]

Hybrid Tea roses, the first being a cultivar named 'La France', were introduced in 1867; they mark the dividing line between old roses and modern roses.[30] There are two *Rosa* 'La France' plants in the Antique and Heritage Rose Garden. Soft colors, delicate fragrance, and ever-blooming habit characterize the popular Hybrid Tea roses, which often grow to large shrubs.[31]

Hybrid Perpetuals have large white, red, or pink fragrant flowers with strong stems. They bloom in both the spring and the fall and were popular through the second half of the nineteenth century. They are crosses between Gallicas, Bourbons, Noisettes, and Damasks.

The beauty and ease of old roses is tempered by their habit of blooming, in most cases, only once per year. To keep year-round interest in this garden, which is a traditional cottage-type garden, the roses have been interspersed with collections of rosemary, lavender, and an assortment of old-fashioned annuals and biennials.

DIOSCORIDES GARDEN

The oldest surviving herbal in the Western world is the five-part *De Materia Medica* of Pedanius Dioscorides, a first-century Greek physician.[32] Dioscorides gathered practical information from written sources as well as generally accepted knowledge, supplementing them with his own experience and observations. In his letter of dedication to his friend and mentor Areius, he described his motivation for compiling the work: "Although many writers of modern times, as well as of antiquity, have composed treatises on the preparation, power, and testing of medicines, I will try to show you that I was not moved to this undertaking by a vain or senseless impulse. It was because some of these authors did not perfect their work, while others derived most of their account from histories."[33]

Dioscorides then turned to the method he had used in putting together *De Materia Medica*. Other writers, he asserted,

> have in a manner deigned to describe familiar facts well known to all, but they have transmitted the powers of medicines and their examination cursorily, not estimating their efficacy by experience, but by vain prating about the cause, have

lifted up each medicine to a heap of controversy: and besides this they have recorded one thing by mistake for another. . . . But I beg that you, and all who may peruse these commentaries, will not pay attention so much to the force of our words, as to the industry and experience that I have brought to bear in the matter. For with very accurate diligence, knowing most herbs with mine own eyes, others by historical relation agreeable to all, and by questioning, diligently enquiring of the inhabitants of each sort, we will endeavour both to make use of another arrangement, and also to describe the kinds and forces of every one of them.[34]

The task that Dioscorides set himself was the collection, proper identification, and arrangement of medicinal substances by origin, form, and use, thereby correcting errors and the poor arrangement found in other works. His particular aversion, as he declared to Areius, was to the alphabetical arrangement of plants, or to systems that separated plants which were closely related in use. Ironically, the surviving copy (incorporated into the Juliana Codex of 512 CE) is organized alphabetically.[35] He assembled information on the medicinal properties of more than a thousand natural products from the plant and animal kingdoms and from minerals. *De Materia Medica* was organized into five books, creating what was essentially a *Physician's Desk Reference* of the time. Book I described aromatic plants, oils, ointments, and trees. Book II was devoted to animal products, milk, grains, and herbs. Book III addressed roots, juices, herbs, spices, and seeds. Book IV continued with roots, berries, flowers, and poisons. Book V discussed wines and metallic ores.

Intended for practical use by physicians, *De Materia Medica* was a revered and frequently consulted text throughout the Middle Ages. Its many translations—Syriac, Arabic, Persian, and Latin, and later German, French, English, Italian, and Spanish—offer ample proof of its wide influence as a medical text.[36] But *De Materia Medica* was also consulted as a botanical reference. Though there is no evidence that the original work was illustrated, subsequent copies over the course of the next fifteen hundred years were illustrated by a succession of botanical artists, each using the style of his day. Even without illustrations, Dioscorides's descriptions of plant materials were so precise that the work was widely consulted for plant identification for centuries.

Meticulous in his descriptions of plant material, Dioscorides declared that "the man who will observe his herbs oftentimes and in divers places, will acquire the greatest knowledge of them."[37] He observed the plants where they grew, noting sprouting, leafing, flowering, and seed-setting times. He made notes on the best times for harvesting, and cautioned that weather and specific locations could have an effect on the strength of various parts of plants.

Dioscorides's contribution to botany was indirect, however, as those more interested in plants than their effects found *De Materia Medica* difficult to consult for purposes of plant identification. As Renaissance botanists soon learned while attempting to match plants in *De Materia Medica* with those being brought back to Europe from voyages of discovery, different parts of the world produced different species of plants. "Out of error truth eventually emerged, and Dioscorides' *De Materia Medica* was the instrument through which it prevailed," Frank Anderson has noted.[38] Ultimately, the science of botany emerged, distinct from that of pharmacy.

Each of the plants in the Dioscorides Garden is described in *De Materia Medica*. While not all of the plants in Dioscorides's work are found in the garden, fifty-one of them are, including black horehound (*Ballota nigra*), which was used with salt and applied to dog bites; teasel (*Dipsacus fullonum*), which was used as a salve for chapped skin; ivy (*Hedera helix*), which was thought to cause sterility when its juice was drunk; and dittany of Crete (*Origanum dictamnus*), which supposedly hastened childbirth when the root was eaten.[39] The Dioscorides Garden at the National Herb Garden recognizes the contributions of Pedanius Dioscorides to the sciences of both botany and pharmacy.

Plants in the Dioscorides Garden at the National Herb Garden

Botanical name	Common name
Acanthus mollis	artist's acanthus
Adiatum capillus-veneris	southern maidenhair
Artemisia pontica	Roman wormwood
Arum maculatum	Lords-and-Ladies
Asarum europaeum	European wild ginger
Aster amellus	Italian aster
Ballota nigra	black horehound
Ballota pseudodictamnus	false dittany
Conium maculatum	poison hemlock
Consolida ambigua	rocket larkspur
Crithmum maritimum	samphire
Daucus carota var. *carota*	Queen Anne's lace
Dipsacus fullonum	teasel
Echinops sphaerocephalus	great globe thistle
Erianthus ravennae	ravenna grass
Euphorbia characias	spurge
Euphorbia lathyris	mole plant
Gladiolus communis	sword lily
Hedera helix	English ivy
Inula helenium	elecampane
Iris ×*germanica* 'Florentina'	orris
Lilium candidum	Madonna lily
Linum usitatissimum	flax
Lychnis coronaria	rose campion
Malva sylvestris	mallow
Myrrhis odorata	sweet cicely
Myrtus communis	myrtle
Narcissus poeticus	poet's narcissus
Nigella sativa	black cumin
Olea europaea	olive
Origanum dictamnus	dittany of Crete
Origanum vulgare subsp. *hirtum*	Greek mountain oregano
Paeonia mascula subsp. *mascula*	peony
Papaver rhoeas	corn poppy

Plants in the Dioscorides Garden (*continued*)

Botanical name	Common name
Papaver somniferum	opium poppy
Phlomis fruticosa	Jerusalem sage
Piper nigrum	black pepper
Polemonium caeruleum	Greek valerian
Ruscus aculeatus	butcher's broom
Ruta graveolens	rue
Salvia officinalis	garden sage
Salvia viridis	Joseph sage
Silybum marianum	milk thistle
Tanacetum parthenium	feverfew
Teucrium chamaedrys	wall germander
Tussilago farfara	coltsfoot
Vinca minor	periwinkle
Vitex agnus-castus	chaste tree

DYE GARDEN

The Dye Garden is a sunny, lively space filled with clashing colors of yellow, red, pink, orange, blue, green, and magenta. It is a perfect spot to identify plants that produce dyes with lush, rich colors. Interestingly, however, a plant's flowers are often no predictors of final dye color. For example, the bright yellow flowers of St. John's wort, *Hypericum perforatum,* produce a red dye, and the roots of the pretty, white-flowered bloodroot, *Sanguinaria canadensis,* make an orange-red dye.[40]

Plants and other natural substances have long been used to create color. Cave paintings that used black, red, white, and yellow pigments have been dated to 15,000 BCE. "With the development of fixed settlements and agriculture around 7000–2000 BCE man began to produce and use textiles, and would therefore add color to them as well."[41] Other instances of the early use of color in textiles include a fragment of fabric dyed with indigo, dated 3500 BCE, found during an excavation in Thebes, and a fragment of madder-dyed cloth from the tomb of Tutankhamen, dated 1350 BCE.[42]

Woad (*Isatis tinctoria*), indigo (*Indigofera tinctoria*), and madder (*Rubia tinctorum*) are among the more illustrious plant dyes, each having a long and intriguing history. Throughout the Middle Ages, woad was used in Europe to produce a rich blue color. Woad required no mordant, or stabilizer, but it did need a complicated and time-consuming process of fermentation, which produced such foul odors that Queen Elizabeth I of England decreed that no dye production would take place within five miles of her residences.[43] In the sixteenth century a new source for a consistently rich blue color was discovered in India and brought to Europe. This new plant, indigo, did not need a lengthy fermentation process to produce a lasting dye. It was immediately seen as a threat to the livelihood of woad dyers, who formed a guild to fight the competition. The guild supported the implementation of laws to ban the importation of the less expensive indigo. Their efforts failed, however, and by the seventeenth century indigo was a major trade item. In 1649, "Europeans attempted to break the Indian monopoly on indigo by planting this species in the New World," where it was eagerly adopted as a potential agricultural crop by American colonists.[44] By 1763, "Louisiana's number one export was indigo, with a value of over $1.2 million."[45] Louisiana's indigo industry was threatened when W. H. Perkins developed the first synthetic dye in 1856.[46] By 1878, indigo's value as an agricultural crop had come to an end in America.[47]

The third time-honored dye plant, madder, was grown throughout Europe and Asia, producing rich reds for those who knew the secrets of releasing the color from its roots. The roots of madder produce alizarin, a clear red that was popularly known as "Turkey red" in the nineteenth century. Madder produces a very stable dye that was used in ancient Egypt, Greece, and Rome. In the eleventh century, madder was later taken to Italy by Crusaders; it was reintroduced into Europe by the thirteenth century. Madder was also the source of the dye used to produce the uniforms of British soldiers in the eighteenth century, thus the term "redcoats."[48]

Most natural dyes, which can be prepared by simply boiling the appropriate plant parts in fresh water, are not colorfast, which means the colors will fade with time and washing. Animal-based fabrics, such as wool or silk, accept color more readily because their fibers expand when heated in a dye bath, thus increasing the surface area available to accept dye. Vegetable-based fabrics, such as linen or cotton, are more resistant to the natural dye process and often result in softer tones.[49] To avoid the problem of fading and to create more vibrant colors, substances called mordants are added to dye baths. Chemicals ranging from alum (aluminium potassium sulfate) to tin, chrome, copper sulfate, and vinegar serve as mordants, many of which will alter the resulting color.[50] Some plants, usually those high in tannins, contain natural mordants, making additives unnecessary. Bedstraw (*Galium verum*) roots and flowers will produce a reasonably stable orange-red. Madder roots will produce a creamy pink, but if chrome is used as a mordant, it will produce a rich brown dye.[51]

Plants are seldom used as a source for dyes any longer, as synthetic versions produce bright, consistent, and affordable colors. Fortunately, some artisans still use natural dyes, continuing an ancient practice and producing fabrics with soft, natural colors. There is history in the Dye Garden, and a wealth of plants to inspire creativity.

Plants in the Dye Garden at the National Herb Garden

Botanical name	Common name	Color (some require mordants)
Achillea millefolium	yarrow	gray-greens
Agrimonia eupatoria	agrimony	yellow, gold
Alchemilla vulgaris	Lady's mantle	yellow, yellow-green
Alkanna tinctoria	alkanet	reddish, red-purple
Allium cepa	onion	gold, orange, rust, olive
Amaranthus cruentus	purple amaranth	reddish
Anthemis tinctoria	golden Marguerite	yellow, yellow-orange
Arctostaphylos uva-ursi	bearberry	yellow, green, gray
Asperula tinctoria	dyer's woodruff	red

Plants in the Dye Garden (continued)

Botanical name	Common name	Color (some require mordants)
Baptisia alba	wild indigo	indigo blue
Basella alba	Malabar spinach	purplish
Bixa orellana	annatto	bright yellow
Calendula officinalis	pot marigold	yellow
Calluna vulgaris	heather	green, yellow, purple, brown
Carthamus tinctorius	safflower	rose, pink, yellow
Chelidonium majus	greater celandine	green
Chenopodium album	lamb's quarters	bright yellows, greens
Coreopsis tinctoria	calliopsis	gold, orange-red, brick red
Cosmos sulphureus	yellow cosmos	rust, brick red
Crocus sativus	saffron crocus	yellow
Curcuma longa	turmeric	yellow
Cytisus scoparius	scotch broom	yellow, yellow-green
Dahlia spp.	dahlia	yellow, bronze, red
Filipendula ulmaria	Queen-of-the-meadow	greenish yellow, black
Galium mollugo	white bedstraw	reds
Galium verum	Lady's bedstraw	red
Genista tinctoria	dyer's greenweed	greenish yellow
Hypericum perforatum	Saint John's wort	red, yellow
Indigofera tinctoria	indigo	blue
Inula helenium	elecampane	blues
Iris pseudacorus	yellow flag	black
Isatis tinctoria	dyer's woad	indigo blue
Lawsonia inermis	henna	orange-red
Mahonia aquifolium	Oregon grape	dull green-yellow
Myrica pensylvanica	bayberry	gray-green, yellow
Perovskia atriplicifolia	Russian sage	soft gray-green
Phytolacca americana	poke	red
Polygonum tinctorium	dyer's knotweed	blue
Pteridium aquilinum	bracken	yellow to olive
Reseda luteola	weld	yellow
Rhus glabra	smooth sumac	gray, black
Rubia tinctorium	madder	red
Sanguinaria canadensis	bloodroot	yellow to green

Plants in the Dye Garden (*continued*)

Botanical name	Common name	Color (some require mordants)
Tagetes spp.	marigolds	yellow, rust, olive green
Tanacetum vulgare	tansy	yellow to green
Verbascum thapsus	mullein	olive to gray
Zinnia spp.	zinnias	yellow

COLONIAL GARDEN

In the shadows of the Colonial Garden are visions of Puritans stepping from boats after long voyages, carrying carefully wrapped packets of their favorite herbs and seeds, which were intended to help them survive and to feel at home in an unfamiliar land. The plants brought to the new land were for the "seasoning and preservation of food, for medical treatment, to attract bees, for fragrance, to repel vermin, and as a source for dyes."[52] These little plants, along with the few belongings the colonists could bring, were all they had to remind them of families and homes left behind.

Colonial families did not have what we think of as an herb garden. Their gardens of vegetables, herbs, and flowers were generally small and close to the house.[53] Most were square or rectangular, divided evenly by walks that were wide enough for two to pass. The walks might have been packed earth, sand, shells, or gravel. The gardens were usually fenced to keep out animals, and herbs and flowers were intermingled with household vegetables. Kitchen gardens were often in the front of the house, making them easy to tend. According to David Tucker, in the early nineteenth century, landscape and horticultural icons such as Bernard McMahon promoted the theories of John Parkinson that "onions and cabbages . . . be offensive in smell and taste for English families," and kitchen gardens were moved to the back of the house.[54] The front garden was reserved for sweet-smelling flowers.

Kitchen gardens were primarily the responsibility of women and children, while husbands spent their time raising cash crops or on other ways of earning a living. "The beginnynge of March or a little afore, is tyme for a wyfe to make her garden, and to gette as many good sedes and herbes as she canne," recommended Master Fitzherbert in his *Book of Husbandry* in 1522.[55] Gardens might have included "strawberries, gooseberries, currants, and raspberries, as well as aromatic shrubs of thyme, savory, and hyssop," in addition to "peas, beans, cabbage, lettuce, endive, potatoes, artichokes, and Jerusalem artichokes."[56] Of the fifty plants recommended for kitchen gardens by William Lawson in *The Country Housewife's Garden* (1617), forty were for "medicine, seasoning, and strewing."[57]

Rue, hyssop, tansy, and lavender were grown to be placed among linens and incorporated into soaps and ointments. A leaf of bay, *Laurus nobilis*, placed in flour and grain bins, repelled weevils. Plants were grown to provide dye for linens, poisons for vermin, and medicine for a variety of ailments, from headaches to heart conditions. Medicinal herbs might have included betony, chamomile, clary sage, foxglove, hyssop, pinks, and valerian.

Fennel, *Foeniculum vulgare,* native to Mediterranean regions, was a favored vegetable and flavoring, and a tea brewed from its leaves or seeds was thought to aid digestion. During the colonial era, the seeds became known as "meeting seeds," as they would quiet a grumbling stomach when chewed during interminably long religious services.[58]

Pot marigold flowers, *Calendula officinalis*, were used to add color to cheese and butter, to thicken soups, and to add spiciness and color to salads. They also were held to have medicinal properties and were often used to prevent or heal skin infections. Lavender, *Lavandula angustifolia*, and rosemary, *Rosmarinus officinalis*, were old favorites; they added fragrance to the home (an especially welcome effect when the house was closed against the weather) and were also used for medicinal purposes.

Over time we have learned that some of the herbs commonly used for medicinal or culinary purposes in the colonial era are not safe for consumption. Borage, *Borago officinalis*, for instance, was favored for its cucumber-flavored leaves and flowers. It was a favorite in salads, soups, and beverages. It was an ingredient of German green sauce, which includes parsley, chervil, chives, sorrel, and salad burnet. It was used as a spring tonic and was believed to be a mood elevator, most likely because the flowers were added to wine. More recently, borage has been found to contain carcinogenic compounds and is no longer recommended for consumption.[59]

Colonial housewives fortunate enough to have brought with them small books of "receipts," which contained recipes for physical ailments as well as favorite dishes, had the wisdom and experience of their mothers and grandmothers to guide them. These receipts ranged from "How to Make a Conserve of Roses" to the most effective remedies for killing lice.[60]

The herbs that came to America with its early European settlers did well in the new soil and climate, and they still grow in our gardens today. Our uses for these plants may have changed over the years, but our affection for them remains. The Colonial Garden is a tribute to our ancestors and to the plants they brought with them to America.

Plants in the Colonial Garden at the National Herb Garden

Botanical name	Common name	Historic use
Achillea millefolium	yarrow	medicinal
Allium schoenoprasum	chives	flavoring
Anethum graveolens	dill	flavoring
Angelica archangelica	angelica	flavoring; sweets
Apium graveolens var. *graveolens*	wild celery	flavoring
Arctium lappa	great burdock	medicinal
Artemisia abrotanum	southernwood	medicinal; insect repellent
Artemisia absinthium	wormwood	medicinal
Atriplex hortensis	orach	medicinal
Borago officinalis	borage*	flavoring; beverage*
Calendula officinalis	pot marigold	flavoring, food coloring
Ceanothus americanus	New Jersey tea	beverage
Chamaemelum nobile	Roman chamomile	beverage; medicinal
Cichorium intybus	chicory	medicinal; salad

Plants in the Colonial Garden (*continued*)

Botanical name	Common name	Historic use
Cnicus benedictus	blessed thistle	medicinal
Convallaria majalis	Lily-of-the-Valley*	medicinal*
Datura stramonium	jimsonweed*	medicinal*
Dianthus caryophyllus	clove pink	flavoring, medicinal
Digitalis purpurea	foxglove*	medicinal*
Dipsacus sativus	fuller's teasel	medicinal; treating wool
Eruca sativa	rocket	salad; cosmetic
Erysimum cheiri	wallflower	medicinal; fragrance
Foeniculum vulgare	fennel	flavoring; salad; medicinal
Genista tinctoria	dyer's greenweed	medicinal; yellow-green dye
Gentiana saponaria	downy gentian	medicinal
Geranium robertianum	herb Robert	medicinal
Geum urbanum	avens	medicinal
Hesperis matronalis	sweet rocket	salad
Hyssopus officinalis	hyssop	flavoring; medicinal
Inula helenium	elecampane	medicinal
Iris ×germanica 'Florentina'	orris*	medicinal; fragrance*
Juniperus communis	juniper	flavoring; medicinal
Lavandula angustifolia	English lavender	fragrance
Leucanthemum vulgare	oxeye daisy	medicinal
Lysimachia nummularia	moneywort	medicinal
Lysimachia punctata	garden loosestrife	medicinal; insect repellent
Malus 'Roxbury'	apple	fruit; medicinal
Malva moschata	musk mallow	medicinal
Mentha pulegium	pennyroyal*	insect repellent; medicinal*
Mentha spicata	spearmint	medicinal; beverage; flavoring
Monarda didyma	bee balm*	beverage; medicinal*
Nepeta cataria	catnip	beverage; medicinal
Origanum majorana	sweet marjoram	flavoring; fragrance; medicinal
Origanum vulgare	wild marjoram	flavoring; medicinal
Petroselinum crispum	parsley	flavoring; medicinal; dye

Plants in the Colonial Garden (*continued*)

Botanical name	Common name	Historic use
Polygonatum multiflorum	Solomon's seal	medicinal
Portulaca oleracea	purslane	salads; pot herb; medicinal
Prunella vulgaris	self-heal	medicinal
Pulmonaria officinalis	lungwort	medicinal
Rosmarinus officinalis	rosemary	flavoring; medicinal; fragrance
Rumex acetosa	garden sorrel	flavoring; pot herb; medicinal
Ruta graveolens	rue*	medicinal*
Salvia officinalis	garden sage	flavoring; medicinal
Salvia sclarea	clary sage*	medicinal; pot herb*
Sanguisorba minor	salad burnet*	flavoring; medicinal*
Santolina chamaecyparissus	lavender cotton	medicinal; insect repellent
Satureja montana	winter savory	flavoring
Saxifraga virginiensis	early saxifrage	medicinal
Sempervivum tectorum	houseleek	medicinal
Sium sisarum	skirret	medicinal; pot herb
Smyrnium olusatrum	alexander	medicinal; salads
Stachys officinalis	betony	medicinal; snuff; beverage
Symphytum officinale	comfrey*	medicinal*
Tanacetum balsamita	costmary	medicinal; fragrance; flavoring
Tanacetum cinerariifolium	pyrethrum	insect repellent
Tanacetum parthenium	feverfew	medicinal; insect repellent
Tanacetum vulgare	tansy	medicinal; insect repellent; dye
Taraxacum officinale	dandelion	medicinal; pot herb
Thymus praecox subsp. *articus*	creeping thyme	flavoring; medicinal
Thymus vulgaris	garden thyme	flavoring; medicinal
Tussilago farfara	coltsfoot*	medicinal*
Valeriana officinalis	valerian	medicinal
Valerianella locusta	corn salad	salads
Verbena officinalis	vervain	medicinal
Vinca minor	periwinkle	medicinal
Viola odorata	sweet violet	salads; sweets; medicinal

*These herbs do not have Generally Recognized as Safe status and should not be consumed or used externally. No herb should be used medicinally without the advice and guidance of a physician.

NATIVE AMERICAN GARDEN

From the frozen tundra of the Alaskan zone 1 to the steamy flatlands of zone 10 Florida, the North American continent provides a wealth of herbs, shrubs, vines, and trees. From this botanical richness, Native Americans took what they needed for food, clothing, shelter, tools, medicine, ceremony, and ornament.

Though many Native American tribes gathered the plants they needed and migrated to harvest leaves, bulbs, roots, and seeds as necessary, gardening and agriculture were also well-established practices by the time of the arrival of European colonists. Native American cultivation of squash, gourds, and pumpkins began as early as ten thousand years ago, followed by corn by about 5000 BCE.[61] Even so, a nineteenth-century Anglo-American viewed Native American gardening with a prejudiced eye: "While they are industrious, these people are not progressive farmers and have learned nothing of modern methods. The same crops are raised continuously until the soil will yield no more or is washed away, when new ground is cleared or broken. The value of rotation and fertilization has not yet been discovered or taught."[62]

In fact, however, thousands of years before the arrival of Europeans in North America, complicated canal irrigation systems were used in the Sonoran desert area by the Hohokam, a prehistoric tribe.[63] Northern Plains Indians, among others, also had successful and sophisticated agricultural systems in place in their permanent villages, as reported by Buffalo Bird Woman, who was born in 1839 and followed centuries-old traditions of gardening. In the early 1900s, she told the story of village life to anthropologist Gilbert Wilson, who observed, "Hidatsa gardeners were sensitive to the ecological demands of the Northern Plains climate. They carved garden plots from wooded and brushy areas in fertile bottomlands, where tillable soil was renewed annually by flooding; they did not try to cultivate on the prairie, which was covered with dry, virtually impenetrable sod. Brush cleared for planting was spread over the plots and burned, for it was conventional wisdom that burning trees and brush 'softened the soil and left it loose and mellow for planting.' It also added nutrients to the soil."[64]

Native Americans, dependent on the land for their survival, were keen observers of nature. The methods they employed in gardening and gathering were based on climate, the local environment, and the needs of the tribe. They also took care not to endanger plants with extinction. Their methods were successful, often producing so much that extra food stores were available for trade.[65]

Without the assistance of the Native Americans, who were considered primitive by many of the same colonists who depended on Native American knowledge for their survival, the successful colonization of America by Europeans may have been long delayed. Nearly 75 percent of the foods that we currently grow, and that form a significant part of our diet, were new to the first Europeans to arrive in America.[66] Corn, beans, squash, pumpkins, tomatoes, peppers, peanuts, many fruits, and sunflowers were all cultivated by Native American tribes, who taught the colonists how to plant, harvest, prepare, and preserve the unfamiliar foods that would sustain them.

Though many of the plants used by Native Americans were for flavoring otherwise bland foods, which is the traditional definition of a culinary herb, the palates of European settlers resisted change. "Their cookery has nothing commendable about it but that it is performed with little trouble," reports Robert Beverly in his 1705 volume describing Native American food.[67] Colonists brought with them their favorite basil, thyme, sage, and other European and Mediterranean herbs as their primary flavoring agents, which they used even with the unfamiliar vegetables, meats, and fowl that they found in their new land.[68] "I doubt not every woman bore with her across seas some little package of seeds and bulbs from her English home garden, and perhaps a tiny slip or plant of some endeared flower," wrote Alice Morse Earle of the Puritans arriving in New England.[69]

Yet Native Americans did use a number of plants as seasonings, including sumac (*Rhus trilobata*), whose bright red berries were used to flavor breads and make a citrusy beverage; Western coltsfoot (*Petasites palmata*), which provided a salty taste from the ash of its slowly burned leaves; wild ginger (*Asarum canadense*) to flavor foods; wild strawberry (*Fragaria virginiana*) to flavor cornmeal mush; wintergreen (*Gaultheria procumbens*) to flavor meat and fish; mountain mint (*Pycnanthemum virginianum*) to flavor meats and soups; and juniper berries (*Juniperus communis*) to flavor game and vegetables.[70]

Of most interest to the newly arrived colonists from Europe, however, were the medicinal botanicals used by Native Americans. These medicines were quickly adopted, both for personal use and for their economic value. As early as the mid-1700s, ginseng (*Panax quinquefolius*) was gathered for export. John Jacob Astor, among many others, started his fortune trading in ginseng. The profits from a shipment by Astor in the late 1780s gave him the resources to invest in New York real estate and to establish his fur-trading business.[71] In 1841, 640,967 pounds of dried, wild-collected ginseng roots were exported, with an average price of $ .71 per pound.[72] Today, dried, wild-collected ginseng brings between $250 and $350 per pound, and it has been overcollected to the point that the plant is threatened with extinction.[73]

By 1820, nearly two-thirds of American medicinals were derived from plants that had been first introduced to Europeans by Native Americans.[74] In the 1830s, the Shaker religious community in Pennsylvania started a thriving business dealing in medicinal botanicals, both collected from the wild and cultivated, many of which were shipped to Europe and Asia.[75]

The Native American Garden is a place to pause and to appreciate the rich resources of the United States. It is a place to learn about the foods, flavorings, sweeteners, dyes, medicines, and more that have been used historically and remain available to us still. The Native American Garden is a tribute to the wealth of the earth and to the Native Americans who graciously shared their knowledge of plants with newcomers from Europe.

Plants in the Native American Garden at the National Herb Garden

Botanical name	Common name	Historic use
Acorus calamus	sweet flag	prevent illness
Actaea racemosa	black cohosh	treat female complaints
Adiantum pedatum	maidenhair fern	darken hair
Allium tricoccum	wild leek	food
Apocynum cannabinum	Indian hemp*	rope and net fiber*
Aquilegia canadensis	wild columbine*	treat intestinal distress*
Arctostaphylos uva-ursi	bearberry*	tobacco additive*
Arisaema triphyllum	Jack-in-the-pulpit*	food*
Asarum canadense	wild ginger	food seasoning, preservative
Asclepias tuberosa	butterfly weed*	treat cuts and wounds*
Aster novae-angliae	New England aster	tobacco additive
Baptisia tinctoria	wild indigo*	blue dye*
Betula lenta	black birch*	syrup*
Blephilia hirsuta	wood mint	treat headache
Caltha palustris	marsh marigold*	spring greens*
Calycanthus floridus	Carolina allspice	treat urinary and bladder complaints
Caulophyllum thalictroides	blue cohosh*	treat menstrual cramps, aid delivery*
Ceanothus americanus	New Jersey tea	treat stomach complaints
Cephalanthus occidentalis	buttonbush*	treat toothache, diarrhea*
Comptonia peregrina	sweet fern	insect repellent
Cornus sericea	red osier	smoking
Corylus americana	hazelnut	tea
Cunila origanoides	American dittany	treat fevers and colds
Diospyros virginiana	persimmon	food
Diphylleia cymosa	umbrella leaf*	diuretic*
Echinacea purpurea	purple coneflower	treat snakebites
Epilobium angustifolium	fireweed	spring vegetable, fiber
Erythronium americanum	trout lily	food, fishing
Euonymus atropurpureus	burning bush*	treat facial sores, eye lotion*
Eupatorium perfoliatum	boneset*	treat colds, fevers*
Eupatorium purpureum	Joe-Pye weed	treat urinary tract infections
Fragaria virginiana	wild strawberry	food

Plants in the Native American Garden (*continued*)

Botanical name	Common name	Historic use
Gaultheria procumbens	wintergreen*	treat rheumatism, fever*
Geranium maculatum	wild geranium	treat hemorrhoids
Geum rivale	purple avens	treat malaria
Gillenia trifoliata	Indian physic*	emetic*
Gnaphalium obtusifolium	sweet everlasting	smoking
Hedeoma pulegioides	American pennyroyal*	treat fever*
Helenium flexuosum	sneezeweed	contraception
Hepatica americana	round-lobed hepatica	treat dizziness
Heuchera americana	rock geranium	astringent
Hierochloe odorata	sweet grass	purification
Hydrastis canadensis	goldenseal*	treat liver and heart conditions; dye*
Ilex vomitoria	yaupon*	beverage*
Iris versicolor	wild blue flag*	poultices for swelling*
Juncus spp.	rush	baskets
Kalmia latifolia	mountain laurel*	suicide*
Lindera benzoin	spicebush	flavoring and breads
Lobelia cardinalis	cardinal flower*	rituals*
Lobelia inflata	Indian tobacco*	smoking, emetic*
Lobelia siphilitica	great blue lobelia*	treat syphilis*
Matteuccia pensylvanica	ostrich fern	food
Mertensia virginica	Virginia bluebells	treat whooping cough, consumption
Mitchella repens	partridgeberry	smoking
Monarda fistulosa	wild bergamot	treat bronchial troubles
Monarda punctata	horsemint	treat chills, fever
Nicotiana rustica	wild tobacco*	smoking, ritual*
Opuntia humifusa	prickly pear	food, poultices
Osmorhiza claytonii	wooly sweet cicely	treat sore throat; aid delivery and weight gain
Osmunda cinnamomea	cinnamon fern*	food*
Panax quinquefolius	ginseng*	fertility, general medicinal*

Plants in the Native American Garden (*continued*)

Botanical name	Common name	Historic use
Phytolacca americana	poke*	treat rheumatism*
Podophyllum peltatum	mayapple*	fruit—food; root—suicide*
Polemonium reptans	Jacob's ladder	emetic
Polygonatum biflorum	small Solomon's seal	restorative (smoke from roots)
Proboscidea parviflora var. *hohokamiana*	devil's claw	food, fiber for basketry
Pteridium aquilinum	bracken*	food*
Pycnanthemum virginianum	mountain mint	flavoring
Rhus glabra	smooth sumac	smoking
Rosa virginiana	pasture rose	treat stomach complaints
Rubus odoratus	flowering raspberry	treat bowel complaints
Sagittaria latifolia	arrowhead	food
Salvia lyrata	lyre-leaved sage	salve
Sambucus canadensis	American elderberry*	food*
Sanguinaria canadensis	bloodroot*	dye, insecticide*
Sassafras albidum	sassafras*	tea*
Satureja douglasii	yerba buena	treat fevers, colds
Smilacina racemosa	false Solomon's seal	restorative (smoke from the roots)
Solidago canadensis	Canada goldenrod	treat fevers
Solidago odora	sweet goldenrod	tea, smoking additive
Spigelia marilandica	Indian pink*	expel worms*
Tiarella cordifolia	foamflower	mouthwash
Tradescantia virginiana	spiderwort	laxative
Trillium grandiflorum	large flowered trillium	treat female diseases
Uvularia perfoliata	strawbell	treat sore throat
Vaccinium angustifolium	lowbush blueberry	food, flavoring
Vaccinium corymbosum	highbush blueberry	food, flavoring
Veratrum viride	green hellebore*	treat wounds*
Veronicastrum virginicum	Culver's root*	emetic*
Xanthorhiza simplicissima	yellowroot	treat sore mouths
Yucca filamentosa	Adam's needle	cordage, twine

*Parts or all of these plants have since been found to be toxic, and in some cases, lethal. Use of any plants for food or for medicine should be made only with research and consultation with knowledgeable botanists and physicians.

MEDICINAL GARDEN

The Medicinal Garden, which contains only a small fraction of the world's plants, boasts a bewildering variety of plants with different textures, colors, sizes, and shapes. How early people learned to use these plants is almost beyond comprehension. It has been suggested that humans may have mimicked animal behavior, observing the plants animals used to heal themselves of wounds, parasites, and the like, and then applied what they observed to their own uses.[76]

Jennifer A. Biser has amassed a number of interesting stories about the use of medicinal plants. As she writes:

> Pausing only to wipe the feverish sweat from her brow, the WaTongwe woman finishes crushing a few leaves and stems a fellow tribe member brought her from the mujonso, or "bitter leaf" tree. She soaks them in a bowl of cold water while her stomach aches with a dull pain. Closing her eyes and grimacing in anticipation of the liquid's foul taste, she holds her nose and gulps down the bitter elixir, hoping this reliable remedy will rid her of the intestinal pain that's plagued her for days.
>
> Nearby, in Tansania's Mahale Mountains National Park, a lethargic chimpanzee suffering from diarrhea and malaise slowly pulls a young shoot off a small tree called *Vernonia amygdalina*. She peels away the shoot's bark and leaves with her teeth, and begins chewing on the succulent pith. Swallowing the juice, she spits out most of the fibers, then continues to chew and swallow a few more stalks for half an hour.
>
> Recovered within 24 hours, both of these females resume business as usual. They were both suffering the effects of an intestinal parasite infection. And, in case you haven't guessed, they both ate from the same tree.[77]

Other examples in Biser's article suggest the use of plants by animals for such purposes as inducing labor, governing the gender of offspring by diet, fighting bacteria, and repelling insects. Whether or not humans learned about the uses of medicinal plants by mimicking animal behavior does not begin to address the question of how animals might have made their discoveries. It does, however, suggest the need for additional study, as well as underscoring the need to preserve the habitats of plants and animals.

As Jules Janick notes, "The prehistoric discovery that certain plants are edible or have curative powers and others are inedible or cause harm is the origin of the healing professions and its practitioners—priest, physician, and apothecary—and the plant sciences—botany and horticulture."[78] Amazingly, of the more than four hundred thousand species of plants on earth, only 2 percent have been thoroughly explored by modern methods for their medicinal properties.[79] How extraordinary that those "primitive" peoples could have discovered which plants would be effective at treating their ailments. Equally astonishing is the fact that their experiences and successes were transmitted through the generations to us, since prior to written history, humans were dependent on the oral transmission of proper plant identification and the purposes to which the plants were put.

Archaeological studies prove the antiquity of the medicinal use of plants by humans. In a burial site dated about sixty thousand years ago, located in what is now Iraq, the remains of eight different flowers were found. Of those eight, seven are still used medicinally or as insect repellents.[80]

One of the earliest works which includes the preparation and use of herbs is attributed to Shen Nung, a Chinese emperor from c. 3500 BCE. He is said to have tasted hundreds of herbs to "test their medicinal value, and is assumed to be the author of *Shen-nung pen ts'ao ching* (*Divine Husbandman's Materia Medica*)."[81] Another early Chinese work is by Huang Ti (c. 2600 BCE), known as the Yellow Emperor and the father of internal medicine, who appointed health ministers to taste herbs and plants and to record herbal formulas.[82]

The most complete early medical document that has survived to this day is the Ebers Papyrus, which has been dated to about 1500 BCE and which was named for George Ebers, who purchased it in 1862. This papyrus contains a collection of 811 prescriptions, with symptoms, diagnoses, and surgical treatments for wounds and sores. The manuscript includes uses for acanthus, acacia, aloe, balsam, barley, caraway, cedar, coriander, crocus, cucumber, date, elderberry, fennel, fig, flax, garlic, grape, juniper, lettuce, linseed, mint, mulberry, nasturtium, onion, palm, papyrus, peppermint, pomegranate, poppy, saffron, watermelon, wheat, willow, and wormwood, as well as various animal and mineral substances.[83] Other early medical papyri contain detailed descriptions of ailments, the proper preparation of prescribed ingredients, and often a magical or religious chant to be recited as the prescription is administered. Though many substances are used in these prescriptions (including the dung of various animals, rotten fish, and worse), about 80 percent of their ingredients were of plant origin.[84]

Several classical writers had a lasting influence on herbal medicine. Hippocrates (c. 400 BCE) promoted healthful living and prescribed natural remedies, often single substances, including vinegar, herbs, and honey. He also encouraged eliminating magic and superstition from the practice of medicine. Theophrastus (c. 340 BCE) described more than five hundred plants in his *Historia Plantarum*, a treatise on medicine and plants. Crateuas (c. 100 BCE) created the first known illustrated herbal. Pliny the Elder (c. 60 CE) compiled in his *Naturalis Historia* the writings of many authors whose works have not survived. He listed more medicinal plants than any of the ancient writers.[85] And, finally, Dioscorides compiled his *De Materia Medica*, discussed above.

Throughout the medieval and early modern period, innumerable treatises on herbs were written in western and eastern Europe, Asia, and the Arab world. Many of these works offer similar prescriptions based on the same plant material, as well as describing plants that are unique to the areas in which their authors lived and worked. Though some of the plants described in these works have since been found to be ineffective or toxic, many are still in use by pharmaceutical companies and herbalists.

Many of these plants are in the Medicinal Garden. Foxglove, *Digitalis purpurea*, is a biennial that grows to about three feet in shades of pink, purple, and yellow. It is the source of digoxin, which is used to create pharmaceuticals that treat heart conditions. German chamomile, *Matricaria recutta*, is a low-growing annual or biennial with small, daisy-like blooms from early summer to the fall; it has been used for centuries for its sedative and carminative qualities. Maidenhair tree, *Ginkgo biloba*, is a stately deciduous tree with easily recognized fan-shaped leaves that turn a brilliant yellow in the fall. The tree is widely known for its medicinal qualities and has recently been studied for use in treating heart disease, stroke, and memory loss. Witch hazel, *Hamamelis virginiana*, fills the air with a tantalizing sweetness as it blooms in late fall or early winter. It is a medium to tall deciduous shrub that is used for the astringent qualities of its leaves and bark.

Tall or small, flashy or plain, herbs are a veritable medicine chest of treatments for the ailments of humans and animals. Nearly 40 percent of medicines manufactured in the United States contain chemicals based on plants, and pharmaceutical companies still seek sources of new medicines in the plant world.[86] Some herbs with long histories of medicinal uses have been found to be toxic, however. Comfrey, *Symphytum officinale*, used externally for its wound-healing qualities, has been found to be carcinogenic, especially when used internally. Greater celandine, *Chelidonium majus*, was long used for toothaches and to remove film from the cornea of the eye, though we now know that the whole plant is poisonous.

The Medicinal Garden contains plants that were used in the past as well as plants in current favor with the pharmaceutical industry. Most of them will grow in your home garden, where you can enjoy their beauty and history and appreciate the new uses being found for them. Still, using plants safely for their medicinal qualities requires a thorough understanding of plants, the human body, and chemistry. It is not for the amateur.

Plants in the Medicinal Garden at the National Herb Garden

Botanical name	Common name	Historic use	Area of origin/ distribution
Aconitum napellus	monkshood*	heart, nervous system*	Europe
Actaea racemosa	black cohosh*	uterine cramps, cough*	Canada; continental United States
Allium sativum	garlic	anti-bacterial	Asia
Aloe vera	true aloe*	burns, irritations of skin*	Spain; Canary Islands
Althaea officinalis	marsh mallow	skin preparations	N Africa; Asia; Europe
Ammi majus	bishop's weed	psoriasis	Africa; Asia; S Europe
Arctostaphylos uva-ursi	bearberry*	bladder, kidney disease*	Asia; Europe; North and South America
Arnica montana	arnica*	pain and inflammation*	Europe
Artemisia annua	sweet wormwood	fevers, dysentery	W Asia; E, S Europe
Asclepias tuberosa	butterfly weed*	lung inflammations*	North America
Atropa belladonna	deadly nightshade*	pain, visions*	N Africa; temp. Asia; Europe
Avena sativa	oats	fevers, inflammation	cultivated only
Berberis aquifolium	Oregon grape	digestive complaints	W Canada; W United States
Bistorta officinalis	snakeweed	diarrhea, gum infections	N Africa; Asia; Europe
Calendula officinalis	pot marigold	skin conditions	unknown
Camellia sinensis	tea	colds, asthma	Asia
Capsella bursa-pastoris	shepherd's purse*	bleeding, cystitis*	unknown
Capsicum annuum	chile pepper*	arthritis, pain*	continental United States; Central America
Catharanthus roseum	Madagascar periwinkle	leukemia, cancers	Europe
Centaurea montana	mountain bluet	upset stomach	Europe
Chelidonium majus	greater celandine*	corns, warts, toothache*	N Africa; Asia Europe
Codonopsis lanceolata	bonnet bellflower	gynecological diseases	Asia
Coffea arabica	coffee*	analgesics*	Ethiopia; Sudan; Kenya
Colchicum autumnale	autumn crocus*	gout*	Europe
Convallaria majalis	lily-of-the-valley*	heart*	temp. Asia; Europe

Plans in the Medicinal Garden (*continued*)

Botanical name	Common name	Historic use	Area of origin/ distribution
Crocus sativus	saffron crocus	heart	cultivated
Cucurbita pepo	summer pumpkin	worms	continental United States
Datura stramonium	jimsonweed*	respiratory ailments*	Mexico
Digitalis purpurea	foxglove*	heart*	N Africa; Europe
Echinacea spp.	purple coneflower	infection, wounds	Canada; continental United States
Eleutherococcus senticosus	Siberian ginseng	preventive, stress	China; Japan; former Soviet states
Eucalyptus globulus	blue gum	antiseptic	Australia
Eupatorium perfoliatum	boneset*	influenza*	Canada; continental United States
Filipendula ulmaria	queen-of-the-meadow	diarrhea, arthritis	temp. Asia; Europe
Gentiana lutea	yellow gentian	bitter tonic	Turkey; Europe
Ginkgo biloba	maidenhair tree	heart, memory	China
Glycyrrhiza glabra	licorice*	laxative, colds*	N Africa; Asia; Europe
Gossypium herbaceum	levant cotton	abortifacient, male contraceptive	S Africa
Hamamelis virginiana	witchhazel	astringent	Canada; continental United States
Helleborus niger	Christmas rose*	heart, nerves*	central, SE Europe
Hydrastis canadensis	goldenseal*	antiseptic, astringent*	Canada; continental United States
Hypericum perforatum	Saint John's wort*	tonic, tranquilizer*	N Africa; Asia; Europe
Inula helenium	elecampane	antibacterial	temp. Asia; E, SE Europe
Leonurus cardiaca	motherwort	heart	Turkey; Europe
Macleaya cordata	plume poppy*	skin, worms, cancer*	China; Japan
Mahonia aquifolium (See *Berberis aquifolium*)			
Marrubium vulgare	horehound*	expectorant*	Africa; Asia; Europe
Matricaria recutita	German chamomile	sedative	temp. Asia; Europe
Mentha ×piperita	peppermint	indigestion	cultivated
Momordica charantia	balsam pear*	viral infections*	Africa; China; trop. Asia; Australia

Plants in the Medicinal Garden (*continued*)

Botanical name	Common name	Historic use	Area of origin/ distribution
Oenothera biennis	evening primrose	asthma, eczema	Canada; continental United States
Panax quinquefolius	ginseng*	general tonic*	E Canada; continental United States
Papaver somniferum	opium poppy*	sedative, pain*	Africa; temp. Asia; SE, SW Europe
Plantago arenaria Waldst. & Kit.	fleawort	laxative	Africa; Asia; central, E Europe
Plantago major	plantain	wounds, eyewash	Eurasia
Plantago psyllium (See *Plantago arenaria*)			
Podophyllum peltatum	mayapple*	purgative, cancer*	E Canada; continental United States
Polygonum bistorta (See *Bistorta officinalis*)			
Rheum palmatum	turkey rhubarb	general tonic, diarrhea	China
Ricinus communis	castor bean*	laxative*	Africa
Rumex crispus	yellow dock*	venereal disease*	N Africa; Asia; Europe
Salix purpurea	purple osier	pain, inflammation	N Africa; Mongolia; Europe
Salvia officinalis	garden sage*	astringent, gargle*	Greece; Italy; Albania; Yugoslavia
Sanguinaria canadensis	bloodroot*	antiseptic, anesthetic*	Canada; continental United States
Scrophularia nodosa	knotted figwort	wounds	temp. Asia; Europe
Senna marilandica	wild senna	laxative	continental United States
Serenoa repens	saw palmetto	prostate problems	SE United States
Silybum marianum	milk thistle	liver	Egypt; Israel; Turkey; SE, SW Europe
Symphytum officinale	comfrey*	skin*	temp. Asia; Europe
Tanacetum parthenium	feverfew	fever, headache, menstrual disorders	SE Europe
Taxus brevifolia	western yew*	cancer*	W Canada; W United States

Plants in the Medicinal Garden (*continued*)

Botanical name	Common name	Historic use	Area of origin/ distribution
Thymus praecox Opitz subsp. *britannicus* (Ronniger) Holub	creeping thyme	digestive, respiratory	Europe
Thymus vulgaris	garden thyme	gastrointestinal	Morocco; Italy; France; Spain
Trichosanthes kirilowii	snake gourd	HIV, diabetes	China; Japan; Korea
Valeriana officinalis	valerian	sedative	temp. Asia; Europe
Viburnum opulus	cranberry bush*	antispasmodic*	temp. Europe; Canada; Asia; continental United States
Zanthoxylum clava-herculis	southern prickly ash	toothache, sore throat	continental United States
Zingiber officinale	ginger	nausea	trop. Asia

*Parts or the whole of these plants have been found to be toxic, with side effects ranging from minor skin irritation to death. In some cases, toxicity depends on dosage. Self-medication is not advised. Always consult a physician before using herbs as medications.

Plant origin information compiled from USDA, ARS, National Genetic Resources Program. *Germplasm Resources Information Network—(GRIN)* [Online Database]. National Germplasm Resources Laboratory, Beltsville, Maryland. http://www.ars-grin .gov/cgi-bin/npgs/html/paper.pl?language=en&chapter=distrib (08 May 2005).

INDUSTRIAL GARDEN

It often comes as a surprise to find that something ephemeral and beautiful in the plant world is useful to the world of heavy industry. The plants on display in the Industrial Garden are not only used in quaint cottage industries where tea is brewed, potpourri blended, and sachets stitched. These plants have also found a place in the raucous world of smokestacks and assembly lines.

For thousands of years, plants have proved their usefulness, providing wood for shelter and fueling the fires that provided humans with their primary source of energy. Flax, cotton, papyrus, and sisal were (and still are) used to create clothing, paper, and rope, not only providing basic amenities but also feeding cultural advancement.[87] Today, lubricants, dyes, and soaps are created from plant oils, coloring our world and ensuring the efficient operation of machinery.

In the early- to mid-twentieth century, the coal and petroleum industries changed the focus of the industrial world, supplying less expensive versions of what previously had been agricultural products. With the oil embargo of the 1970s came a renewed interest in alternative, renewable sources for fuel and industrial oils. The Agricultural Research Center of the U.S. Department of Agriculture began exploring new crops for their potential use in industry, eventually evaluating "8,000 species of plants for seed oils, 600 for paper fiber, and thousands for medicinal or insecticidal activities."[88]

In spite of the success of the efforts of the Agricultural Research Center and the willingness of American farmers to invest in alternative crop production, the proposed users of these supplies—the chemical industry—have resisted the change, citing cost and supply uncertainties. Nonetheless, a stroll through the Industrial Garden provides a fascinating introduction to the incredibly diverse uses of herbs in industry, ranging from cosmetics, plastics, sponges, fibers, and lubricants to dentifrices and radiation indicators.

The next time you select a plant for your garden, try one of these, and think about the power that is packed into that small, often beautiful, plant.

Plants in the Industrial Garden at the National Herb Garden

Botanical name	Common name	Historic use
Abelmoschus esculentus	okra	fiber
Abelmoschus moschatus	musk mallow	perfumes
Abutilon theophrasti	china jute	fiber
Allium sativum	garlic	flavoring, germicide
Aloe vera	true aloe	ointments, lotions
Althaea officinalis	marsh mallow	emollient, paper
Arachis hypogaea	peanut	oil, soaps, paints, dye
Arbutus unedo	strawberry tree	tanning

Plants in the Industrial Garden (*continued*)

Botanical name	Common name	Historic use
Arctostaphylos uva-urso	bearberry	tanning
Argemone mexicana	Mexican prickly poppy	soap
Asclepias syriaca	milkweed	mattress stuffing, rubber
Asclepias tuberosa	butterfly weed	agricultural products
Beta vulgaris	beet	sugar, livestock feed
Boehmeria nivea	ramie	fabric, fire hose, nets
Calendula officinalis	pot marigold	agricultural products
Camellia oleifera	tea oil plant	tea oil
Capsicum annuum	chile pepper	medicines, foods
Capsicum frutescens	Tabasco pepper	hot sauce
Carthamus tinctorium	safflower	dye, oil, paint, varnish
Cistus ladanifer	labdanum, crimson-spot rockrose	perfume fixative
Corchorus capsularis	jute	burlap, webbing, twine
Crambe abyssinica	crambe	lubricants, plasticizers
Crotalaria juncea	sunn hemp	fishing nets, cordage
Cuphea spp.	cuphea	lubricants, surfactants
Cyamopsis tetragonolobus	guar	mining, cosmetics, drugs, foods
Derris elliptica	tuba root	insecticide
Dimorphotheca sinuata	cape marigold	surface coatings, plastic foams, lubricants
Echinacea angustifolia	purple coneflower	insecticide
Eucalyptus globulus	blue gum	dentifrices, medicinals
Eucommia ulmoides	hardy rubber tree	rubber
Euphorbia lathyris	mole plant	alternative fuels
Foeniculum vulgare	fennel	nylon, plasticizers, urethane foams, lubricants
Glaucium flavum	horned poppy	soap
Glycine max	soybean	glycerine, paints, varnish, printing inks, foods
Glycyrrhiza glabra	licorice	flavoring for tobacco, medicine, confections
Gossypium hirsutum	upland cotton	fabrics
Hedera helix	English ivy	insect repellent
Helianthus annuus	sunflower	oil for food and burning

Plants in the Industrial Garden (*continued*)

Botanical name	Common name	Historic use
Hevea brasiliensis	Para rubber tree	rubber, oil for soap and paint
Hibiscus cannabinus	kenaf	fiber for fabric, paper
Hibiscus sabdariffa	roselle	cordage
Hordeum vulgare	barley	brewing industry
Humulus lupulus	hops	brewing industry
Iris ×germanica 'Florentina'	orris	perfumery
Lantana camara	yellow sage	paper, rubber, insect control
Lavandula angustifolia	English lavender	perfumery
Levisticum officinale	lovage	flavoring
Limnanthes alba	meadowfoam	liquid wax
Linum usitatissimum	flax	linen, linseed oil
Luffa aegyptiaca	loofah	loofah sponges, filters
Medicago sativa	alfalfa	paint manufacture, chlorophyll
Melissa officinalis	lemon balm	perfumery, furniture polish
Mentha ×piperita	peppermint	flavoring for food, medicine, tobacco
Monarda didyma	bee balm	perfumery
Nicotiana rustica	wild tobacco	tobacco industry
Nicotiana tabacum	tobacco	cigars, cigarettes, pipe tobacco, insecticide
Ocimum tenuiflorum	holy basil	insecticide
Parthenium argentatum	guayule	rubber
Perilla frutescens	perilla	paint, varnish, ink, linoleum
Pimpinella anisum	anise/aniseed	medicines, dentifrices, perfumery, beverages, "licorice" candy
Pinus palustris	longleaf pine	timber, turpentine, resin, wood pulp, varnish, ink, wax, lubricants
Quillaja saponaria	soap-bark tree	soap
Ricinus communis	castor bean	castor oil; lubricants, soap, synthetic rubber, oilcloth, plastics, nylon
Rosmarinus officinalis	rosemary	perfumes, soaps, shampoo
Ruta graveolens	rue	perfumery, oil
Saccharum officinarum	sugarcane	sugar, molasses; explosives, synthetic rubber, wax
Salvia officinalis	garden sage	antique fabric cleanser

Plants in the Industrial Garden (*continued*)

Botanical name	Common name	Historic use
Sesamum indicum	sesame	edible oil; soaps, cosmetics, insecticides
Simmondsia chinensis	jojoba	liquid wax, cosmetics, drugs, plastics, lubricant
Sorghum bicolor	sorghum	fiber for brooms; wax
Stevia rebaudiana	stevia	sugar substitute
Stokesia laevis	Stokes' aster	stabilizer for vinyl plastics
Tagetes spp.	marigold	insecticide
Tanacetum cinerariifolium	pyrethrum	insecticide
Tanacetum coccineum	pyrethrum	insecticide
Tanacetum vulgare	tansy	insecticide
Thymus vulgaris	garden thyme	soaps, perfumes, mouthwash
Tradescantia ×*andersoniana*	Virginia spiderwort	radiation indicator
Triticum aestivum	wheat	foods, beverages, fabric sizing
Zea mays	corn	corn oil for linoleum, paint, varnish, soft soap, oilcloth

FRAGRANCE GARDEN

On a warm summer day the Fragrance Garden beckons with its siren call of aromas. Fragrance has long been an important part of life, for practical, religious, and sensual purposes. As far back as 6000 BCE, musk, "the best of all fixatives and quite indispensable in every fine perfume," was in use by Egyptian and Asiatic cultures.[89] A fixative is a substance added to a perfume to stabilize the volatile oils of the fragrant ingredients. In addition to musk, ambergris from whales and orris root from iris rhizomes (*Iris* ×*germanica* 'Florentina' or *Iris* ×*pallida* 'Dalmatica') are commonly used as fixatives.[90]

Greeks and Romans both made copious use of perfumes, adding fragrance to bath water, clothing, shoes, linens, and hair. They coated their pets' hair with pomades and used their favorite fragrances to scent the water in their fountains.[91] Roman soldiers doused themselves with thyme water for courage and carried scented flags into battle. Even in the most sophisticated cities—those that had some rudimentary sewer systems—open trenches for the emptying of "night jars" made potpourri, perfume, incense, and strewing herbs household necessities, especially on warm, humid days.[92]

Our word *perfume* is from the French *parfum,* which is in turn from the Latin *per,* thoroughly, and *fumar,* to smoke or expose to fumes, indicating the early and continuing use of fragrance in religious ritual. Prayers and incantations were seen to waft heavenward on wisps of burning incense, while "fragrance evoke[d] religious feeling through the most directly emotional of all the senses."[93] Flowers and fragrance remain a part of our spiritual lives, adorning births, weddings, life celebrations, illness, and death.

From the earliest records of gardens, often taken from tomb paintings and pottery fragments from before 2000 BCE, it is apparent that gardens were for more than food production. Although early walled gardens, which gave protection from animals and strong dry winds, were primarily utilitarian, they "emphasized the contrast between two separate worlds: the outer one where nature remained awe-inspiringly in control and an inner artificially created sanctuary."[94] In addition to trees for shade and plants for food and medicine, these gardens incorporated flowers, which carried spiritual meanings and added a sensual quality to these private areas.

For the same reasons, we still add fragrant plants to our own gardens, creating oases of peace in an increasingly turbulent world. Fragrance calls to mind times and places of the past, in ways that are often beyond our understanding or even our conscious awareness. Patchouli (*Pogostemon cablin*) and lavender (*Lavandula* spp.) conjure up images of old-fashioned ladies in fussy dresses; lily-of-the-valley (*Convallaria majalis*) and gardenia (*Gardenia jasminoides*) bring to mind June brides; and rosemary (*Rosmarinus officinalis*), for remembrance, is associated with weddings and funerals.

During the Elizabethan era, and possibly long before that, sweet bags were carried when out on the streets of towns, often held to the nose to mask unpleasant odors. John Parkinson, in his *Paradisi in Sole Paradisus Terrestris* (1629), describes these useful little dainties as filled with sweet marjoram, costmary, and lavender, all tied up in small bundles for their "sweet sent [sic] and savour."[95]

Potpourri (mixtures of fragrant petals) and tussie-mussies (small bouquets of fragrant blooms and herbs) are still popular with herb gardeners today. Most contemporary potpourri mixtures consist of dried fragrant flower petals, a few spices, and a fixative, with the addition of a few drops of essential oils to boost the fragrance. Victorian-era potpourri was often described as a "moist mixture" with more attention to resulting fragrance and less to appearance.

If purchasing potpourri in department or specialty stores, read the ingredients carefully, or try to determine by appearance what is being sold. Many potpourri blends are made with cheap materials that are completely devoid of fragrance. Wood shavings and dried weeds dyed in colors to suit the season make up the bulk of potpourri, even some of the quite expensive blends. They rely on fragrant oils and an occasional spice to perfume the ingredients. Be careful to keep such blends out of the reach of children and pets and to dispose of them carefully.

The fragrance of dried flowers can be quite long-lived. Lavender wands, for example, have been known to retain their fragrance for as many as ten years; they are often discarded more because they become shopworn than because they lose their fragrance. Lavender wands are usually made with thirteen to fifteen tall stems of lavender, with the stems bent backwards over the flowering tops, which are then woven with ribbon or raffia to encase the flowers in a little basket-like shape. Lavender wands are often used to keep lingerie and linen fresh.

Tussie-mussies are often wrapped with a lacy handkerchief or carried in elegant little silver holders. Just a few snips of small herbs and blossoms are enough to fill these holders and create a lovely fragrance to take with you on a busy day.

The Fragrance Garden is a mélange of flowers that might have been used centuries ago and are still used today, some of which you may remember from a garden of your childhood.

Some plants are used strictly for their fragrance and beauty in the garden, others for use as cut flowers, and still others for multiple purposes: in perfumes, as flavorings for food and beverages, or for potpourri and sachets. Some of these plants have great economic value (*Nicotiana* spp.) and some are nearly forgotten (mignonette, *Reseda odorata*). All of the plants in the Fragrance Garden will please those who take the time to walk slowly through the garden, brushing against the plants to release their scent or smelling the varied flowers.

Plants in the Fragrance Garden at the National Herb Garden

Botanical name	Common name
Abeliophyllum distichum	Korean abelia leaf
Abelmoschus moschatus	musk mallow
Agastache foeniculum	anise hyssop
Aloysia citriodora	lemon verbena
Angelica archangelica	angelica
Artemisia abrotanum	southernwood
Artemisia annua	sweet wormwood
Artemisia ludoviciana 'Silver Queen'	silver queen
Artemisia schmidtiana	silver mound
Boronia megastigma	scented boronia
Buddleia davidii	butterfly bush
Caryopteris ×*clandonensis*	blue mist
Cedronella canariensis	canary balm
Centranthus ruber	red valerian
Chimonanthus praecox	wintersweet
Choisya ternata	Mexican oregano
Cistus ladanifer	labdanum
Citrus aurantium	sour orange
Clethra alnifolia	sweet pepper bush
Convallaria majalis	lily of the valley
Cymbopogon citratus	lemongrass
Daphne odora	winter daphne
Dianthus caryophyllus	clove pink
Dianthus plumarius	cottage pink
Dictamnus albus	gas plant

Plants in the Fragrance Garden (*continued*)

Botanical name	Common name
Erysimum cheiri	wallflower
Eucalyptus citriodora	lemon scented gum
Fothergilla gardenii	dwarf fothergilla
Galium odoratum	sweet woodruff
Gardenia jasminoides	gardenia
Geranium macrorrhizum	big root geranium
Helichrysum italicum subsp. *italicum*	curry plant
Heliotropium arborescens	heliotrope
Hierochloe odorata	sweet grass
Hyacinthus orientalis	hyacinth
Hyssopus officinalis	hyssop
Illicium verum	star anise
Iris ×*germanica* 'Florentina'	orris
Jasminum grandiflorum	royal jasmine
Lavandula ×*intermedia*	lavandin
Lindera umbellata	lindera
Matricaria recutita	German chamomile
Matthiola incana	stock
Mentha spp.	field mint
Myrtus communis	myrtle
Narcissus spp.	daffodils
Nicotiana spp.	tobacco
Ocimum basilicum	sweet basil
Origanum vulgare	wild marjoram
Pelargonium spp.	scented geraniums
Perovskia atriplicifolia	Russian sage
Petunia ×*hybrida*	garden petunia
Philadelphus spp.	mock orange
Pogostemon cablin	patchouli
Polianthes tuberosa	tuberose
Primula vulgaris	English primrose
Pycnanthemum spp.	mountain mints
Reseda odorata	mignonette
Rosmarinus officinalis	rosemary
Salvia clevelandii	blue sage

Plants in the Fragrance Garden (*continued*)

Botanical name	Common name
Salvia dorisiana	fruit-scented sage
Salvia elegans	pineapple sage
Salvia leucantha	Mexican bush sage
Salvia sclarea	clary sage
Salvia uliginosa	bog sage
Santolina chamaecyparissus	lavender cotton
Santolina virens	green santolina
Scabiosa atropurpurea	sweet scabious
Teucrium fruticans	tree germander
Thymus camphoratus	camphor thyme
Thymus ×citriodorus	lemon thyme
Thymus herba-barona	caraway thyme
Thymus praecox subsp. *articus*	creeping thyme
Thymus vulgaris	garden thyme
Valeriana officinalis	valerian
Vetiveria zizanioides	vetiver
Viburnum farreri	fragrant viburnum
Viola odorata	sweet violet
Vitex agnus-castus	chaste tree

ASIAN GARDEN

Heady fragrances, brilliant flowers, and stately shapes hint at the exotic appeal of the plants in the Asian Garden. Many are significant for their medicinal properties, others for their culinary value, and some simply for their beauty.

It is fitting that the National Herb Garden should have a theme garden dedicated to Asian herbs, as Chinese herbalism "has the longest unbroken history of recorded knowledge."[96] China claims 35,000 species of plants, with 5,000 of those dedicated to medicinal use. Similarly, India boasts the use of 600 native medicinal plants.[97] The wealth of knowledge from these regions, as well as southeast Asia, and the great diversity of plant material indigenous to those areas, eventually made their way to North America, where many of the plants have been incorporated into our pharmaceutical industry. As a bonus, many of the plants that give a distinctive taste to Asian cuisine were also brought to our shores.

Garlic chives (*Allium tuberosum*) have the wonderful flavors of garlic and chives all in one. Lemongrass (*Cymbopogan citratus*) has subtle and soft lemon tones that make soups and desserts truly intoxicating. The sweet spice of cardamom (*Ellettaria cardamomum*) makes itself invaluable in both the savory and sweet cuisine of southeast Asia. Vietnamese or field mint (*Mentha canadensis*) has peppermint overtones, while holy basil (*Ocimum tenuiflorum*) is predominately spicy with overtones of clove. Vietnamese coriander (*Polygonum odoratum*) has a very strong cilantro-like taste and was used interchangeably with holy basil, though is no longer recommended, for it lacks Generally Recognized as Safe status.

Many of the plants traditionally used in Asian medicine are now grown in our country as ornamentals, including Korean angelica (*Angelica gigas*) which is a stately architectural plant with bold leaves and clusters of purple flowers in midsummer. The orange speckled flower of the blackberry lily (*Belamcanda chinensis*) is a sight, and the gardener is surprised in the fall to see its ripened black seeds exposed in clusters atop the flower stalk waving high above the foliage.

Most woodland gardens are not complete without cinnamon fern (*Osmunda cinnamomea*) which gives the garden a wonderful airy texture; it was used to treat fevers and nausea. Its long stalks of brown continue to make this plant interesting long after its foliage is dormant. Tree peonies (*Paeonia suffruticosa*) are increasingly popular for their elegant beauty. These shrubs, with their gorgeous flowers (from pale whites to deep reds and purples), make any garden a thing of delight. The bark and roots of tree peonies have been used medicinally in China and Tibet for centuries. Strawberry geraniums (*Saxifraga stolonifera*) make an incredible ground cover in shady areas. The thick foliage of this striking perennial adds wonderful texture to a garden, and it has flowers in variations of yellow, pink, white, and green.

So whether you grow some of the ornamental medicinal plants or want to experiment with their exotic flavors, include in your own garden some of the plants you see on your visit to the Asian Garden at the National Herb Garden.

Plants in the Asian Garden at the National Herb Garden

Botanical name	Common name	Historic use
Adonis amurensis	Amur adonis	medicinal
Agastache rugosa	wrinkled giant hyssop	medicinal
Allium thunbergii	Japanese onion	medicinal
Allium tuberosum	Chinese chive, garlic chive	culinary, medicinal
Alpinia galanga	greater galangal	culinary, medicinal
Amaranthus tricolor	Joseph's coat	medicinal, culinary
Anemone ×hybrida	Japanese anemone	medicinal
Angelica gigas	Korean angelica	medicinal
Aralia elata	Japanese angelica tree	medicinal
Arctium lappa	great burdock	medicinal, culinary
Astilbe chinensis	Chinese astilbe	tonic
Belamcanda chinensis	blackberry lily	medicinal
Boehmeria nivea	ramie	fiber, medicinal
Callicarpa bodinieri	beautyberry	medicinal
Camellia japonica	camellia	medicinal, cosmetic
Camellia sasanqua	sasanqua camellia	cosmetic
Celosia argentea	quail grass	medicinal
Centella asiatica	water pennywort	culinary, medicinal
Coix lacryma-jobi	Job's tears	medicinal
Cryptotaenia japonica	Japanese wild chervil	medicinal, culinary
Curcuma longa	turmeric	medicinal, culinary
Cymbopogon citratus	lemongrass	medicinal, culinary
Dendranthema indicum	wild chrysanthemum	medicinal
Dianthus superbus	fringed pink	medicinal
Elettaria cardamomum	cardamom	culinary, medicinal
Epimedium grandiflorum	longspur	medicinal
Equisetum hyemale	horsetail	medicinal
Fritillaria verticillata var. thunbergii	fritillary	medicinal

Plants in the Asian Garden (*continued*)

Botanical name	Common name	Historic use
Gardenia jasminoides	gardenia	medicinal
Glycine max	soybean	culinary, medicinal, industrial
Gomphrena globosa	globe amaranth	medicinal
Gypsophila oldhamiana	Oldham gypsophila	medicinal
Hemerocallis fulva	tawny daylily	medicinal, culinary
Hydrangea macrophylla	Hortensia	medicinal
Iris ensata	Japanese iris	cosmetic, medicinal
Leonurus artemisia	motherwort	medicinal
Lilium auratum	goldband lily	culinary
Liriope spicata	creeping lilyturf	medicinal
Lithospermum officinale	Gromwell	medicinal
Luffa aegyptiaca	loofah	culinary, industrial
Lycoris squamigera	magic lily	medicinal
Mentha canadensis	field mint	medicinal
Momordica charantia	balsam pear	medicinal, industrial
Nandina domestica	heavenly bamboo	medicinal, industrial
Ocimum tenuiflorum	holy basil	medicinal, culinary
Oenanthe javanica	water dropwort	medicinal, culinary
Ophiopogon japonicus	dwarf lilyturf	medicinal
Osmunda cinnamomea	cinnamon fern*	culinary*
Paeonia suffruticosa	tree peony	medicinal
Perilla frutescens	perilla	medicinal
Perilla frutescens 'Atropurpurea'	beefsteak plant*	culinary*
Petasites japonicus	sweet coltsfoot	medicinal, culinary
Physalis alkekengi	Chinese lantern	medicinal
Platycodon grandiflorus	balloon flower	medicinal
Polygonum odoratum	Vietnamese coriander*	culinary*, medicinal
Poncirus trifoliata	hardy orange	medicinal
Sanguisorba officinalis	great burnet	medicinal
Saxifraga stolonifera	strawberry geranium	medicinal, culinary
Scutellaria baicalensis	skullcap	medicinal
Sesamum indicum	sesame	culinary, medicinal, industrial

Plants in the Asian Garden (*continued*)

Botanical name	Common name	Historic use
Tetrapanax papyriferus	rice paper plant	industrial, medicinal
Thalictrum minus	meadow rue	medicinal
Thymus quinquecostatus	Asiatic thyme	culinary
Trigonella foenum-graecum	fenugreek	medicinal, culinary, industrial
Zanthoxylum piperitum	Asian pepper	culinary, medicinal
Zingiber officinale	ginger	culinary, medicinal

*These herbs do not have Generally Recognized as Safe status and are not recommended for consumption.

BEVERAGE GARDEN

A steamy cup of amber-colored tea, with its essence of warm summer days wafting upward, makes a cold, gray day bearable. Likewise, a bracing sip of a spring green tonic can chase the winter cobwebs from your head and bones. The plant labels in the Beverage Garden contain a wealth of information about some of the easiest and most pleasant ways to enjoy herbs. The leaves, flowers, or seeds of the plants in this garden all have a history of use for beverages. Many also have medicinal properties.

According to legend, the mythical Chinese emperor Shen Nong discovered tea around 2700 BCE when a leaf of *Camellia sinensis* fell from a bush into his pot of boiling water. He praised the medicinal powers of the resulting brew, and the drinking of tea began.[98] By the 1600s, tea was one of China's most important exports. Countries around the world demanded regular supplies of leaves, which made beverages that were relaxing or stimulating, and enjoyable in either case. Black tea refers to leaves that have been selected, rolled, fermented, and fired for a short period before storing. Green tea, which usually has a sharper taste and more antioxidants, has not been fermented. Oolong tea combines elements of both black and green teas.

A purist will refer to a brew only from the leaves of the *Camellia sinensis* as tea, while a beverage made from herbs is more properly called an infusion or a tisane. Tisanes generally are intended for medicinal purposes. It is possible that herbal tisanes developed first as medicinal brews and were later enjoyed as beverages for pleasure. We use the generally accepted term *herb tea* to refer to those beverages enjoyed simply for their taste and aromas. Herb teas are always best, and most flavorful, if the entire leaf is used. When the leaves are dried and crumbled, their oil glands are exposed and subject to faster evaporation of the volatile oils, leaving dull shreds for your teacup.

Some herbs make wonderfully flavorful teas on their own, including peppermint (*Mentha ×piperita*), chamomile (*Chamaemelum nobile*), and ginger (*Zingiber officinale*), while others are more palatable in combinations. Any number of recipes can be followed, but it is just as easy to try your own. All you need is fresh, boiling water (use bottled or filtered water for the best tea), a tablespoon or two of fresh leaves (or a teaspoon or so of dried, if you must), and about four to five minutes to allow the leaves to steep. Pour the freshly boiled water over the herbs in your teacup, or increase the amount of herbs and make a pot of tea. Do not boil the herbs and water together, or all of the lovely flavor of your herbs will evaporate into the rising steam. Strain your tea, perhaps add a little honey and lemon, and enjoy this simple indulgence.

America created its own blend of tea in the 1770s. China tea had become the standard in England by 1650, and the colonists brought the habit of drinking tea with them to their new country.[99] But by 1773, the taxes imposed on tea were so great that the colonists revolted, dumping 342 chests of tea into Boston Harbor. That left housewives scrambling to create a palatable—and patriotic—alternative to China tea. Bee balm, *Monarda didyma*, was one of the most popular herbal choices, along with New Jersey tea, *Ceanothus americanus*, blackberry and raspberry leaves (*Rubus* spp.). After the end of the Revolutionary War, herbs again took second place to China tea for those who could afford it.

Herbs have been used in beverages in other ways as well and are easy for people to try on their own. A time-honored tradition is the addition of herbs to wine. In fact, wine can be made entirely from herbs. This is an old tradition in England, where the results are known as English country wines. Elder-flower (*Sambucus nigra*) champagne and dandelion wine are probably the best known of these wines. Other favorites include hops (*Humulus lupulus*), rose hip (*Rosa* spp.) or poppy (*Papaver* spp.) wine, as well as mead, which is honey wine blended with fruits and flowers. As the herbal ingredients are fermented raw, some of their medicinal properties are retained, giving tonic qualities to some of the resulting wines.[100]

An easier, and equally delicious, process is to steep a few herbs in a favorite bottle of wine. Dianthus flowers will lend a slight clove-like fragrance to a wine, and sweet woodruff gives a faint hint of vanilla to traditional recipes for Mai wine. Just add the herbs to your bottle of wine, replace the cork, and allow the bottle to sit for several hours or overnight. Strain the herbs and serve the wine, perhaps with a dainty flower floating on top.

For the more adventurous, herbal liqueur is a delightful way to preserve the flavor of your herbs and provide for pleasant winter evenings. The simplest recipes for liqueurs call for a good-quality vodka or brandy, to which is added a simple sugar syrup and a selection of herbs, flowers, fruits, or seeds. The liqueur is allowed to age for two to eight weeks; it is then strained and filtered to remove all traces of the herbs before being decanted into glass bottles.

The best-known herbal liqueurs are Chartreuse and Benedictine. Created during the Renaissance era by a Venetian monk, Dom Bernardo Vincelli, at the abbey of Fécamp, Benedictine is an elixir of twenty-seven plants and spices. Only Benedictine monks produced this liqueur until the end of the eighteenth century, but since that time others have also marketed liqueurs made from the same recipe.[101] Chartreuse has an equally impressive history. In 1605, monks at the Chartreuse monastery in Vauvert, France, received an ancient manuscript titled "An Elixir of Long Life." In 1737 the monastery's apothecary, Frère Jerome Maubec, interpreted the manuscript and created the Chartreuse liqueur, using an extraordinary 130 herbs and spices. Other recipes are now available, but the original is still manufactured by Chartreuse monks as Elixir Vegetal de la Grande-Chartreuse.[102]

One other herb-based liqueur that deserves mention, mostly for its notorious history, is absinthe, also known as the Green Fairy, Opaline, and Green Devil. Absinthe, around which an entire counterculture evolved, was the beverage of choice for many in the years between 1800 and 1915, including Vincent Van Gogh, Édouard Manet, and Henri de Toulouse-Lautrec. *Artemisia absinthium* is the ingredient from which the liqueur takes its name, and around which a controversy over the drink evolved. Thujone, one of the major components of *A. absinthium,* is a chemical that may cause hallucinations and convulsions. A definitive link between thujone and these deleterious physical effects has never been fully confirmed, but it nonetheless resulted in a nearly worldwide ban on absinthe beginning around 1915. Many claimed that the liqueur's high alcohol content or adulterants added to it were to blame for the bizarre behavior exhibited by those who regularly consumed the beverage. Others thought that such behavior was simply due to the alcoholic proclivities or unstable personalities of those involved.

Absinthe has a very bitter taste, and most people cut it with water and a little sugar to make it drinkable. Numerous recipes exist for the liqueur, adding, in addition to *A. absinthium,* anise, fennel, mint, coriander, angelica root, and sometimes even spinach, all of which contribute to its emerald color. Absinthe can be found in London again, and other areas around the world are considering lifting the ban on it. Regardless of the liqueur's legal status, *A. absinthium,* which was once used medicinally to expel intestinal worms, still has a thujone content, making the advisability of its consumption questionable.[103]

The Beverage Garden displays many of the plants that have been used in beverages in one form or another over the years. The best way to decide which ones you prefer is to experiment with them, starting with those that have the most appealing scent. Take note, however, that some of the plants in this garden are no longer considered safe for consumption or should be consumed only in moderation.

Plants in the Beverage Garden at the National Herb Garden

Botanical name	Common name	Historic use
Agrimonia eupatoria	agrimony	tea
Aloysia citriodora	lemon verbena	tea
Angelica archangelica	angelica*	alcoholic beverages*
Artemisia absinthium	wormwood*	absinthe*
Borago officinalis	borage*	wine cups*
Calluna vulgaris	heather	tea, mead
Camellia sinensis	tea	tea
Carum carvi	caraway	liqueur
Catha edulis	Arabian tea	tea
Cedronella canariensis	canary balm	tea
Centaurium erythraea	centaury	vermouth, liqueur
Chamaemelum nobile	Roman chamomile	tea
Cichorium intybus	chicory	coffee substitute
Coffea arabica	coffee	coffee, liqueur
Coriandrum sativum	coriander, cilantro	gin, vermouth, liqueur
Crocus sativus	saffron crocus	liqueur, milk
Ficus carica	fig	wine, brandy
Filipendula ulmaria	queen-of-the-meadow	herb beer, tea
Foeniculum vulgare	fennel	tea, liqueur
Fragaria vesca	alpine strawberry	tea, Crème de Fraises
Galium odoratum	sweet woodruff	Mai wine
Geum urbanum	avens	ale, liqueur
Glycyrrhiza glabra	licorice	soft drinks, beer, liqueur
Hibiscus sabdariffa	roselle	tea, wine
Humulus lupulus	hops	beer, tea
Hyssopus officinalis	hyssop	tea, liqueur
Ilex paraguariensis	maté	tea (contains caffeine)
Juniperus communis	juniper	gin, liqueur, soft drinks**
Laurus nobilis	sweet bay	tea, soft drinks, liqueur
Levisticum officinale	lovage	tea, liqueur
Marrubium vulgare	horehound*	ale, liqueur*
Matricaria recutita	German chamomile	tea, Benedictine
Medicago sativa	alfalfa*	tea*
Melissa officinalis	lemon balm	tea, liqueur, cold drinks

Plants in the Beverage Garden (*continued*)

Botanical name	Common name	Historic use
Mentha ×*piperita*	peppermint	tea, cold drinks, liqueur
Mentha spicata	spearmint	tea, cold drinks, liqueur
Monarda didyma	bee balm*	tea*
Myrrhis odorata	sweet cicely*	liqueur*
Nepeta cataria var. *citriodora*	lemon catnip*	tea*
Pimpinella anisum	anise	tea, liqueur
Prunus mume	Japanese apricot	liqueur
Punica granatum	pomegranate	fruit drinks, wine, grenadine
Salvia officinalis	garden sage	tea, ale**
Salvia sclarea	clary sage	wine, beer, ale
Solidago odora	sweet goldenrod	tea
Stachys officinalis	betony	tea, tonic
Tanacetum balsamita	costmary	ale, beer, tea
Taraxacum officinale	dandelion	tea, beer, wine
Teucrium scorodonia	wood germander	ale
Thymus ×*citriodorus*	lemon thyme	tea
Thymus vulgaris	garden thyme	tea, liqueur
Trifolium pratense	red clover	tea
Zingiber officinale	ginger	tea, brandy, ale, beer

*No longer considered safe for consumption

**For consumption in moderation

CULINARY GARDEN

Nestled at the center of the theme gardens, with a backdrop of tall boxwoods (*Buxus* spp.) and framed with pawpaw (*Asimina triloba*) and jujube trees (*Ziziphus jujube*), is the Culinary Garden. It is filled with flavorful plants—some popular and well-known, others rarely seen in home gardens—all of which complement and enhance a variety of foods. Most can be grown in the average garden in the United States.

Fresh herbs subtly increase the appeal of most foods. How humans came to incorporate these plants into foods is nearly as curious as how they came to be used medicinally. The use of herbs most likely evolved over hundreds of thousands of years. They may have been used first as foods and then as medicines as their beneficial effects were noticed; perhaps it was the reverse. However the process occurred, it gave rise to cultural variations in cuisine that we still enjoy today.

Little remains to document the earliest uses of herbs. In part this is because food containers were made from vegetable or animal substances—such as wood, basket material, or animal parts—that deteriorated rapidly. Archaeological digs have unearthed pottery jars that were in use c. 2500 BCE, near Knossos, on the island of Crete. These jars contain traces of olive oil "perfumed with herbs from the hillsides."[104]

By the first century CE, and probably thousands of years earlier, cooking was quite sophisticated and trade in herbs and spices was widespread. This trade, which dealt in cinnamon, nutmeg, cloves, black pepper, cardamom, and other spices, led to great wealth for some traders, to outbreaks of hostilities, and to high-priced spices, making them accessible primarily to those of wealth and position.[105] Herbs grown closer to home, being more readily available to the average household, were used instead of more precious spices. Cooks eventually began using foods that did not call for disguise by the use of spices, but that "could be combined with the light touch—of unspoilt nature, garden, and meadow—that goes with herbs, especially when they are fresh."[106]

The first extant cookbook is attributed to a first-century Roman, Apicius, and includes a recipe for a sauce for roasted meat: "One quarter ounce each of pepper, lovage, parsley, celery seed, dill, asafetida root, hazelwort, cyperus, caraway, cumin, and ginger, plus a little pyrethrum, 1 1/4 pints of liquamen, and 2 1/2 fluid ounces of oil."[107] Liquamen was a fermented sauce, based on fish and salt, that required months to prepare and was often produced as an industry giving some indication of the mastery of herbs and spices.

The spice trade was governed by economics and world politics. Vast fortunes were made by controlling the movement of spices, and as new routes were found that resulted in less expensive spices, power and politics reared their unruly heads and shut down those same routes. "Pepper has been so scarce at times and is so expensive that one pound was considered a royal present, and was used like money as a medium of exchange," according to W. M. Gibbs.[108] With the fall of Rome, civilized cooking fell as well, and those who assumed power kept their less-refined ways of eating. Always more available to upper classes than to the general populace, spices were now even more difficult to procure. Food was bland. "The Huns from central Asia kept their beef under their horse-saddles, to be seasoned with the animals' sweat," notes J. O. Swahn.[109] With the paucity of spices came an interest in the flavoring ability of fresh herbs, however.

With the beginning of the Crusades in 1095, the European appetite for spices was reawakened.[110] Once again, the spice trade became a force for expanding both culture and cuisine. Constantinople, Alexandria, Genoa, and Venice profited and continued to grow from the trade in spices. The appetite for spices in European kitchens gradually returned, at least to those who could afford the luxury items. To those who could afford few or none, the growing use of herbs was a consolation.

A list for a 1328 funeral feast in Sweden included "500 grams of cinnamon, 700 of saffron, one kilogram of ginger, three of pepper, five of caraway, and forty of almonds" for its preparation. When the sailor Vasco de Gama arrived in India in 1498, the "spice trade, and international maritime traffic as a whole, were instantly transformed."[111] By the sixteenth century, the spice trade crisscrossed the globe, creating a new economic center in Europe equal to that of Asia.

Most of the herbs and spices used in premodern Europe were of Mediterranean origin. Christian monasteries played a role in carrying on the herbal tradition, for they often kept gardens to supply their own needs as well as for their neighbors. Herbs that had been brought from far-off locales found a place in monastery gardens, among the trees, vines, roots, and vegetables grown by the monks. Herbs eventually moved from monastery gardens into home gardens, where they were appreciated for their flavor and usefulness.

Tastes continue to change, moving from sophisticated to plain and back again. Today we are experiencing a growing interest in the use of herbs. Even in the early 1980s, it was a challenge to find herb plants, and the herbs sold in little glass jars in grocery stores were faintly reminiscent of the fresh plant. Now lush herb plants can be found in almost every plant nursery, even in large chain stores. Fresh herbs can be bought by the bunch in many supermarkets, not just specialty stores. Meanwhile, demand only continues to grow.

For those willing to put forth a minimum of effort, many different kinds of herbs—from the ordinary to the exotic—can be grown at home. At the right time of year, you may see the pods open on sesame (*Sesamum orientale*), spilling their seeds and giving rise to the "Open sesame!" of *Ali Baba and the Forty Thieves* legend. The caper bush (*Capparis spinosa*) with its buds spilling over a rock wall, turmeric (*Curcuma longa*) with its small seeds embedded in a cone left by its fading flower, and horseradish (*Armoracia rusticana*) with its long tapering leaves all grow abundantly in the garden. Even dandelion (*Taraxacum officinale*), used in salads, wine, and as a vegetable, has a place in the garden.

On a sunny summer day, with its riot of blooms and tantalizing fragrances of basil, mint, and roses, a garden provides a visual and olfactory feast. Parsley, sage, rosemary, and thyme are all here, for they have long been favored as garnishes and flavoring agents. Clove pinks (*Dianthus caryophyllus*) with the bitter white bases of the petals removed, lend a sweet clove-like flavor to fruit, wine, salads, and syrups. Hyssop flowers (*Hyssopus officinalis*) have been used for centuries to flavor game. Pot marigold (*Calendula officinalis*) adds flavor and a golden color to soups, cakes, and muffins. Lavender flowers (*Lavandula angustifolia*) flavor desserts, wine, and baked goods.

Happily, we have learned from the ancients and from our more recent ancestors how best to take advantage of the fresh and appealing flavors that plants lend to our foods. We have easy access to these plants and, more important, can grow them in our own gardens. Experimenting with unfamiliar plants is a pleasant pastime with a tasty reward.

Plants in the Culinary Garden at the National Herb Garden

Botanical name	Common name	Primary use
Allium spp.	onions, garlic, chives	salads, soups, meats, vegetables, vinegar
Aloysia citriodora	lemon verbena	salads, desserts, sauces
Alpinia spp.	galangals	curries, meats, soup, fish
Amaranthus cruentus	purple amaranth	leaves—vegetables; grain—flour
Anethum graveolens	dill	bread, cheese, fish, sauces
Anthriscus cerefolium	chervil	sauces, egg dishes, vegetables, meat, salads
Armoracia rusticana	horseradish	relish
Artemisia dracunculus 'Sativa'	French tarragon	sauces, chicken, fish
Asimina triloba	pawpaw	fresh as a fruit
Borago officinalis	borage*	garnish*
Brassica spp.	mustards	meats, cheese, eggs, vegetables
Calendula officinalis	pot marigold	flavor and color
Capparis spinosa	caper bush	sauces, fish, meat, eggs, butters
Capsicum spp.	chile peppers	soups, stews, meats, vegetables
Carum carvi	caraway	bread, cheese, sausage, cabbage, desserts
Centranthus ruber	red valerian*	salads, soups*
Chenopodium ambroisiodes	epazote*	beans, stews, shellfish*
Cinnamomum zeylanicum	cinnamon	savory and sweet dishes
Coriandrum sativum	coriander, cilantro	seeds—savory and sweet dishes; fresh—Middle Eastern, Asian, Latin American dishes
Crocus sativus	saffron crocus	rice, soups, breads, pastries
Cuminum cyminum	cumin	breads, vegetables, meats
Curcuma longa	turmeric	curries, sauces, pickles, rice
Cymbopogon citratus	lemongrass	fish, pork, chicken, beverages
Dianthus caryophyllus	clove pink	garnish, beverages, lamb
Eruca sativa	rocket	salads, vegetable, soups
Eryngium foetidum	culantro*	raw or steamed; fish, beans, soups*
Ferula assa-foetida	asafoetida	lentils, sauces, vegetarian
Foeniculum vulgare	fennel	leaves—soup, fish, salads; seeds—sweets, sausage, cheese
Hyssopus officinalis	hyssop	game, salads, soups

Plants in the Culinary Garden (*continued*)

Botanical name	Common name	Primary use
Laurus nobilis	sweet bay	soups, stews, sauces, meats, some sweets
Lavandula angustifolia	English lavender	salads, dressings, desserts
Levisticum officinale	lovage	vegetables, soups, breads, liqueur
Lippia graveolens	Mexican oregano*	southwestern dishes*
Melissa officinalis	lemon balm	beverages, vegetables, meats, grains
Mentha aquatica	orange mint	desserts
Mentha spicata	spearmint	vegetables, beverages, mint sauce, desserts
Mentha ×villosa var. *alopecuroides*	apple mint	sweet dishes
Mespilus germanica	medlar	jams, jellies
Monarda fistulosa var. *menthifolia*	oregano de la Sierra	game, meats, semi-soft cheese
Myrrhis odorata	sweet cicely*	salads, fruit, stews, garnish*
Nigella sativa	black cumin	breads, cakes, vegetables, curries
Ocimum basilicum	sweet basil	pesto, tomato dishes, vegetables, meats, eggs
Origanum majorana	sweet marjoram	meat, game, fish, soup, cheese, eggs, vegetables
Origanum ×majoricum	hardy sweet marjoram	meats, eggs, soup, vegetables
Origanum onites	Greek oregano	vegetables and meats, pastas
Origanum vulgare subsp. *hirtum*	Greek mountain oregano	classic Greek cuisine, Italian dishes
Papaver rhoeas	corn poppy	baked goods, soups, stews
Pelargonium graveolens	rose geranium	jellies, sugar, desserts, fruits
Petroselinum crispum	parsley	soups, stews, meats, salads, vegetables
Pimpinella anisum	anise	baked goods, salads, stews, vegetables
Plectranthus amboinicus	Cuban oregano*	meat dishes, black beans*
Poliomintha bustamanta	Mexican oregano*	meats, soups, vegetables*
Polygonum odoratum	Vietnamese coriander*	fish, poultry, meat, vegetables, rice*

Plants in the Culinary Garden (*continued*)

Botanical name	Common name	Primary use
Rosa rugosa	Japanese rose	salads, jelly, syrup
Rosmarinus officinalis	rosemary	meats, soups, sauces, breads, vinegar
Rumex acetosa and *R. scutatus*	French sorrel, garden sorrel	salads, soups, sauces, veal, poultry, fish
Salvia elegans	pineapple sage*	fruits, desserts, beverages*
Salvia officinalis	garden sage	games, poultry, apples, onions, potatoes
Sanguisorba minor	salad burnet*	salads, soups, beverages*
Satureja hortensis	summer savory	stews, soups, beans, eggs
Satureja montana	winter savory	beans, vegetables, meats
Tagetes lucida	Mexican tarragon*	salads, sauces, beverages *
Taraxacum officinale	dandelion	salads, or as vegetable
Thymus ×citriodorus	lemon thyme	poultry, fish
Thymus pulegioides 'Oregano-scented'	oregano scented thyme	meats, fish, vegetables
Thymus vulgaris	garden thyme	soups, stews, roasts, vegetables
Trigonella foenum-graecum	fenugreek	curries
Tropaeolum majus	nasturtium	salads, soups, garnish
Tulbaghia violacea	society garlic	soups, salads
Viola odorata	sweet violet	salads, sweets, jelly, syrup
Zingiber officinale	ginger	curries, baked goods, beverages
Ziziphus jujube	jujube	fresh in breads, cakes, puddings, soups

*These herbs do not have Generally Recognized as Safe status and are not recommended for consumption.

Notes

···

Growing and Using Herbs

1. Henry Beston, *Herbs and the Earth* (1935; reprint, Boston: David R. Godine, 1990), 10.

2. HSA National Herb Garden committee, Minutes, April 24, 2006, The Herb Society of America, Kirtland, Ohio.

3. Arthur O. Tucker and Thomas DeBaggio, *The Big Book of Herbs: A Comprehensive Illustrated Reference to Herbs of Flavor and Fragrance* (Loveland, Colo.: Interweave Press, 2000), 87.

Herbs in the Culinary Garden

1. Tucker and DeBaggio, 477.

2. Maud Grieve, "Anise," in *A Modern Herbal* (1931), botanical.com/botanical/mgmh/a/anise040.html.

3. Mike Laverty and Luhr Jensen, "Oils, Aminos, Plants, Phermones, and Mr. Steelhead," www.activeangler.com/articles/freshwater/articles/trout/luhr_jensen/oils_pheromones.asp.

4. Tucker and DeBaggio, 266.

5. Gernot Katzer, "Asafetida, *Ferula Assa-foetida* L.," *Spice Pages,* www.uni-graz.at/~katzer/engl/Feru_ass.html; India Agro Industry, "Asafoetida," www.agriculture-industry-india.com/spices/asafoetida.html.

6. Tucker and DeBaggio, 394.

7. Ibid., 310.

8. Isaiah 28:25–27 (King James version).

9. Robert W. Lebling and Donna Pepperdine, "Natural Remedies of Arabia," *Saudi Aramco World* 57, no. 5, www.saudiaramcoworld.com/issue/200605/natural.remedies.of.arabia.html.

10. Tucker and DeBaggio, 320.

11. American Spice Trade Association, ASTA Online, www.astaspice.org/faq/.

12. Reay Tannahill, *Food in History* (New York: Stein and Day, 1973), 47.

13. J. O. Swahn, *The Lore of Spices: Their History, Nature, and Uses around the World* (London: Grange Books, 1992), 176.

14. Quoted in W. M. Gibbs, *Spices and How to Know Them* (Buffalo, N.Y.: Matthews-Northrup Works, 1909), 66.

15. Tucker and DeBaggio, 249.

16. Ibid., 250.

17. James Duke, *The Green Pharmacy* (Emmaus, Pa.: Rodale Press, 1997), 337.

18. Tucker and DeBaggio, 299.

19. Jekka McVicar, *Herbs for the Home: A Definitive Sourcebook to Growing and Using Herbs* (New York: Viking Studio Books, 1995), 95.

20. Tucker and DeBaggio, 300.

21. Quoted in Lesley Bremness, *The Complete Book of Herbs: A Practical Guide To Growing and Using Herbs* (New York: Viking Studio Books, 1988), 88.

22. Nicholas Culpeper, *Culpeper's Color Herbal,* ed. David Potterton (New York: Sterling Publishing, 1983), 110.

23. Quoted in Eleanor Sinclair Rohde, *Herbs and Herb Gardening* (New York: Macmillan, 1937), 119.

24. Rohde, 119.

25. Tannahill, 16, 25.

26. Swahn, 26.

27. Tannahill, 220.

28. Ibid., 165.

29. Bremness, 60; Swahn, 26 (quote).

30. Deni Bown, *The Herb Society of America New Encyclopedia of Herbs & Their Uses,* rev. ed. (New York: DK Publishing, 2001), 147.

31. Swahn, 27.

32. Gibbs, 167.

33. Tucker and DeBaggio, 561.

34. Ibid., 193.

35. Roy Genders, *Garden Pinks* (London: John Gifford, 1962), 13.

36. Tucker and DeBaggio, 257.

37. Lady Rosalind Northcote, *The Book of Herb Lore* (1912; reprint, New York: Dover, 1971), 171.

38. Gernot Katzer, "Rosemary (Rosmarinus officinalis L.)," *Spice Pages,* http://www.uni-graz.at/~katzer/engl/Rosm_off.html.

39. Duke, 13, 60–61, 85–86, 128–29.

40. Northcote, 133.

41. Quoted ibid., 130.

42. Tucker and DeBaggio, 246.

43. Ibid., 542.

44. Ibid., 537.

45. Ibid., 557.

46. "The Babylonian 'Epic of Creation, Enuma Elish,'" third tablet, lines 40–45, The Plesiosaur Site, www.plesiosaur.com/creationism/creationmyths/myths_16.php.

47. Tucker and DeBaggio, 558–60.

48. See the American Violet Society webpage, www.americanviolet.org (accessed November 6, 2006).

Herbs without Generally Regarded as Safe (GRAS) Status

1. U.S. Food and Drug Administration, Center for Food Safety and Applied Nutrition, Office of Food Additive Safety, "Frequently Asked Questions about GRAS," www.cfsan.fda.gov/~dms/grasguid.html.

2. Tucker and DeBaggio, 28.

3. "Botanicals Generally Recognized as Safe," www.biologie.uni-hamburg .de/b-online/ibc99/dr-duke/gras.htm. A list of botanicals included in the Code of Federal Regulations, title 21, parts 172, 182, 184, and 186. This list may be dated, but it is a good place to start.

4. McVicar, 122.

5. Tucker and DeBaggio, 374.

6. Carolyn Neithammer, *American Indian Cooking: Recipes from the Southwest* (Lincoln: University of Nebraska Press, 1999), 117.

7. Jeff Hart, *Montana Native Plants and Early Peoples* (Helena: Montana Historical Society and Montana Bicentennial Administration, 1976), 12–13.

8. Melvin R. Gilmore, *Uses of Plants by the Indians of the Missouri River Region*, enlarged ed. (Lincoln: University of Nebraska Press, 1991), 59.

9. Gregory L. Tilford, *Edible and Medicinal Plants of the West* (Missoula, Mont.: Mountain Press, 1997), 18.

10. Christine Wittman, "Early American Tea Herbs," *The Herb Companion* 4, no. 2 (December 1991/January 1992): 20–24.

11. Tucker and DeBaggio, 191.

12. Ibid., 490.

13. McVicar, 209.

14. Northcote, 16.

15. Quoted in Rohde, 123.

16. From Sir Francis Bacon's essay, "Of Gardens" (1625). The full text of this essay can be found online: www.gardenvisit.com/t/bacon.htm.

17. Maud Grieve, "Sweet Cicely," in *A Modern Herbal* (1931), botanical .com/botanical/mgmh/c/cicswe67.html.

Herbal Trees

1. The Spice House, "Cinnamon," www.thespicehouse.com/category/product _type_Cinnamon.php. The various types of cinnamon discussed here were ordered from this site.

2. California Rare Fruit Growers, "Jujube," www.crfg.org/pubs/ff/jujube .html.

3. Ibid.

4. Adel A. Kader, "Chinese Jujube (Chinese Date): Recommendations for Maintaining Post Harvest Quality," Postharvest Technology Research Information Center, University of California–Davis, postharvest.ucdavis.edu/Produce/ProduceFacts/Fruit/jujube.shtml.

5. "Public Health Statement for Cyanide," Agency for Toxic Substances and Disease Registry, Centers for Disease Control, www.atsdr.cdc.gov/toxprofiles/phs8.html.

6. Ivan Day, "Theodore Garrett's Medlar Cheese," *Historic Food*, www.historicfood.com/medlar%20cheese%20recipe.htm.

7. Paw Paw Foundation, www.pawpaw.kysu.edu/pawpaw/ppf/about.htm.

8. Alice B. Russell et al., "Poisonous Plants of North Carolina," Cooperative Extension Service, North Carolina State University, www.ces.ncsu.edu/depts/hort/consumer/poison/poison.htm.

9. Charles E. Johnson, with Allen D. Owings and Bob Mirabello, "Pawpaws for Ornamental Use Being Researched," LSU Agricultural Center, text.lsuagcenter.com/en/lawn_garden/commercial_horticulture/ornamentals/Pawpaws+for+Ornamental+Use+Being+Researched.htm.

10. Susan Gaidos, "Pawpaw Shows Promise in Fighting Drug-Resistant Tumors," based on an interview with Jerry McLaughlin, www.scienceblog.com/community/older/1997/B/199701156.html.

11. Snake C. Jones and Desmond R. Layne. "Pawpaw Description and Nutritional Information," Paw Paw Foundation, www.pawpaw.kysu.edu/pawpaw/cooking.htm.

The National Herb Garden: America's Garden

1. Patrick Taylor, *Planting in Patterns* (New York: Harper & Row, 1989), 45.

2. U.S. National Arboretum, "A Capitol Idea," www.usna.usda.gov/Gardens/collections/columns.html.

3. The Knot Garden measures 53' 10" by 24' 10".

4. Richard Ober, ed., *The National Herb Garden Guidebook* (Springfield, Va.: Potomac Unit, The Herb Society of America, 1996), 1.

5. Penelope Hobhouse, *Gardening through the Ages* (New York: Simon & Schuster, 1992), 11.

6. "Hypnerotomachia Poliphili," University of Glasgow Library, Special Collections Department, special.lib.gla.ac.uk/exhibns/month/feb2004.html.

7. Hobhouse, 151.

8. Ibid., 163–87.

9. Alice Morse Earle, *Old Time Gardens Newly Set Forth* (New York: Macmillan, 1901), 54–59.

10. Ralph Dutton, *The English Garden* (London: B. T. Batsford, 1950), 33.

11. Ibid., 50.

12. Joseph Wood Krutch, ed., *The Gardener's World* (New York: G. P. Putnam's Sons, 1959), 92.

13. Michael Weishan, "Knots and Parterres," *Country Living Magazine*, magazines.ivillage.com/countryliving/garden/your/articles/0,12922,284660_294160,00.html

14. Sir Francis Bacon, "Of Gardens" (1625), www.gardenvisit.com/t/bacon.htm.

15. Horace Walpole, "On Modern Gardening," *Gardens Guide*, http://www.gardenvisit.com/t/w4.htm.

16. A. J. Downing, *A Treatise on the Theory and Practice of Landscape Gardening, Adapted to North America; with a View to the Improvement of Country Residences*, 4th ed. (New York: George P. Putnam, 1849), 31.

17. Ibid., 63.

18. Ober, 1.

19. Bown, 346 (quote)–47.

20. Ober, 2.

21. George Nicholson, *The Illustrated Dictionary of Gardening: A Practical and Scientific Encyclopedia of Horticulture for Gardeners and Botanists*, vol. 4 (London: L. Upcott Gill, 1887), 315.

22. Ibid., 319.

23. Ober, 2.

24. Louise Bechtel and Edwin DeT. Bechtel, "Old Roses and Their Influence on Modern Varieties," *The Herbarist* 23 (1957): 15.

25. Arthur K. Wheelock, Jr., *From Botany to Bouquets: Flowers in Northern Art* (Washington, D.C.: National Gallery of Art, 1999). See Fig. 31, Abrosius Bosschaert the Elder, *Vase of Roses in a Window*, 1618–1619, oil on copper, p. 41; Fig. 41, Jan Phillips van Thielen, *Roses and Tulips and Jasmine in a Glass with a Dragonfly and a Butterfly*, 1650s, oil on panel, p. 53; and Fig. 60, Jan van Huysum, *Still Life with Flowers and Fruit*, c. 1715, oil on panel, p. 69.

26. Elizabeth Scher, "Historic Roses," *The Herbarist* 38 (1972): 54.

27. "Varieties of Antique Roses," *Guide to Antique Roses*, www.roseinfo.com/rose_guide.html.

28. Ober, 3.

29. Ibid.

30. Ibid.

31. "Varieties of Antique Roses," www.roseinfo.com/rose_guide.html.

32. Frank J. Anderson, *An Illustrated History of the Herbals* (New York: Columbia University Press, 1977), 10. Dioscorides's original work no longer exists, but a copy from 512, discovered in Turkey in 1562, is held in the Austrian National Library. The Latin translation of the Greek title is further translated into English as *The Materials of Medicine*.

33. Pedanius Dioscorides, *De Materia Medica*, http://www.heronbotanicals.com/links/hblinks.html.

34. Ibid.

35. Anderson, 11; Ober, 1.

36. Anderson, 10.

37. Pedanius Dioscorides, "Introduction," *De Materia Medica*, www.heronbotanicals.com/links/hblinks.html.

38. Anderson, 15.

39. Ober, 6–14.

40. Malcolm Stuart, *The Encyclopedia of Herbs and Herbalism* (New York: Crescent Books, 1987), 100.

41. Siobhan nic Dhuinnshleibe, "A Brief History of Dyestuffs & Dyeing," Society for Creative Anachronism Web site, kws.atlantia.sca.org/dyeing.html.

42. Ober, 21; Lynn Ertle, "Mad about Madder," *The Herb Quarterly* 88 (Winter 2001): 26.

43. Arthur C. Gibson, "Woad Is Me," from a series of lectures entitled "Plants and Civilization," delivered at the University of California–Los Angeles, www.botgard.ucla.edu/html/botanytextbooks/economicbotany/Isatis/.

44. Anne Mattson, "Indigo in the Early Modern World," www.bell.lib .umn.edu/Products/Indigo.html.

45. Gary Noel Ross, "Indigo—Mysterious Dye," *Louisiana Environmentalist,* May–June 1995, www.leeric.lsu.edu/le/special/indigo.htm.

46. Stuart, 100.

47. Ross, "Indigo—Mysterious Dye."

48. Ertle, 29.

49. Stuart, 99.

50. Bremness, 198.

51. Stuart, 100.

52. Anne Bishop, "Herbs and the Colonial Woman," *The Herbarist* 51 (1985): 38.

53. Earle, 38–53; David Tucker, *Kitchen Gardening in America: A History* (Ames: Iowa State University Press, 1993), 27.

54. Tucker, 33.

55. Quoted in Dutton, 38. There is debate regarding the identity of Master Fitzherbert and the authorship of the *Book of Husbandry.* The work is generally attributed to John Fitzherbert, a farmer, but some have argued that it may have been written by John's brother, who was a lawyer. See www.ling .upenn.edu/hist-corpora/PPCEME-RELEASE-1/info/fitzh.e1.htm.

56. Tucker, 33.

57. Ibid., 20.

58. Kay Sanecki, *The Book of Herbs: How to Plant, Grow, and Harvest Your Own Herbs* (London: Magna Books, 1988), 48.

59. Tucker, and DeBaggio, 191.

60. Elaine Dow, *Simples & Worts: Being All about the Herbs of Our Puritan Forefathers (and Mothers), with Additional Seventeenth- and Eighteenth-Century Miscellany* (Topsfield, Mass.: Historical Presentations, 1982), 6.

61. E. Barrie Kavasch, *Native Harvest: American Indian Wild Foods and Recipes* (New York: Dover, 2005), xxvi.

62. James Mooney, *Myths of the Cherokee and Sacred Formulas of the Cherokees* (1887–90; reprint, Nashville, Tenn.: Charles and Randy Elder, 1972), 179.

63. John Mazzeo, "Ethnography, Ethnology, and Ethnohistory," www .ic.arizona.edu/~anth4206/206/module_01pr.htm.

64. Gilbert L. Wilson, *Buffalo Bird Woman's Garden: Agriculture of the Hidatsa Indians* (St. Paul: Minnesota Historical Society Press, 1987), xx.

65. Elliott Coues, ed., *The History of the Expedition under the Command of Lewis and Clark Expedition,* vol. 1 (1893; facsimile reprint, New York: Dover, 1965), 164.

66. Kavasch, xxvi.

67. Quoted in in Ann Leighton, *American Gardens in the Eighteenth Century* (Amherst: University of Massachusetts Press, 1986), 17.

68. Richard M. Bacon, *The Forgotten Art of Growing, Gardening, and Cooking with Herbs* (Dublin, N.H.: Yankee, 1972), 6–9.

69. Earle, 2.

70. Edith Allen Murphey, *Indian Uses of Native Plants* (1958; reprint, Glenwood, Ill., Meyerbooks, 1990), 17, 25–26; Ober, 45, 49; "Wintergreen Hides in Snow," Traditional Herbal and Plant Knowledge, Identifications, www.kstrom.net/isk/food/wintergr.html; "Juniper: Tribal Uses," www.kstrom.net/isk/food/juniptri.html.

71. Val Hardacre, *Woodland Nuggets of Gold: The Story of American Ginseng Cultivation* (Northville, Mich.: Holland House Press, 1968), 50.

72. Ibid., 318.

73. Sumner, 64–65, 190–91.

74. Tilford, 2.

75. Bown, 22.

76. Judith Sumner, *The Natural History of Medicinal Plants* (Portland, Ore.: Timber Press, 2000), chap. 7.

77. Jennifer A. Biser, "Really Wild Remedies—Medicinal Plant Use by Animals," *ZooGoer* 27, no.1 (1998), nationalzoo.si.edu/Publications/ZooGoer/1998/1/reallywildremedies.cfm.

78. Jules Janick, "Herbals: The Connection between Horticulture and Medicine," www.hort.purdue.edu/newcrop/history/lecture23/lec23l.html.

79. David Bramwell, "How Many Plant Species Are There?" *Plant Talk* 28 (April 2002), www.plant-talk.org/stories/28bramw.html.

80. Richard Evans Schultes, "The Medicine Man: Herbalist Supreme," *The Herbarist* 53 (1987): 1–6.

81. "Classics of Traditional Chinese Medicine," National Library of Medicine, History of Medicine Division, www.nlm.nih.gov/hmd/chinese/emperors.html.

82. C. Kwong-Robbins, "The Art and Science of Chinese Herbal Medicine," *U.S. Pharmacist* 28:03, www.uspharmacist.com/index.asp?show=article&page=8_1040.htm.

83. Janick, "Herbals: The Connection between Horticulture and Medicine."

84. Sir Ernest Wallis Budge, *Herb Doctors and Physicians in the Ancient World* (Chicago: Ares, 1978), 27.

85. Christopher Hobbs, "An Outline of the History of Herbalism," *Health World,* www.healthy.net/scr/article.asp?ID=901.

86. Medicinal Plants Working Group, "Green Medicine," Plant Conservation Alliance, National Park Service, www.nps.gov/plants/medicinal.

87. L. H. Princen, "New Industrial Crops," *The Herbarist* 60 (1994): 26.

88. Ibid., 27.

89. Grace Chess Robinson, "Flowers and Perfume," *The Herbarist* 32 (1966): 15.

90. Tucker and DeBaggio, 303.

91. Beata Hayton, "The Perfumed World of Caesar and Cleopatra," *The Herbarist* 56 (1990): 114.

92. Ibid, 115.

93. Ibid., 112.

94. Hobhouse, 11.

95. Quoted in Northcote, 118.

96. Bown, 14.

97. Ibid., 32

98. Nancy Friedman, ed., *The Book of Tea and Herbs: Appreciating the Varietals and Virtues of Fine Tea and Herbs* (Santa Rosa, Calif.: The Cole Group, 1993), 44.

99. Wittman, 22.

100. Robert K. Henderson, "O, Thou Invisible Spirit," *The Herb Companion* 13, no.1 (October/November 2000): 60.

101. "Benedictine: A Zest for Eternity," www.benedictine.fr/anglais/homepage.html.

102. "History of the Chartreuse Liqueurs," *The Homeland of Chartreuse*, www.chartreuse.fr/pa_history3_uk.htm; Madalene Hill and Gwen Barclay, "Herbal Liqueurs: More Than One Way to Enjoy Dessert," *The Herb Companion* 3, no. 2 (December/January 1991): 50.

103. Tucker and DeBaggio, 176–77.

104. Tannahill, 77.

105. Rita Buchanan, "A Chronicle of Herbs and Spices: Seasoning Reasoning through the Ages," *The Herb Companion* 9, no. 1 (October/November 1996): 28.

106. Swahn, 70.

107. Tannahill, 95.

108. Gibbs, 36.

109. Swahn, 14.

110. Claire Loewenfeld and Philippa Back, *The Complete Book of Herbs and Spices*, 2d, rev. ed. (Newton Abbot: David & Charles, 1978), 18.

111. Swahn, 15 (first quote), 17 (second quote).

Bibliography

Agricultural Research Service. *Botanicals Generally Recognized as Safe.* Module 19. www.ars-grin.gov/duke/syllabus/gras.htm (accessed October 11, 2006).

American Spice Trade Association. ASTA Online. www.astaspice.org/faq/ (accessed September 8, 2006).

Anderson, Frank J. *An Illustrated History of the Herbals.* New York: Columbia University Press, 1977.

"The Babylonian 'Epic of Creation, Enuma Elish,'" third tablet, lines 40–45, The Plesiosaur Site, www.plesiosaur.com/creationism/creationmyths/myths_16.php (accessed November 6, 2006).

Bacon, Sir Francis. "Of Gardens" (1625), www.gardenvisit.com/t/bacon.htm (accessed November 6, 2006).

Bacon, Richard. *The Forgotten Art of Growing, Gardening, and Cooking with Herbs.* Dublin, N.H.: Yankee, 1972.

Bechtel, Louise, and Edwin DeT. Bechtel. "Old Roses and Their Influence on Modern Varieties." *The Herbarist* 23 (1957): 10–20.

"Benedictine: A Zest for Eternity." www.benedictine.fr/anglais/homepage.html (accessed September 8, 2006).

Beston, Henry. *Herbs and the Earth.* 1935. Reprint, Boston: David R. Godine, 1990.

Beverly, Robert. *The History and Present State of Virginia,* edited by Louis B. Wright. In Ann Leighton, *American Gardens in the Eighteenth Century.* Amherst: University of Massachusetts Press, 1986. 17–34.

Biser, Jennifer A. "Really Wild Remedies—Medicinal Plant Use by Animals." *ZooGoer* 27, no.1 (1998), nationalzoo.si.edu/Publications/ZooGoer/1998/1/reallywildremedies.cfm (accessed October 11, 2006).

Bishop, Anne. "Herbs and the Colonial Woman." *The Herbarist* 51 (1985): 37–40.

"Botanicals Generally Recognized as Safe." www.biologie.uni-hamburg.de/b-online/ibc99/dr-duke/gras.htm (accessed November 6, 2006).

Bown, Deni. *The Herb Society of America New Encyclopedia of Herbs & Their Uses.* Rev. ed. New York: DK Publishing, 2001.

Bramwell, David. "How Many Plant Species Are There?" *Plant Talk* 28 (April 2002), www.plant-talk.org/stories/28bramw.html (accessed September 8, 2006).

Bremness, Lesley. *The Complete Book of Herbs: A Practical Guide to Growing & Using Herbs.* New York: Viking Studio Books, 1988.

Buchanan, Rita. "A Chronicle of Herbs and Spices: Seasoning Reasoning through the Ages." *The Herb Companion* 9, no. 1 (October/November 1996): 26–29.

Budge, Sir Ernest Wallis. *Herb Doctors and Physicians in the Ancient World.* Chicago: Ares, 1978.

California Rare Fruit Growers Web site. "Jujube." www.crfg.org/pubs/ff/jujube.html (accessed September 8, 2006).

"Classics of Traditional Chinese Medicine." National Library of Medicine, History of Medicine Division. www.nlm.nih.gov/hmd/chinese/emperors.html (accessed November 8, 2006).

"Compounds from the Pawpaw Tree." Complementary Approaches. *Artemis.* The Avon Foundation Breast Center at Johns Hopkins. www.hopkinsbreastcenter.org/artemis/199807/comp.html (accessed October 11, 2006).

Coon, Nelson. *Gardening for Fragrance.* New York: Hearthside Press, 1967.

Coues, Elliott, ed. *The History of the Expedition under the Command of Lewis and Clark.* 3 vols. 1893. Facsimile reprint, New York: Dover, 1965.

Culpeper, Nicholas. *Culpeper's Color Herbal.* Ed. David Potterton. New York: Sterling Publishing, 1983.

Day, Ivan. "Theodore Garrett's Medlar Cheese." *Historic Food.* www.historicfood.com/medlar%20cheese%20recipe.htm (accessed September 8, 2006).

Dioscorides, Pedanius. *De Materia Medica.* www.heronbotanicals.com/links/hblinks.html (accessed September 8, 2006).

Dow, Elaine. *Simples and Worts: Being All about the Herbs of our Puritan Forefathers (and Mothers), with Additional Seventeenth- and Eighteenth-Century Miscellany.* Topsfield, Mass.: Historical Presentations, 1982.

Downing. A. J. *A Treatise on the Theory and Practice of Landscape Gardening, Adapted to North America; with a View to the Improvement of Country Residences.* 4th ed. New York: George P. Putnam, 1849.

Duke, James A. *The Green Pharmacy.* Emmaus, Pa.: Rodale Press, 1997.

Dutton, Ralph. *The English Garden.* London: B. T. Batsford, 1950.

Earle, Alice Morse. *Old Time Gardens Newly Set Forth.* New York: Macmillan, 1901.

Ertle, Lynn. "Mad About Madder." *Herb Quarterly* 88 (Winter 2001): 24–30.

Fernald, Merrit Lyndon, and Alfred Charles Kinsey. *Edible Wild Plants of Eastern North America.* 1958. Reprint, New York: Dover, 1996.

Friedman, Nancy, ed. *The Book of Tea and Herbs: Appreciating the Varietals and Virtues of Fine Tea and Herbs.* Santa Rosa, Calif.: The Cole Group, 1993.

Gaidos, Susan. "Pawpaw Shows Promise in Fighting Drug-Resistant Tumors." Based on an interview with Jerry McLaughlin. www .scienceblog.com/community/older/1997/B/199701156.html (accessed November 6, 2006).

Garland, Sarah. *The Herb Garden: A Complete Guide to Growing Scented, Culinary and Medicinal Herbs.* New York: Penguin Books, 1984.

Genders, Roy. *Garden Pinks.* London: John Gifford, 1962.

Gibbs, W. M. *Spices and How to Know Them.* Buffalo, N.Y.: Matthews-Northrup Works, 1909.

Gibson, Arthur C. "Woad Is Me." From a series of lectures entitled "Plants and Civilization," delivered at the University of California–Los Angeles. www.botgard.ucla.edu/html/botanytextbooks/ economicbotany/Isatis/ (accessed October 9, 2006).

Gilmore, Melvin R. *Uses of Plants by the Indians of the Missouri River Region.* 1977. Enlarged ed. Lincoln: University of Nebraska Press, 1991.

Grieve, Maud. "Anise." In *A Modern Herbal* (1931). botanical.com/ botanical/mgmh/a/anise040.html (accessed November 2, 2006).

———. "Sweet Cicely." In *A Modern Herbal* (1931). botanical.com/ botanical/mgmh/c/cicswe67.html (accessed November 6, 2006).

Hardacre, Val. *Woodland Nuggets of Gold: The Story of American Ginseng Cultivation.* Northville, Mich.: Holland House Press, 1968.

Hart, Jeff. *Montana Native Plants and Early Peoples.* Helena: Montana Historical Society and Montana Bicentennial Administration, 1976.

Hayton, Beata. "The Perfumed World of Caesar and Cleopatra." *The Herbarist* 56 (1990): 110–16.

Henderson, Robert K. "O, Thou Invisible Spirit." *The Herb Companion* 13, no. 1 (October/November 2000): 60–61.

Hill, Madalene, and Gwen Barclay. "Herbal Liqueurs: More Than One Way to Enjoy Dessert." *The Herb Companion* 3, no. 2 (December/ January 1991): 50–53.

———. *Southern Herb Growing.* Fredericksburg, Tex.: Shearer Publishing, 1987.

"History of the Chartreuse Liqueurs." *The Homeland of Chartreuse.* www.chartreuse.fr/pa_history3_uk.htm (accessed September 7, 2006).

Hobbs, Christopher. "An Outline of the History of Herbalism." *Health World*. www.healthy.net/scr/article.asp?ID=901 (accessed September 7, 2006).

Hobhouse, Penelope. *Gardening through the Ages: An Illustrated History of Plants and Their Influence on Garden Styles from Ancient Egypt to the Present Day*. New York: Simon & Schuster, 1992.

"Hypnerotomachia Poliphili." University of Glasgow Library, Special Collections Department. special.lib.gla.ac.uk/exhibns/month/feb2004.html (accessed October 11, 2006).

India Agro Industry. "Asafoetida." www.agriculture-industry-india.com/spices/asafoetida.html (accessed November 2, 2006).

Janick, Jules. "Herbals: The Connection between Horticulture and Medicine." www.hort.purdue.edu/newcrop/history/lecture23/lec23l.html (accessed September 7, 2006).

Johnson, Charles E., with Allen D. Owings and Bob Mirabello. "Pawpaws for Ornamental Use Being Researched." LSU Agricultural Center. text.lsuagcenter.com/en/lawn_garden/commercial_horticulture/ornamentals/Pawpaws+for+Ornamental+Use+Being+Researched.htm (accessed September 7, 2006).

Jones, Snake C., and Desmond R. Layne. "Pawpaw Description and Nutritional Information." Paw Paw Foundation. www.pawpaw.kysu.edu/pawpaw/cooking.htm (accessed September 7, 2006).

"Juniper: Tribal Uses." www.kstrom.net/isk/food/juniptri.html (accessed November 8, 2006).

Kader, Adel A. "Chinese Jujube (Chinese Date): Recommendations for Maintaining Post Harvest Quality." Postharvest Technology Research Information Center. University of California–Davis. postharvest.ucdavis.edu/Produce/ProduceFacts/Fruit/jujube.shtml (accessed October 11, 2006).

Katzer, Gernot. "Asafetida (*Ferula Assa-foetida* L.)." *Spice Pages*. www.uni-graz.at/~katzer/engl/Feru_ass.html (accessed November 2, 2006).

———. "Rosemary (*Rosmarinus officinalis* L.)." *Spice Pages*. www.uni-graz.at/~katzer/engl/Rosm_off.html (accessed September 7, 2006).

Kavena, Juanita Tiger. *Hopi Cookery*. Tucson: University of Arizona Press, 1990.

Kavisch, E. Barrie. *Native Harvest: American Indian Wild Foods and Recipes*. New York: Dover, 2005.

Kowalchik, Claire, and William H. Hylton, eds. *Rodale's Illustrated Encyclopedia of Herbs*. Emmaus, Pa.: Rodale Press, 1987.

Krutch, Joseph Wood, ed. *The Gardener's World*. New York: G. P. Putnam's Sons, 1959.

Kwong-Robbins, C. "The Art and Science of Chinese Herbal Medicine." *U.S. Pharmacist* 28:03. www.uspharmacist.com/index.asp?show =article&page=8_1040.htm (accessed September 7, 2006).

Laverty, Mike, and Luhr Jensen. "Oils, Aminos, Plants, Phermones, and Mr. Steelhead." www.activeangler.com/articles/freshwater/ articles/trout/luhr_jensen/oils_pheromones.asp (accessed September 7, 2006).

Lebling, Robert W., and Donna Pepperdine. "Natural Remedies of Arabia." *Saudi Aramco World* 57, no. 5, www.saudiaramcoworld.com/ issue/200605/natural.remedies.of.arabia.html (accessed November 8, 2006).

Leighton, Ann. *American Gardens in the Eighteenth Century.* Amherst: University of Massachusetts Press, 1986.

Loewenfeld, Claire, and Philippa Back. *The Complete Book of Herbs and Spices.* 2d, rev. ed. Newton Abbot: David & Charles, 1978.

McVicar, Jekka. *Herbs for the Home: A Definitive Sourcebook to Growing and Using Herbs.* New York: Viking Studio Books, 1995.

Mattson, Anne. "Indigo in the Early Modern World." www.bell.lib.umn .edu/Products/Indigo.html (accessed September 7, 2006).

Mazzeo, John. "Ethnography, Ethnology, and Ethnohistory." www.ic .arizona.edu/~anth4206/206/module_01pr.htm (accessed September 7, 2006).

Medicinal Plants Working Group. "Green Medicine." Plant Conservation Alliance. National Park Service. www.nps.gov/plants/medicinal (accessed September 7, 2006).

Meuninck, Jim. *Basic Essentials: Edible Wild Plants and Useful Herbs.* Old Saybrook, Conn.: Globe Pequot Press, 1999.

Mooney, James. *Myths of the Cherokee and Sacred Formulas of the Cherokees.* Nashville, Tenn.: Charles and Randy Elder, 1982.

Murphey, Edith Van Allen. *Indian Uses of Native Plants.* 1958. Reprint, Glenwood, Ill.: Meyerbooks, 1990.

National Library of Medicine, History of Medicine Division. "Classics of Traditional Chinese Medicine." www.nlm.nih.gov/hmd/chinese/ emperors.html (accessed September 7, 2006).

Neithammer, Carolyn. *American Indian Cooking: Recipes from the Southwest.* Lincoln: University of Nebraska Press, 1999.

nic Dhuinnshleibe, Siobhan. "A Brief History of Dyestuffs & Dyeing." Society for Creative Anachronism Web site. kws.atlantia.sca.org/ dyeing.html (accessed October 9, 2006).

Nicholson, George. *The Illustrated Dictionary of Gardening: A Practical and Scientific Encyclopedia of Horticulture for Gardeners and Botanists.* Vol. 4. London: L. Upcott Gill, 1887.

Northcote, Lady Rosalind. *The Book of Herb Lore*. 1912. New York: Dover, 1971.

Ober, Richard, ed. *The National Herb Garden Guidebook*. Springfield, Va.: Potomac Unit, The Herb Society of America, 1996.

Ottesen, Carole. *The Native Plant Primer*. New York: Harmony Books, 1995.

Paw Paw Foundation. www.pawpaw.kysu.edu/ppf/about.htm (accessed September 7, 2006).

Princen, L. H. "New Industrial Crops." *The Herbarist* 60 (1994): 26–34.

"Public Health Statement for Cyanide." Agency for Toxic Substances and Disease Registry. Centers for Disease Control. www.atsdr.cdc .gov/toxprofiles/phs8.html (accessed November 6, 2006).

Riddle, John M. *Dioscorides on Pharmacy and Medicine*. Austin: University of Texas Press, 1985. From an online excerpt. www.tiscalinet.ch/ materiamedica/Volltext/Dioskurides.htm.

Robinson, Grace Chess. "Flowers and Perfume." *The Herbarist* 32 (1966): 8–19.

Rohde, Eleanor Sinclair. *Herbs and Herb Gardening*. New York: Macmillan, 1937.

Ross, Gary Noel. "Indigo—Mysterious Dye." *Louisiana Environmentalist*, May–June 1995. www.leeric.lsu.edu/le/special/indigo.htm (accessed September 7, 2006).

Russell, Alice B., et al. "Poisonous Plants of North Carolina." Cooperative Extension Service. North Carolina State University. www .ces.ncsu.edu/depts/hort/consumer/poison/poison.htm (accessed September 7, 2006).

Sanecki, Kay. *The Book of Herbs: How to Plant, Grow, and Harvest Your Own Herbs*. London: Magna Books, 1988.

Scher, Elizabeth. "Historic Roses." *The Herbarist* 38 (1972): 49–55.

Schultes, Richard Evans. "The Medicine Man: Herbalist Supreme." *The Herbarist* 53 (1987): 1–6.

Spice House. "Cinnamon." www.thespicehouse.com/category/product _type_Cinnamon.php (accessed September 7, 2006).

Stuart, Malcolm, ed. *The Encyclopedia of Herbs and Herbalism*. New York: Crescent Books, 1987.

Sumner, Judith. *The Natural History of Medicinal Plants*. Portland, Ore.: Timber Press, 2000.

Swahn, J. O. *The Lore of Spices: Their History, Nature, and Uses around the World*. London: Grange Books, 1992.

Tannahill, Reay. *Food in History*. New York: Stein and Day, 1973.

Taylor, Patrick. *Planting in Patterns*. New York: Harper & Row, 1989.

Tilford, Gregory L. *Edible and Medicinal Plants of the West.* Missoula, Mont.: Mountain Press, 1997.

Tucker, Arthur O. "The Strange History of the Musk Plant." *The Herbarist* 54 (1988): 60–67.

Tucker, Arthur O., and Thomas DeBaggio. *The Big Book of Herbs: A Comprehensive Illustrated Reference to Herbs of Flavor and Fragrance.* Loveland, Colo.: Interweave Press, 2000.

Tucker, David. *Kitchen Gardening in America: A History.* Ames: Iowa State University Press, 1993.

U.S. Department of Agriculture. Natural Resources Conservation Service. "Plants Database." www.plants.usda.gov (accessed September 7, 2006).

U.S. Food and Drug Administration, Center for Food Safety and Applied Nutrition, Office of Food Additive Safety. "Frequently Asked Questions about GRAS." www.cfsan.fda.gov/~dms/grasguid.html (accessed October 11, 2006).

U.S. National Arboretum. www.usna.usda.gov (accessed September 7, 2006).

———. "A Capitol Idea." www.usna.usda.gov/Gardens/collections/columns.html (accessed November 10, 2006).

"Varieties of Antique Roses." *Guide to Antique Roses.* www.roseinfo.com/rose_guide.html (accessed September 29, 2006).

Walpole, Horace. "On Modern Gardening." *Gardens Guide.* www.gardenvisit.com/t/w1.htm (accessed September 8, 2006).

Weishan, Michael. "Knots and Parterres." *Country Living Magazine.* magazines.ivillage.com/countryliving/garden/your/articles/0,12922,284660_294160,00.html (accessed September 8, 2006).

Westland, Pamela. *The Herb Handbook.* New York: Gallery Books, W. H. Smith, 1991.

Wheelock, Arthur K., Jr. *From Botany to Bouquets: Flowers in Northern Art.* Washington, D.C.: National Gallery of Art, 1999.

Wilson, Gilbert L. *Buffalo Bird Woman's Garden: Agriculture of the Hidatsa Indians.* St. Paul: Minnesota Historical Society Press, 1987.

"Wintergreen Hides in Snow." Traditional Herbal and Plant Knowledge, Identifications. www.kstrom.net/isk/food/wintergr.html (accessed November 8, 2006).

Wittman, Christine. "Early American Tea Herbs." *The Herb Companion* 4, no. 2 (December 1991/January 1992): 20–24.

Contributors

Jim Adams has been a member of The Herb Society of America for several years and is the recipient of the Nancy Putnam Howard Award for Excellence in Horticulture. He served as the curator of the National Herb Garden from 1996 to 2005 and is currently horticulturist at the British Embassy in Washington, D.C. He contributed the articles on bay, capers, caraway, cardamom, chives, and anise hyssop.

Caroline Amidon and **Joyce Brobst** are both past presidents of The Herb Society of America. They have published articles on species of *Pelargonium* in *The Herbarist* and *Green Scene*. They have also collaborated with Pat Crocker on a book, *Pelargoniums: 2006 Herb of the Year* (Riversong Studios, 2006). Caroline is a member of the Philadelphia Unit, and Joyce is a member of the Pennsylvania Heartland Unit. They contributed the article on scented geraniums.

Barbara Brouse is a longtime member of The Herb Society of America. She has served on its national board of directors and, for four years, on the National Herb Garden committee. She was founder of the Colonial Triangle of Virginia Unit and is currently a member of the Virginia Commonwealth Unit. She has lectured widely on cooking with herbs. She assisted with the Colonial Garden section.

Madalene Hill is a member of The Herb Society of America, serving as president from 1986 to 1988. She is co-author, with her daughter Gwen Barclay, of *Southern Herb Growing* (Shearer Publishing, 1987). Widely respected for her knowledge and love of plants, she has written many articles and has lectured all across America for more than forty years. With Art Tucker, she contributed the article on mint.

Sandy Salkeld deHoll has served on the national board of The Herb Society of America and on the National Herb Garden committee, serving as its chair for six years. She is a member of the Philadelphia and North Carolina Units. She contributed the articles on clove pink, society garlic, and red valerian.

Lorraine Kiefer has been a member of The Herb Society of America for twenty-five years and a member of the National Herb Garden committee for eight years. She lives in Franklinville, New Jersey, with her husband Ted, where they have the Triple Oaks Nursery and Herb Garden. She is a lecturer, garden writer, and horticulturist throughout the Delaware Valley, where her garden columns appear weekly in more than a dozen papers. She contributed or assisted with the development of articles on the Fragrance Garden, arugula, cilantro, dandelion, dill, edible flowers, lemon balm, lemon grass, lemon verbena, lovage, parsley, saffron, sorrel, tarragon, Mexican tarragon, and Vietnamese coriander.

Scott Kresge, a member at large from the Mid-Atlantic District of The Herb Society of America, served on the National Herb Garden committee for six years. He is the owner of Emily Mae's Garden Stop, a nursery specializing in herbs. He has lectured on herbs for over ten years and holds several national herb collections with the HSA. He graduated with high honors from the Culinary Institute of America. He contributed to articles on the Asian Garden, fenugreek, pot marigold, and *Lippia graveolens*.

Lori Schaeffer, member of the Pennsylvania Heartland Unit of The Herb Society of America, served on the National Herb Garden committee for two years. She assisted with the Medicinal Garden section.

Katherine K. Schlosser has been a member of the North Carolina Unit of The Herb Society of America for sixteen years and also served on the HSA's national board of directors. She has served on the National Herb Garden committee for eight years, currently as the chairperson. She is the author of many articles on herbs and native plants, and has been a speaker on herb and native plant topics for ten years. She contributed "Growing and Using Herbs"; articles on the Entrance Garden, Knot Garden, Historic and Species Rose Garden, Dioscorides Garden, Dye Garden, Industrial Garden, Native American Garden, Medicinal Garden, Fragrance Garden, Beverage Garden, and Culinary Garden; articles on purple amaranth, anise, asafoetida, basil, black cumin, chervil, chile peppers, cumin, fennel, galangal, ginger, horseradish, hyssop, lavender, mustard, nasturtium, paprika, poppies, rosemary, sage, savory, sesame seeds, turmeric, and violet; articles on borage, Cuban oregano, culantro, epazote, *Monarda,* pineapple sage, *Poliomintha bustamanta*, salad burnet, and sweet cicely; articles on cinnamon, jujube, medlar, and pawpaw; the section on GRAS status; and all the plant tables. She also provided the photographs, the Knot Garden sketch, and the skeleton key illustration.

Rexford H. Talbert has been a member of The Herb Society of America for forty years, serving on the national board and a number of national-level committees. He is the author of numerous articles appearing in *The Herbarist, Herb Companion, The Gilded Herb, Kitchen Gardens, Proceedings of the International Herb Association*, and similar publications. He has been a widely sought speaker on herbal subjects for over forty-seven years. He contributed the articles on oregano, thyme, and za'atar.

Arthur O. Tucker is research professor and co-director of the Claude E. Phillips Herbarium at Delaware State University in Dover. He is also co-author, with Tom DeBaggio, of *The Big Book of Herbs* (Interweave, 2000). He has served on the national board of directors of The Herb Society of America and is one of the Society's most respected herb authorities. With Madalene Hill, he contributed the article on mint.

Recipe Authors

The following persons contributed recipes for this book. For reasons of space and, in some cases, similarity of recipes, not all could be included. Without the generosity of each of these persons, the book would not have been possible, for each and every recipe, whether or not it is included here, served as inspiration. The enthusiastic and creative cooks listed below are deserving of special acknowledgment.

Anne Abbott
Debby Accuardi
Ellen Adams
Jim Adams
Caroline Amidon
Gwen Barclay
Billie Beadle
Carol Beckman
Susan Belsinger
Gwen Betor
Carol H. Biester
Barbara Ann Blackburn
Dorothy Bonitz
Deni Bown
Harriet Boyer
Pat Brabazon
Anita Bradley
Barbara Brawley
Devah Brinker
Joyce Brobst
Cathy Brooks-Fine
Barbara Brouse
Gloria Brouse
Jenefer Brouse-Schmidt
Donna Brown
Lillian Campbell
Bobbie Champaign
Marsden Champaign
Virginia Chaney
Al Chewning

Lola Cleavinger
Gail Colbeth
Peggy Conway
Becky Cortino
Elyse Cramer
Beverly Credle
Judy Creighton
Pat Crocker
Eleanor Davis
Irene Davis
Sandy Salkeld deHoll
Alma de la Guardia
Gladys Denham
Pat Dennis
Liz DiPiero
Lory Doolittle
Margaret M. Dutch
Bea Elliot
Margaret (Peggy) Ellmore
Mrs. Robert Evans (Sara)
Marion Foster
Marie G. Fowler
Linda Franzo
Jill Friestad
Dell Gabb
Nancy B. Hanst
Edith Hiett
Madalene Hill
Mary Nell Jackson
Mary J. Johnson

Mary L. Jones
Jennifer F. Jordan
Carol Jordan
Joan Jordan
Adrianne Kahn
Pat Kerber
Laurel Keser
Lorraine Kiefer
Elaine Kimmerly
Joan King
Betty Klingaman
Adele Klingberg
Scott Kresge
Marilyn Kushner
Geri Laufer
Susan Lennox
Mary E. Leslie
Sarah Liberta
Adrienne Lind
Elaine Livingston
Rosalinda R. Madara
Grace Madeira
Dolores Maioriello
Elaine H. McCall
Gloria McClure
Martha McFarland
Shad R. McLennan
Mattie McReynolds
Henrietta McWillie
Rose Miller
Dolores Misiewicz
Joe Money
Christine Moore
Betty Muench
Joan Musser
Scott Norton
Marilyn O'Conner
Betty Odom
Myra O'Neill
Ruth Mary Papenthien

Billi Parus
Jeanne Pettersen
Lane Pierrot
Ed Pierzynski
Priscilla Plucinsky
Amy Pollock
Arlene Popko
Mark Ragland
Betty Rea
Ed Rea
Anna Reich
Terri Reiman
Marilyn Rhinehalt
Louise Richards
Shirley A. Ricketts
Hope Riley
Sue Rountree
Charlene Rupp
Pat Sagert
Rita Salman
Nancy Samson
Ellen Scannell
Lori Schaeffer
Amy Willard Schiavone
Katherine K. Schlosser
Gail Seeley
Debra Seibert
Jo Sellers
Nancy Settel
Phyllis Sharpe
Donna Shelley
Rita Sillivan-Smith
Marilyn Sly
Dorothy Spencer
Janet Stevenson
Deborah J. Stiffler
Anita Sundberg
Mary Swain
Rexford H. Talbert
Jane Taylor

Jane Thomson   Paula Weiss
Pam Trissel   Ann Wilson
Vivian Utko   Edna Wilson
June Vercellotti   Nannette Wilson
Kay Wagstaff   Melinda Winans
Janet Walker   Kelly Wisner
Joy H. Walworth   Mary Remmel Wohlleb
Jamie Jo Washburn   Mary Young

In addition, many kind and generous members of the HSA and the U.S. National Arboretum donated their time and talents—and their families and friends—to test every recipe that was received.

General Index

Mabel Grey Pound Cake with
    Limoncello, 214
Mace, 101
Madder, 267–70
Mai Wine, 130
Mai Wine Ice Ring, 130
Mango Apple Chutney, 226
March, Skip, xiv, xvi, xxi
Marjoram, 55, 256, 274, 295,
    297, 312
Martha's Shrimp, 181
Martin, Joy Logee, xvi
Mayan Hot Chocolate, 129
Mazes, 257
McDowell, Ruth, xv
McIlhenny family, xv
Medicinal Garden, xv, 282,
    285–89
Medlar, 106–107, 110, 312
Melissa officinalis. See Lemon
    balm
Mentha spp. *See* Mint
Mespilis germanica. See Medlar
Mexican oregano
—*Lippia graveolens,* 91, 312
—*Poliomintha bustamanta,* 92, 312
Mexican Potato Cake, 185
Mexican Summer Vegetables, 202
Mexican tarragon, 93, 313
Meyer, Dr. Fred, xv
Mint, 50, 274, 287, 292, 297, 299,
    301, 303, 307, 312
Mint Chocolate Pound Cake, 215
Mint Liqueur, 128
Minted Grain Salad, 158
Mixed Herb Crackers, 121
Monarda didyma, 84, 274, 292,
    303, 307
Monarda spp. *See* Bee balm
Monardes, Nicholas, 84
Mondale, Joan, xvii
Mordants, 269, 270, 271
Mother's Plum Catsup, 230
Mustard, 33, 51–53, 76, 101, 311
Mustard Dill Sauce, 230

My Secret Herb Butter, 230
Myrrhis odorata. See Sweet cicely

Nancy Howard's Opal Basil
    Jelly, 240
Nannette's Orzo Salad, 156
Nasturtium, 36, 54, 284, 313
Native American Garden, 15,
    276–81
New England Unit, xv
New York Unit, xv
Nigella sativa. See Black cumin
Nigella Stuffed Eggs, 243
Nonpareilles, 25
Nutmeg, 8, 29, 101, 308

Ober, Dick, xviii
Ocimum spp. *See* Basil
O'Connor, Audrey, xiv
Onslow Slumgullion, 201
Oregano, 9, 13, 55, 79, 266, 274,
    297, 312
Origanum spp. *See* Oregano
Orris root, 293
Our Favorite Rosemary Chicken,
    176
Oven-Fried Summer Squash, 202
Oysters Lara, 181

Pansies. See *Viola* spp.
Papaver spp. *See* Poppies
Paprika, 8, 9, 30, 56, 286, 291
*Paradisi in Sole, Paradisus Terres-
    tris* (Parkinson), 257, 294
Parkinson, John, 257, 271, 294
Parsley, 6, 10, 28, 57, 273, 274,
    308, 310, 312
Parsley Salad Dressing, 163
Parterres, 256–57
Pasta Provençal, 186
Pawpaw, 108–109, 110, 307, 311
Peasant Rye Dip, 117
Pelargonium spp. *See* Scented
    geranium
Peppermint, 284, 287, 292, 303, 307

The Perfect Marriage, 223
Pesto and Cream Cheese Round,
    114
Pesto Genovese, 234
Petroselinum crispum. See Parsley
Philadelphia Unit, xv
Pimpinella anisum. See Anise;
    Aniseed
Pineapple sage, 94, 298, 313
Pink, 36, 58, 272, 274, 296, 300,
    304, 310, 311
Piquant Green Sauce for Meats,
    231
Pivarnik, Bernice, xix, xxiv
Plectranthus amboinicus. See Cu-
    ban oregano
Plimpton, Susan, xv
Pliny the Elder, 284
Polenta Triangles with Rosemary
    and Walnuts, 122
Poliomintha bustamanta. See
    Mexican oregano
Polygonum odoratum. See Viet-
    namese coriander
Poppies, 59, 265, 266, 288, 304,
    312
Poppy seeds, 113
Port Orange Beef Stew, 165
Portobello Pasta Casserole, 186
Pot marigold, 36, 61, 270, 272,
    273, 286, 291, 310, 311
Potato Salad with Horseradish,
    160
Potato Salad with Lovage, 161
Potomac Unit, xiii, xv, xviii
Potpourri, 45, 67, 69, 260, 261,
    289, 294, 295, 296
Purslane, 275
Pyracantha Berry Jelly, 240

Rabbit Run Spinach Pie, 187
Rady, Virginia, xv
Rainbow Salsa, 225
Rea, Betty, xv, xvi, xxi, xxiv
Red Hibiscus Pepper Jelly, 242

Index of Recipes by Herb

BLACK CUMIN

Nigella Stuffed Eggs, 243

CALENDULA

Dandelion Salad with Citrus
     Dressing, 153
Fresh Herbed Spring Rolls, 119
Herbal Garlic Soup, 142
Herbal Shortbread Cookies, 207
Lemon Broccoli Marigold, 193

CAPERS

Arugula Cappellini with Lemon
     Caper Sauce, 183
Fresh Tuna Salad Pita, 149
Herbed Olives, 120

CARAWAY

Beef Tenderloin Tips with Cara-
     way and Marjoram, 165
Garam Masala, 245
Lemon Caraway Cake, 213

CARDAMOM

Cardamom Apples with Bay
     Leaf Cream, 211
Garam Masala, 245
Spice Liqueur, 129

CHERVIL

Cream of Chervil Soup, 140
Early Spring Omelet with
     Chervil, 190
Inbakad Lax, 120
Martha's Shrimp, 181
Piquant Green Sauce for
     Meats, 231
Spring Pesto with Chervil and
     Pine Nuts, 236
Vinaigrette Carrots, 194
Zesty Spring Dressing, 163

CHILE PEPPERS

Arugula Cappellini with Lemon
     Caper Sauce, 183

Bird's Eye Boursin, 113
Cilantro Salad Dressing, 162
Crab Casserole, 180
Cranberry Salsa, 225
Creole Crab Bisque, 140
Fresh Herbed Spring Rolls, 119
Grilled Corn Dip, 117
Herbal Asian Chicken Salad
     with Noodles and Peanut
     Dressing, 173
Herbed Olives, 120
Lamb with Tomatoes and
     Marjoram, 170
Lebanese Onion Sauce, 229
Lime Vinaigrette, 229
Mango Apple Chutney, 226
Mayan Hot Chocolate, 129
Mexican Potato Cake, 185
Mexican Summer Vegetables, 202
Onslow Slumgullion, 201
Rainbow Salsa, 225
Red Hibiscus Pepper Jelly, 242
Red Pepper Relish, 227
Rice Paper Salmon with Fresh
     Herbs, 182
Roasted Red Pepper Soup with
     Basil, 145
Rosemary Cheddar Bite-Sized
     Bars, 122
Rosemary White Bean Puree, 116
Sage Relish, 227
Sautéed Spicy Collards, 195
Savory Oven-Roasted Potatoes, 199
Southwest Fried Corn, 195
Spicy Tomato Grits, 203
Stuffed Chicken Casserole, 177
White Chili, 188

CHIVES

Cauliflower Vichyssoise, 139
Cold Tomato Soup, 139
Crab Casserole, 180
Cucumber Dill Salsa, 119
Dandelion Salad with Citrus
     Dressing, 153

Early Spring Omelet with
     Chervil, 190
Fresh Herb Cheesecake, 116
Grilled Corn Dip, 117
Mixed Herb Crackers, 121
Nannette's Orzo Salad, 156
Parsley Salad Dressing, 163
Piquant Sauce for Meats, 231
Port Orange Beef Stew, 165
Portobello Pasta Casserole, 186
Potato Salad with Lovage, 161
Rabbit Run Spinach Pie, 187
Savory Herb Biscuits, 134
Scalloped Potatoes, 199
Soupe Verte, 146
Tarragon Goat Cheese Mousse, 118
Thymely Morels, 196
Vinaigrette Carrots, 194
Warm Wild Rice and Barley
     Salad, 159

CILANTRO

Avocado Cilantro Pesto, 234
Cilantro Salad Dressing, 162
Cilantro Tomato Pasta Salad, 153
Cranberry Salsa, 225
Fresh Herbed Spring Rolls, 119
Grilled Pork Back Ribs with
     Asian Gremolata, 179
Herbal Asian Chicken Salad
     with Noodles and Peanut
     Dressing, 173
Mexican Summer Vegetables, 202
Rainbow Salsa, 225
Red Lentil Soup with Cilantro
     and Cumin, 144
Rice Paper Salmon with Fresh
     Herbs, 182
Sofrito, 233
Southwest Fried Corn, 195
Southwestern Corn, 196
White Chili, 188

CINNAMON

Apple, Sage, and Squash Bread, 135

Apple Sage Bread, 135

Carrie's Plum Pudding and
Sauce Delicious, 216

Garam Masala, 245

Ginger Cookies, 207

Harvest Mashed Potatoes, 198

Lebanese Onion Sauce, 229

Mayan Hot Chocolate, 129

Mint Chocolate Pound Cake, 215

Mother's Plum Catsup, 230

Rhubarb Custard Pie, 221

Rosemary Fruit, 162

Saffron Cake, 215

Spice Liqueur, 129

Stuffed Eggplant, 167

Warm Brie with Blueberry
Thyme Chutney, 123

CLOVES

Apple, Sage, and Squash
Bread, 135

Carrie's Plum Pudding and
Sauce Delicious, 216

Garam Masala, 245

Mother's Plum Catsup, 230

Rosemary Fruit, 162

Saffron Cake, 215

CORIANDER

Chicken with Lime and Spices,
172

Garam Masala, 245

Lemon Pepper Seasoning Mix, 246

Mexican Summer Vegetables, 202

CUMIN

Chicken with Lime and Spices,
172

Mexican Summer Vegetables, 202

Red Lentil Soup with Cilantro
and Cumin, 144

Sautéed Spicy Collards, 195

Southwest Fried Corn, 195

Stuffed Chicken Casserole, 177

Tofu Chili, 187

Vegetarian Harvest Bowls with
Ginger Tahini Sauce, 189

White Chili, 188

DANDELION

Arugula, Spinach, Dandelion,
and Feta Salad, 151

Dandelion Salad with Citrus
Dressing, 153

Herbal Garlic Soup, 142

Lorraine's Chicken Soup with
Dandelion and Violets, 143

DILL

Cilantro Salad Dressing, 162

Cucumber Dill Salsa, 119

Fresh Tuna Salad Pita, 149

Herb and Onion Bread, 136

Jamie's Dill Dip Mix, 245

Mustard Dill Sauce, 230

Peasant Rye Dip, 117

Piquant Green Sauce for
Meats, 231

Potato Salad with Horseradish,
160

Savory Herb Biscuits, 134

Scalloped Potatoes, 199

Stuffed Cabbage, 166

Zesty Spring Dressing, 163

EDIBLE FLOWERS

Dandelion Salad with Citrus
Dressing, 153

Fresh Herbed Spring Rolls, 119

Herb Honey, 238

Herbal Garlic Soup, 142

Herbal Shortbread Cookies, 207

Lavender Cookies, 208

Lavender Ice Cream, 217

Lavender Jelly, 239

Lavender Raspberry Cheesecake,
218

Lemon Broccoli Marigold, 193

Lorraine's Chicken Soup with
Dandelion and Violets, 143

Mai Wine, 130

Rose Petal Jam, 241

Rose Petal Trifle, 222

Savory Herb Biscuits, 134

FENNEL

Cheese Tortellini with Fennel
Cream Sauce, 183

Chicken Linguine with Fennel
and Tarragon, 170

Fall Garden Salad, 154

Feta and Fennel Potatoes, 197

Red Pepper Relish, 227

Rose Hip Herbal Tea, 125

GINGER

Geri's Good-on-Anything
Cranberry Chutney, 226

Ginger Cookies, 207

Ginger Pudding Pie, 220

Gingered Butternut Squash
Soup, 141

Gingered Earl Grey Scones, 134

Green Tomato Bread, 136

Grilled Pork Back Ribs with
Asian Gremolata, 179

Herbal Asian Chicken Salad
with Noodles and Peanut
Dressing, 173

Herbal Shortbread Cookies, 207

Honey Mint Carrots, 194

Mango Apple Chutney, 226

Red Lentil Soup with Cilantro
and Cumin, 144

Rice Paper Salmon with Fresh
Herbs, 182

Rose Hip Herbal Tea, 125

Sesame Ginger Sauce, 233

Sugar-Free Ginger Pudding Pie,
222

Vegetarian Harvest Bowls with
Ginger Tahini Sauce, 189

Warm Brie with Blueberry
Thyme Chutney, 123

Wild Strawberry Ginger Jam, 242

Focaccia with Herbs and Tomatoes, 137
Fresh Herb Cheesecake, 116
Fresh Tuna Salad Pita, 149
Gingered Butternut Squash Soup, 141
Grilled Vegetable Sandwich with Red Onion Marmalade, 148
Harvest Bake, 201
Harvest Vegetable Bake, 184
Herbal Garlic Soup, 142
Leg of Lamb Coating, 246
Lemon Broccoli Marigold, 193
Lemon Pepper Seasoning Mix, 246

Lime Chicken with Thyme, 174
Mixed Herb Crackers, 121
My Secret Herb Butter, 230
Nannette's Orzo Salad, 156
Onslow Slumgullion, 201
Oysters Lara, 181
Port Orange Beef Stew, 165
Portobello Pasta Casserole, 186
Rice Pilaf with Herbs, 200
Ricotta and Herb Frittata, 191
Roasted Tomato Pasta Sauce with Fresh Herbs, 232
Rosemary Chicken, 175
Saffron Soup, 146

Savory Herb Biscuits, 134
Thymely Morels, 196
Tuscan Stew, 147
Warm Brie with Blueberry Thyme Chutney, 123
Wild Strawberry Ginger Jam, 242
Zucchini "Crab" Cakes, 203
Zucchini Saga Soup, 147

TURMERIC

Chicken with Lime and Spices, 172
Red Lentil Soup with Cilantro and Cumin, 144
Rosemary Walnuts, 123